LITURGICAL RESOURCES
FOR LENT AND EASTERTIDE

To Wilfrid Harrington OP,
friend and colleague,
for many years' encouragement.

Thomas O'Loughlin

Liturgical Resources
for Lent and Eastertide

the columba press

First published in 2004 by
the columba press
55A Spruce Avenue, Stillorgan Industrial Park,
Blackrock, Co Dublin

Cover by Bill Bolger
Origination by The Columba Press
Printed in Ireland by ColourBooks Ltd, Dublin

ISBN 1 85607 478 1

Acknowledgement

Many items now brought together in this book first appeared in
Scripture in Church over the past ten years. Other pieces appeared in
earlier forms in *The Furrow, Doctrine and Life, New Liturgy,* or *Scripture
Bulletin.* I would like to express my thanks to the editors of these journals
for many useful suggestions they made during the process of public-
ation.

I would also like to acknowledge the feedback I have had from so many
people – priests in parishes, musicians, liturgists, scripture scholars,
and most importantly many who 'sit in the pews' – to the materials
printed here during the time that I was putting together this collection
of resources.

Table of Contents

Preface

The gathering for the Eucharist on Sunday is, and always has been, the central event of the life of the People of God. That gathering for a meal – a practice in direct continuity with all the meals during the lifetime of Jesus which formed his new community and imparted to it his style – is characterised by its encounter with the risen Christ in a variety of ways. First, in the gathering together of the baptised which makes a single group from people who are scattered during the week, and establishes that gathering as a single body in Christ. Gathered at the tables of word and sacrament we become visibly the identity we claim: brothers and sisters in, and parts of, Christ's body. Secondly, there is the encounter with Christ through the communal recollection of the memory of God's works from the community's own 'memory banks'. The scriptures are the communities' book. They are truly known when read in the communities, and understood within the whole memory of the People of God. The living God cannot be contained in a lifeless form such as a book, but rather lives in the living memory of the church animated by the Spirit; but the reading of those ancient books jogs that memory into consciousness, reflection, new understandings, and action. Readings, homilies, and common prayers have been part of the communal activity of the followers of the Way since the outset. Thirdly, there is the encounter in the act of thanksgiving to the Father whereby, in eating and drinking at the Lord's table, we share in the Lord's body and blood.

This weekly gathering is presided over by one of the community whom the church has empowered to act in the name of the whole People of God on earth, and in every moment of the celebration the actions of the one who presides can add to the effectiveness of the whole event, in making this gathering into an encounter with Christ. This act of presiding week after week is a demanding task, and one that few presbyters can undertake without looking for ideas from others, even if it is only to inspire them to appreciate that their own ideas are better than most of those around! To preach and teach, particularly in a culture like ours that finds religious affirmation difficult and experiences distance from many of the historical rituals and narratives of Christianity, is something that demands all the resources of the individual's own experience, study, prayer, and reflection. However, it is also one where gathering ideas and hints from others is clearly required as well. The good teacher brings out what is both old and new, and does not refuse to consider hints from anyone. Here is the purpose of this book: it is a collection of ideas, hints, suggestions that I have put together as part of an attempt to help fellow disciples derive food from their participation in the liturgy, and I offer them now to you. If they help you, and those who minister with you, to enhance your celebrations by picking and choosing from them, that is good. If they inspire you to produce even more effective ways to make the Word present in your gatherings, then that is better.

There is no overall theme to these resources. I have tried to draw from as wide and catholic an experience of the liturgy as possible. There is, however, a guiding notion. Whenever possible the resources are self-referential to the actual event being celebrated: a Eucharist. So whenever a suggestion might help a community have a deeper appreciation of what they are doing, there and then, this has been preferred. The Eucharist is an activity ('Do this in memory'), and the more a community appreciates what it is doing together, the more the action is enhanced and the purpose of all liturgy realized.

To conclude, please reflect on this passage from the *General Instruction on the Roman Missal* (n. 5, Missal, p. xx), which has continually rumbled in the back of my mind:

> The celebration of the eucharist, and the entire liturgy, is carried out by the use of outward signs. By these signs faith is nourished, strengthened, and expressed. It is very important to select and arrange the forms and elements proposed by the church, which, taking into account individual and local circumstances, will best foster active and full participation and promote the spiritual welfare of the faithful.

Ash Wednesday A, B, C

Note

A key notion in Lent, and therefore today's liturgy, is that it is the season of the community's preparation for the event of the Paschal Mystery of rebirth (the rebirth of the newly baptised, the renewal of rebirth for the rest of the church) at Easter. So it is not an individual's sense of having gone astray or an individual's act of repentance or an individual's determination to begin afresh that is being highlighted, but the action of the whole church. We as a people – through the actions of individuals and as a group – have sinned, have caused evil and suffering, have failed to stand up for the truth, the poor, the oppressed; and so we now need to acknowledge our failings and begin a process of re-training *(didache/disciplina)* and renewal *(metanoia/conversio)*. We find ourselves caught up in a solidarity of evil founded in selfishness – and far less than what we claim to be as the people of God. Lent is presented by the liturgy as the gift of a season where that dark world is challenged by the solidarity of grace which is found in Christ. Christ presents to his people reconciliation with the Father, and we become the renewed people (not just a collection of renewed individuals) in accepting his reconciliation and extending that reconciliation to the world (see today's second reading).

This ecclesial dimension of Lent is something that our individualist society in the West can barely appreciate: one of our delusions is that selfishness even reaches into the spiritual sphere: 'I am saved,' 'I can be reconciled apart form the community,' 'I can relate to God without that demanding responsibility in the human community.' But presenting Lent in terms of individual penitence and religious duty further erodes the loss of the ecclesial dimension. This may seem 'to work' if it produces a queue outside the confessional, but such an emphasis comes at a

high price if we as the People of God do not have a deeper sense
of who we are as a single body at the end of Lent. During today's
liturgy the note to sound is that we need to renew ourselves, we
need to become more aware of ourselves as a body and who we
are in Christ, and how we must act as a people charged with a
mission of reconciliation and renewal.

Introduction to the Celebration

In just over six weeks time we will rededicate ourselves as the
church when we recall our Lord's death and victory over death,
and then we shall also welcome new brothers and sisters in the
Lord's body. So that we can do this, we begin today to take stock
of how we are living as Christ's presence in this society; and by
placing ashes on our foreheads we are making a common commitment to become a more perfect church and a more credible
witness to God's love for humanity in this season of renewal.

Penitential Rite

There is none. The liturgy moves directly from the words greeting and introduction to the Opening Prayer.

Headings for Readings
First Reading

Today we are proclaiming a fast and gathering in a solemn assembly to mark the beginning of a season of collective renewal
and spring-cleaning which will lead to an act of collective rededication here in a few weeks time when we renew our baptismal promises at the Easter Vigil. The reading from Joel is the
great solemn proclamation to mark the beginning of this season.

   Note: This reading functions in today's liturgy not just as a
reading on penitence, but as a proclamation that a season has
begun: it is ritually akin to the solemn statement made at the
opening of the Olympic Games calling for a period of peace. If it
is read as a text in the normal way it simply offers some food for
reflection on its message, and its power to mark the beginning of
the season is lost. This piece of Joel each year announces Lent's

start, so it can be marked by asking the congregation to stand, or remain standing, for this reading, by having the lector then process with some solemnity to the ambo and then reading it in a tone of proclamation. If this can be done well, then an introduction is unnecessary or perhaps the reading needs only a cue: 'Let us stand for the proclamation of Lent.'

Second Reading
In Jesus we have been offered reconciliation with the Father, now is the time when we must embrace that re-union with God; and we must take on the task given to us by Christ to reconcile the whole creation. We are called to act as his ambassadors, making peace and renewing the bonds of love in society at large.

Note: the layout of the reading in the Lectionary does not help the Lector to make sense of it. 6:2 is a quotation from Is 49:8 and the 'he' is God – the reading is made far more comprehensible is the Lector's voice indicates who 'he' is, and that at that point Paul is quoting a prophesy.

The Gospel
Prayer, fasting, and almsgiving – these are the three great paths towards overcoming evil: attention to God through prayer; attention to disorder in our own lives through fasting; and attention to the needs of the poor through giving. But we must be careful not to delude ourselves by making these actions into sources of pride or material self-advancement.

The Distribution of the Ashes
Part of the ritual power of this day to mark a moment in the year – even for many for whom the liturgical year is no longer part of their annual time-scape – is the strength of ashes as a sign: they can be touched, smelled, felt as they are placed on the forehead, the slight sting for a few moments afterwards, and then the consciousness that they are visible on our foreheads to those who look at us – they produce for a moment a strange religious self-consciousness. The community who has received the ashes has

become consciously disfigured: it has, literally, dirt on its public face. This disfigurement of the our faces for a day is a perfect sacramental expression of our disfigurement as the People of God in need of renewal: we who are to express the love, peace, and reconciliation of God in how we live and act in the world, have become scandals that bring the name of Christ and his movement into disrepute. Our inward disfigurement needing renewal (Lent) and rededication (Easter) is matched by our outward disfigurement today: taking ashes is taking on board our share in the responsibility for the sins of the whole people, and declaring that we will work together toward renewal.

However, the ashes ceremony is not ritually imposing, so that 'getting the ashes' can be perceived as just 'going to get something'. The Missal states that the ashes are obtained from the previous year's palms and this can be the cue to make the ceremony far more impressive: burn the dried palms and make the ashes after the gospel and before the blessing. This is very simply done. Use a pyrex bowl as the urn and set fire to the dried palms. After a year's drying they burn easily and only a small amount are needed to make more than sufficient ashes. People can be asked to bring the palms they still have at home which provides another way of showing that this is a community event. The burning itself takes only moments and provides a spectacular focus on the ashes and their significance. While the burning is taking place there is an excellent opportunity for a 'few words' on the day and the season or on the use of ashes during the time before Christ.

Since this is a community event, just as the Eucharist is brought to the sick from the Sunday gathering, so ministers should be commissioned today to bring the ashes to those members of the community unable to gather today.

When giving the ashes the phrase from Mk 1:15 is much to be preferred because (1) it is the beginning of the kerygma as recalled by Mark and so marks a new beginning, (2) Jesus saw his call to turn from sin as the call to Israel to become the new regathered people, (3) its structure is that of the baptismal event for which we are now preparing, (4) the purpose of Lent is to renew us as the gospel people whose lives proclaim not sin but the good news, and (5) the Genesis verse presents ashes as symbolising mortality rather than renewal, and derives from a late medieval spirituality that did not understand Christ's call positively nor communally.

Prayer of the Faithful
Those given for 'Lent I' (Missal, pp. 998-9) are ideal for today.

Eucharistic Prayer
The Missal prescribes Preface of Lent IV (P11); note how this preface presents Lent as the collective work of the community: '... our observance ... our faults ... our minds ... help us grow ... offer us the reward ...'. This theme can then be followed by using Eucharistic Prayer II: '... we thank you for counting us worthy to stand in your presence ... may all of us who share ... be brought together in unity ...'.

Invitation to the Our Father
Let us ask the Father to forgive our sins and to bring us to forgive those who sin against us.

Sign of Peace
We are ambassadors charged with a mission to be agents of reconciliation. Let us begin this ministry now by expressing the bonds of peace and forgiveness that must exist among all who share in this holy table.

Invitation to Communion
Behold the Lamb of God, behold him who ate with sinners and called them to a new life, behold him who eats with us now and calls us to a new life in this holy season.

Communion Reflection

Lent is the season of Christian 'training' – which is what the word 'discipline' really means. So as we begin our period of collective training it is interesting to listen to the opening words of the earliest Christian training manual – in use within twenty years of the crucifixion – and which is older than any of our gospels.

> There are two very different ways: the way of life and the way of death!
> The way of life is this:
> First, you shall love the God who made you.
> Second, you shall love your neighbour as yourself,
> And the things you would not want someone to do to you,
> Do not do such things to one another.
> So that we can carry out this way of life, this is how we train:
> We must speak well of those who speak badly of us!
> We must pray for our enemies!
> And we must fast for those who persecute us.
> (*Didache* 1:1-2 – slightly adapted to render the Greek second person plural in English).

Dismissal

Prayer over the People 6 (Missal, p. 380) is most appropriate; but any one of the following Prayers is also suitable for today: 4, 13, 14, or 23.

COMMENTARY

First Reading: Joel 2:12-18

The book was probably written sometime between the rebuilding of the Temple (515) and 343 at a time when life in the whole of Judah and the city of Jerusalem was threatened by an attack of locusts which could easily bring famine in its wake. This threat was seen as a call to repent and the people to turn again to Yahweh since his 'day' [of judgement] was at hand. The text we read is the prophetic summons to the people in the city to repent. It is a call to the whole community – priests, elders, brides and infants (2:16-17) – to turn as one back to the Lord. It is significant that this call to repent is to be answered not by the king on behalf of the people (for kingship was probably in abeyance at the time of writing) but by the whole collection of people of every rank and class acting as the Lord's people. It is also worth noting that there is no hint in the text of any divine disapproval of the temple cult, but rather that the proper performance of the cult be matched by interior renewal. Because of this – it is the call for the interior renewal of the People of God so that they might be worthy of the cult in which the publicly share – it is a text ideally suited to announce the church's Lent.

Psalm : 50: 3-6, 12-14, 17; R/ v.3

This is the penitential psalm *par excellence*, and is an individual lament for sinfulness. Traditionally this was presented as David's lament when challenged by Nathan after his adultery with Bathsheba (see the story found in 2 Sam 11-12). This focus on individual lament is altered by the liturgy in the response: 'on *us* for *we* have sinned'.

Second Reading : 2 Cor 5:20-6:2

This reading belongs to a larger unit, 5:11-6:10, where Paul presents a theology of reconciliation and of the ministry reconciliation that is given to Christians. Reconciliation is given to us by God in Christ: God reconciles us, and we accept reconciliation – hence the command in the passive voice, 'Be reconciled to God.' This notion of reconciliation is only found in the NT in Paul and is built on the image of being joined back, reconnected, restored bonds of love, or of realignment of disjointed parts. And this is the time in the history of the universe when this possibility is available to humanity, and in this the prophesy of Isaiah is fulfilled. This is the mission on which Christ has been sent, and this mission is prolonged in that we are sent as a delegation, an embassy, a mission, a group of representatives (*presbeuomen*) to assist in the reconciliation of the world. Note that for Paul this is a basic collective activity of each church that will read his letter.

This reconciliation of the world is a task that Christians have to perform before God as part of their participation in Christ. His readers live at the very moment when they have to get on with the ministry of reconciliation and thus make Christ present.

Gospel: Mt 6:1-6, 16-18

These verses, located by Matthew within the Sermon on the Mount (4:23-7:29) form a unit devoted to Christian training in a form that is derived from the earliest Jewish-Christian communities. The text as it is edited in the liturgy is built around three smaller units that are very similar in structure: vv. 2-4 on almsgiving; vv. 5-6 on prayer; and vv. 16-18 on fasting – and the repetitive structure and instruction shows it was part of a single piece of oral training. Thus it is the text as read today, without the intrusion of the Our Father (vv. 7-15), that was the original text of Matthew; the text as read in the received gospel must be the work of a second redaction.

It is frequently noted that this piece of instruction in Matthew on 'community discipline' is 'without synoptic parallel' – in so far as there are no verbal parallels in either Luke [Q] or Mark (where we usually look to see how the early community adapted teaching to its needs and situation). However, when we state that the disciplines recounted in these verses were central planks in the training of new gentile Christians prior to their assimilation into a Jewish-Christian church we are on far surer ground than usual. We know from the *Didache* – which is earlier than Matthew – that these exact practices are the prescribed necessary training for anyone, Jew or Gentile, who wished to become a follower of 'The Way of Life.' The difference between the training as presented in the *Didache* and in Matthew is that in the *Didache* these practices are simply demanded as part of the community's rule whereas by Matthew's time they are being placed directly on the lips of Jesus – and thus given the highest authority as their source. It is this influence of memorised oral training – either from our extant *Didache* or, more probably, an oral text parallel to it – on Matthew that probably explains why this unit of training is interrupted by the Our Father in the received text – for that prayer too was part of the oral training, but in the *Didache* it is simply prescribed for daily use without any source/authority being attributed to it, while in Matthew's received text it has been given the highest authority as its source. The reference to the need to pray in vv. 5-6 is the cue for the insertion of the community's most basic prayer. The Ouyr Father was taught in the initiation process of Christians, and was recited three times a day as the community's prayer.

When the church Fathers, notably Augustine, presented prayer, fasting and almsgiving as a single 'three-horse chariot' in training Christians so that they could 'progress along the road to Christian completeness', they were not reducing 'evangelical freedom' to rules and training as many scholars in the wake of the Reformation argued, but rather continuing to witness to a practice of actual training that goes back to the Jewish roots of the very first communities of Christians and a practice that is witnessed first in the extant *Didache* and then a few decades later by Matt hew as we have his text.

HOMILY NOTES

1. If the liturgy conveys the basic message of today (i.e. that we (1) as a community (2) begin today a season/period in which we undertake (3) a journey and process of renewal that (4) makes us more fully the Body of Christ and (5) leads others to the moment of baptism, then a homily need only be a word or two in length while the ashes are being made by burning last year's palms.

2. To see this season as a gift/opportunity is very difficult for us as we are still burdened with half-remembered images of long ago when dancing, weddings, and eggs and lard were forbidden. Penitence which is just an attempt 'to make up' for sins by voluntary sufferings so as to avoid penalties post mortem has the effect of placing God's justice and human retributive justice on the same plane – and thus denying the

graciousness of God as seen in Christ's reconciliation. So the task is to present Lent as the time for re-building bonds, becoming joined back to God and neighbour, for overcoming strife and working for peace and justice, and renewing 'the bonds of peace' (cf Eph 4:3) and love.

3. Renewing ourselves as the people chosen as God's own, recovering the image of Christ soiled by sin, rebuilding the links with those we have injured and scandalised is not something that can happen in a moment: it requires time, patience, effort, and the commitment of resources. This is why we have a season and not just some quick ceremony: reconciliation is always a longer process than the impression given in our rites of reconciliation, whether individual or collective. The resources needed may be emotional – speaking again to someone who has offended us or crossing boundaries that keep us apart in warring tribes; political – advocating policies based on the fact that we believe Christ has commissioned us to minister reconciliation to the world; spiritual – time needed to serve the community, to pray, or to grow in understanding of Christ's way through taking part in a 'Lenten Group'; and financial – using our material resources to help build the kingdom of justice, love, and peace.

4. We are involved in two solidarities: in that of sin that disfigures the world and the image of God in each of us; and in the community of grace through baptism. Lent is the time when we re-align ourselves and seek to oppose sin in every sphere with love.

First Sunday of Lent Year A

Note

For many people, today, rather than Ash Wednesday, is their first encounter with the season of Lent. It is therefore worthwhile presenting today as the introduction to the whole season. However, the difficulty is that 'Lent' must not be presented as a season on its own, possibly with Easter as sequel; rather it has to be seen as a stage in the annual season of renewal, the celebration of death of the old person – resurrection to new life, that is central to the whole time between Lent's beginning and Pentecost.

Introduction to the Celebration

We are the people who have been baptised into Christ and share in his new life. But we are also a people still in need of repentance and renewal. Today we begin a season that leads us through Christ's death to his resurrection and onwards to our celebration of the Spirit dwelling within us at Pentecost. Today we begin a season of renewal in that new life, we start to take stock of the state of our discipleship as individuals and as a people. During the coming weeks we will focus on the core of our faith and our dedication to building the new kingdom announced by Jesus.

Rite of Penance

Option c. iv (Missal, p. 393) is appropriate.

Opening Prayer

The alternative opening collect is better today as it opens up a theme that is picked up in the first reading.

Headings for Readings
First Reading

As Christians we believe that God is the sovereign creator and
that all that he made is good; we also know that in our world
and in our own lives there is disruption, decay, and evil. Part of
the difficulty of believing is that we have to face both these realities – that God is good, but there is evil in the world – without
ignoring or denying either of them. Now we are going to read an
ancient story that attempts to explain how both these apparently
contradictory 'facts' can exist side-by-side.

Second Reading

Paul took the historical existence of Adam as a fact, and tried to
understand the significance of Jesus by contrasting him with
Adam. Even if we do not think of Adam as an historical individual, the state of sinfulness in which we humans find ourselves is
a fact; and faced with this human situation, we believe that Jesus
offers us forgiveness and a life that cannot be destroyed by evil
or death.

Gospel

Matthew presents the temptation of Jesus as occurring at the
outset of his public ministry for which Jesus was preparing by a
period of forty days of prayer and fasting. We are now entering
a time of preparing to do the Father's will more closely by a similar time of prayer and fasting. We too must be alert to the reality
of temptations that would call us away from the Way of Christ.

Prayer of the Faithful
President

As we begin our annual period of renewal in the risen life of the
Lord, let us ask the Father for our needs, the needs of all the
churches, and the needs of all humanity.

Reader (s)

1. For the whole Church of God, that this period of prayer and

fasting will prepare us to enter into the new life of Christ at Easter.

2. For all [especially those in this community] who are beginning their final period of preparation for baptism; that their initiation into the People of God may bring them joy and peace in their lives.

3. As we renew ourselves through reconciliation with our sisters and brothers and with the Father, let us pray that the Light of truth and the Spirit of reconciliation will be present in the hearts of all peoples and in all who have duties of leadership in the world.

4. As we begin our time of fasting, let us pray for all who do not have a fair share of the world's resources and for all who are hungry, that the Father will give them hope and move human hearts to help them.

5. *Local needs.*

6. For ourselves, that we as a community will have the strength to avoid temptation, and serve the Father with pure hearts.

President

Father, your Son was tempted in every way that we are but did not sin. Grant us the grace and strength we need to reject sin and to serve you with all our hearts and skills, for we ask this through Christ, your Son, our Lord. Amen.

Eucharistic Prayer

The preface for this Sunday (P12) relates directly to today's gospel.

Invitation to the Our Father

As we begin this time when we will seek forgiveness for our sins, let us ask the Father to forgive us our trespasses as we forgive those who trespass against us:

Sign of Peace
Today we are committing ourselves to renewing our commitment to be the people of peace, let us begin by offering a token of
reconciliation and peace to each other.

Invitation to Communion
Behold the bread of life, the Lord's loaf broken so that each of us
can share its sustenance; happy are we who are called to this
banquet.

Communion Reflection
Robert Herrick's poem, 'To keep a true Lent,' makes a fine reflection for this Sunday. The text is in the Breviary, vol 2, pp.
612*-613* (Poem n 77).

Dismissal
Prayer over the people, n 4 (Missal, p. 380).

COMMENTARY

First Reading: Gen 2:7-9, 3:1-7
This is an abbreviated form of the 'Fall Story'. But we should
first note that by Jesus's time there were several schools of interpretation regarding this story, and that for which Paul opted –
which interpreted it as a 'fall' and a fall from divine favour (Rom
5) – was just one of the ways that this story was used. Paul seems
to have adopted his position as it was that found in the circles in
which he was trained in Jewish thought, but it is unclear
whether he continued to use it when he became a follower of
Jesus, because it could be used to show why a 'redeemer' was
necessary; or whether, since he was using the 'fall' interpretation, he then had to present Jesus using the notion of a redeemer.
However, this does mean that the Fall has stood very close to the
centre of most Christian theology for most of our history. This
Fall 'downwards' then became the basis for the explanation of
the fact of evil in a good creation as being accounted for by

Original Sin. That, in turn, became the basis for a particular theology of grace: we can only do good (due to the presence of Original Sin) through the assistance of God.

Given the history of the tradition that has brought the text to our attention, this chain of thought cannot be avoided by the Christian reader, but it is interesting to note that the story has been interpreted in many other ways. One of these is that God placed Adam and Eve in a protected environment, but then through the experience of temptation they had to become aware of their own abilities and the need to act responsibly: in the testing they were forced to become fully human and grown up and capable of a more significant relationship with God as they were now moral agents. Hence, 'their eyes were opened' and they became the key actors among all the living beings, through moral responsibility and through work.

If you do mention this reading in detail in your comments or homily, then take care to avoid dated clichés (e.g. 'our first parents') which can give the impression that this text is an historical account of the earliest human history. If you do mention it, it is worth mentioning that it is not to be considered as 'a revealed alternative' to the investigations of empirical science, but a rich religious myth which seeks to explain the presence of evil, suffering, the goodness of God, and also the hiddenness of God.

However, although the first and second readings today do form a famous theological doublet, one should try to limit the extent that that pairing sets the tone for the liturgy. In today's liturgy – as opposed to the history of Christian theology – the story of Adam and Eve is, in effect, a counterpoint to the gospel: and the gospel and the first reading should be read against each other. Jesus is tempted, but resists, he challenges the promises of the tempter, hence the tempter leaves and angels console him. Adam and Eve acquiesce with the tempter and are left severely alone with the need to defend themselves in the world. This interpretation does not do justice to Genesis, but it does highlight the gospel (which was written with an awareness of this Genesis story) and its message: temptation is there as a fact in the world and can be resisted. However, it is best to observe a silence as to how temptation is resisted because in answering that question the western churches have expended too much labour and, indeed, blood: it is the question that sparked off the whole debacle about actual grace, human initiative, and the ability to imitate Christ. In Genesis there is an awareness of temptation, and that succumbing to it leads to greater misery; part of Matthew's message is that because Jesus resisted temptation, so we too can resist.

Psalm: 50:3-6, 12-14, 17. R/ cf v.3
See the comment on the psalm for Ash Wednesday.

Second Reading: Rom 5:12-19
This reading forms the perfect sequel to the first reading as it is here that Paul takes the Adam and Eve story and interprets it as the origin of the 'fall', thereby explaining to himself and his audience how he makes sense of the need for Jesus's life and death. The churches have invested so much energy into the edifice of (1) the theology of Original Sin, (2) this Pauline theology of redemption, and (3) the theology of grace that is ultimately based on these verses of Paul, that it is well nigh impossible to unpack these verses without at the same time unpacking the whole edifice.

The key point to note is that Paul's starting point appears to be the fact of the gift of God that is Jesus, and Jesus is the one who opens up a way to the Father. The interpretation of Genesis then follows as a means to explain why humanity needed this new gift. So if now a way is opened, then formerly it must have been closed, so how did it come to be closed, and so there must have been a 'fall', and so forth. We should not think of Paul as setting forth a series of doctrines (e.g. 'the Fall', 'Original Sin', a theory of transmission, or a doctrine of grace) so that Christians could know these facts. Such interpretations view doctrines as if they are religious facts about the nature of the universe in the same way that the 'law of gravity' is a fact about the physical universe. However, this is how this text has been preached in all the western churches in recent centuries – e.g. the 'Monogenism' debate within Catholicism in the 1950s – and to some extent this is how it is still presented by many Christians. Rather, we should think of Paul trying to make sense of what he believes has happened in Jesus Christ – in him a new way of being at rights with God has been opened up – and if he is to fit this with what he already believes, then one way of doing that is to link it to a complex understanding of the effects of a fall at the very beginning of human history which must be still having an effect. The key thing is to focus on Paul's starting point – Jesus offers us a new way to God – rather than to get tied up in the logic by which he wants to explain this to himself and make it fit with his background.

Gospel: Mt 4:1-11

For Matthew's community (1) it is in the experience of fasting that one confronts the basic questions of faith – it is a practice of great religious worth, and (2) there is an implicit belief in the presence of the devil as a tempter, and (3) in the presence of angels as those tasked by God to help people. All three of these assumptions are likely to be alien to many in your congregation and this will inhibit the extent to which they can 'hear' this text.

In the early church a fast prepared people for baptism or for taking on any specific ministry, so Matthew presents Jesus as the model for this practice: to prepare for his ministry (remember this passage comes from the beginning of the gospel, while we – because our period of fasting comes just before Easter – imagine it coming towards the end, just before Holy Week), Jesus prepares himself by a fast for the 'perfect' period: forty days. During this time of preparation – achieved by fasting – he is offered three temptations: material comforts, supernatural abilities, and power/glory/status. Matthew's church are, by the account of Jesus's rejections of these temptations, encouraged to persevere in their fasting, to be assured that they can resist temptations, and that they have divine help – angels with them – in rejecting the snares of the devil.

HOMILY NOTES

1. We speak much about 'discipleship' and about 'being disci-
    ples'; we also speak about the 'discipline of Lent,' but rarely
    do we link discipleship with discipline, fixed training
    regimes, and building up skills through practice. In our cult-
    ure discipline belongs to dieting, skills training belongs to
    sporting activities, and warm feelings belong to religious dis-
    cipleship. Earlier Christians took a far more practical ap-
    proach to living a Christian life and discipleship: it required
    disciplined training, skills acquisition, mentoring by more
    experienced members of the community (surviving vestigially
    in 'God parents'), regular practice, and periodic renewal and
    servicing. Here lies one of the origins of Lent and it became
    linked to preparing for baptism since the prospective mem-
    bers of the community had to have learned the basic skills.
2. From the outset, three skills were seen as essential. First, the
    ability to pray: both alone and in a willingness to take part in
    the liturgy. One cannot be a Christian without prayer, nor
    call yourself one unless you gather with the Christians for
    prayer.
3. Second, a Christian must have the ability to fast. Fasting is a
    private and a public act. Private in that it touches one person-
    ally and makes one conscious of what one is about, literally
    in the pit of the stomach. This is felt religion, not an engage-
    ment with warm abstractions. Fasting is also communal in
    that it is done at fixed times of the week and year, and when
    one fasts as a part of a group, one identifies with them by
    sharing their practice. Then one is not acting alone, but it is
    the whole group that is imploring heaven collectively for
    their needs by fasting. Fasting without the dimension of
    prayer is simply dieting; prayer without fasting (or some
    other collective activity that 'touches' us), may be little more
    than repetitive sounds.
4. Third, giving to the poor (almsgiving) is a basic Christian act-
    ivity, and any notion that Christian belief can be separated

from care for justice and development would involve imagining Christianity as a philosophical system and divorce it from its roots – although this is a way of viewing Christian belief that is today quite common. Early Christians assumed that it was no use thanking God for his gifts and asking for his mercy, unless they were prepared to divert their gifts, resources, and mercy to the poor. To acknowledge God as our creator implies a care for all in need. And to acknowledge need and not do something about it is hypocrisy. Now that we have a global consciousness (just turn on the radio and listen to the news: details from every place on the planet where something bad, good, or interesting has happened over the last 12 hours), our almsgiving must have a global reach, hence the importance during Lent of thinking about world poverty, supporting development agencies, and taking some action to remove injustice: this is not a parallel activity to Lent, but part of its core. But remember, prayer and fasting without care for the poor turns faith into a private affair or a 'holy huddle', but almsgiving without prayer and fasting while noble, also fails to acknowledge the larger mystery that envelops all creation.

5. Lent is a time for polishing up basic Christian skills:
   • Prayer: on one's own and with the group;
   • Fasting: practising simplicity of lifestyle with the group;
   • Almsgiving: making with other Christians a real contribution to making the world a better place for all God's children.

First Sunday of Lent Year B

Note

See Year A.

Introduction to the Celebration

At the beginning of Lent we hear the call that introduces the message of Jesus: 'Repent and believe in the Good News.' This next few weeks will be a time of refreshment, a time of repentance that prepares us for Easter when we will renew our commitment to believing in the Good News of God's love. So now, let us pause and take heed that we are entering Lent and ask ourselves whether we are open to be really changed as people over the next few weeks.

Rite of Penance

Lord Jesus, you call us to repentance and belief, Lord have mercy;

Lord Jesus, you call us to turn from selfishness, Christ have mercy;

Lord Jesus, you show us the way to the Father, Lord have mercy.

Headings for Readings

First Reading

This is a time when we remember how often we have broken our relationships and betrayed those who have trusted us: God, those we love, our friends, or other people. But we have a relationship with God – a covenant – so that even if we are unfaithful, God is always faithful: a fact that we should be reminded of each time we see a rainbow. Because God is faithful, he welcomes us when we turn back to him.

Second Reading

We become the people of Christ through baptism. This is a time when we prepare to welcome new members into our community at the Easter Vigil, and a time when we prepare to renew ourselves and renew our baptismal commitment.

Gospel
This is the opening message of Jesus to all who listen to him: turn around in your lives; begin to live in a new way.

Prayer of the Faithful
Use the Sample Prayer of the Faithful n 5 (Lent 1), (Missal, pp. 998-999).

Eucharistic Prayer
Since Mark does not dwell on the temptations of Jesus in the desert, the preface for the First Sunday of Lent (P12) does not work well in year B. It is better to replace it with Preface of Lent I (P8) that surveys the whole message of the season now beginning.

Invitation to the Our Father
The Father has established a covenant with us in Jesus, so now we can pray:

Sign of Peace
To follow Jesus is to dare to live in a new way: a way of trust and generosity, a way of reconciliation and peacemaking. Let us show each other that this is our desired lifestyle.

Invitation to Communion
This is the Lamb of God who calls us to repent and believe in the Good News. Happy are we who stand around his table.

Communion Reflection
We are now the body of Jesus Christ.
We are no longer isolated units.
We are each distinct members of the one body of the Lord.

We have been called by Christ.
We have been gathered into one.
We are no longer scattered and lost.

We are invited to repent.
We are challenged to believe the Good News.
We are strengthened to begin afresh.
We have shared one loaf.
We have drunk from one cup.
We have been guests around Christ's table.

We must now be Christ's presence in the creation.
We share our sufferings with him and his with us.
We are the witnesses to his resurrection.
We must convey his call to repentance.
We must proclaim his reconciliation.
We must make known his Good News to all creation.

Dismissal
Prayer over the People n 6 (Missal, p. 380).

COMMENTARY

First Reading: Gen 9:8-15
This is presented in Genesis as the first universal covenant made
by God after the first lapse by humanity. Noah is presented as
the father of all humanity (one son was the progenitor of all
Asiatic peoples, one of all African peoples, and one of all
European peoples), and accordingly the testimony to this
covenant must be visible to everyone – hence the choice of the
rainbow. This passage in Genesis fulfils, within the scheme of
the Redactor, a crucial purpose: the message of the God of Israel
is not limited to one people or culture, but is universal in its embrace. God is sovereign Lord of all peoples, lands, the whole of
creation. And, so its claim about the nature of the covenant
makes a fundamental statement: God is steadfast faithfulness,
and all humanity can return to him.

Second Reading: 1 Pet 3:18-22
This is part of an early homily on Easter/baptism. It seeks to give an account of the paschal Mystery (including 'the descent into hell') and to link that with an understanding of baptism. The imagery depends on recognising that the audience lived in a three-deck universe. The living humans dwell on the middle tier, those who had died without baptism lived on a lower tier ('in prison') and awaited release, while Christ and all who are one with him through baptism live, or can live, on an upper tier at God's right hand in a 'place' that is higher than that occupied by 'the angels, dominations, and powers' (i.e. those celestial beings who never had to live on the middle, earthly tier).

The reading should remind us that in every age and culture we have to imagine what we mean by the Paschal Mystery anew.

Gospel: Mk 1:12-15
This is the stark opening call in Mark. The word we render as 'repent' (earlier Catholic translations insisted that it had to be rendered 'Do penance' – and so it set the tone for penitential activities in Lent) would probably be better translated as 'turn around,' or 'start living in a new way,' or 'change your ways.'

The relationship between John and Jesus is a complex one – only in Luke do we find an attempt to make the two preachers come into complete harmony of message and work through his story of a family connection between them. Jesus appears to have been originally part of John's movement. John appears to have preached the fast approach of the kingdom, but it is a kingdom that will usher in, except for the repentant, the time when God will chastise Israel, or all humanity, for its unfaithfulness. But Jesus broke with John's movement by proclaiming a soon coming kingdom, but one where God would not come to punish but rather welcome home sinners and offer a new life. From other places in the gospels we can detect that this break with John, and the beginning of his own preaching, occurred while John was still alive. That Mark places the beginning of Jesus's preaching after John's arrest shows that already by Mark's time the memory of the community of Jesus was harmonising both the messages and ministries of John and Jesus – a process that reached its climax in the stories of Mary and Elizabeth/ Zechariah in Luke 1.

HOMILY NOTES

1. It is sobering to note that most of those who train people in communications or teaching techniques regard the standard format of the homily/sermon as the least useful way to teach. They usually give these reasons: (1) people have a felt expectation that the sermon is going to be 'boring' or of little value; (2) the group are passive listeners; (3) the structure of the ritual allows little variation; (4) there is often a culture gap between the preacher and the majority of the congregation; (5) you have only, usually, your voice without other props or communications tools to convey your message; (6) there is such a wide range of people and expectations that inevitably some will believe that you are irrelevant, 'over their heads' or, conversely, patronising; and (7) the time allowed is neither short enough for a 'quick thought for the day' (which inevitably then is lost amid the other words of the Liturgy of the Word) nor long enough to produce a succinct piece of teaching. We have inherited the format of the homily at the Eucharist from a different communications culture and from the age before print, and so we are stuck with it; we would never invent it or anything like it today.

2. It can, therefore, be valuable on occasion to break with the homily format altogether and embark on a completely different communications strategy. The brevity and directness of today's gospel make it a good day to try out this method (common in almost every other face-to-face communication environment today) whose aim is to awaken people to the importance they attach to a particular topic in their lives. Ask each person to turn to someone near them, preferably not someone they are related to, and express to that person (1)

what Lent means to them, and (2) what Jesus's opening call means to them. Tell them that after five minutes you will ring the sanctuary bell to end the discussion.

3. This method will shock some, embarrass others, and infuriate those who imagine Christian faith as simply down-loading 'facts' from a professional, or imagine liturgy as a purely private affair where they can ignore others in the assembly in the same way we ignore people with whom we have to share a bus. However, it should make many aware that it is only by thinking and talking about most aspects of life that we begin to understand and see what must be done. This activity of sharing may make more learning and understanding take place than any amount of preaching by a preacher.

4. Conclude by acknowledging that it may have been difficult, while reminding everyone that they are the people chosen to proclaim Christ's call to repent and believe, and that it is a task for life and not just five minutes. But make sure that your closing statement takes no more than a minute or you will be giving, in effect, a minor homily.

First Sunday of Lent Year C

Note
See Year A.

Introduction to the Celebration
In every area of our lives there are periods of mending, renewing, and refocusing. We talk about 'spring cleaning', 'annual reviews, and 'in-service training'. Now we enter a period to renew our discipleship prior to celebrating the death and resurrection of Jesus at Easter. So now can we spend some moments considering how God our creator made us and has provided for us. Let us recall that God our saviour has called us to live in a new way and to build a world of justice and peace. Let us remember how God our inspiration offers us strength for our discipleship.

Rite of Penance
Option c. iv (Missal, p. 393) is appropriate.

Headings for Readings
First Reading
This is the account of a central memory of the people of Israel: the Lord delivered his people from slavery. We have a similar central memory about Jesus: he has delivered us from slavery to sin and has given us new life.

Second Reading
Paul sets out the core of our creed in one line: if your lips confess that Jesus is Lord and if you believe in your heart that God raised him from the dead, then you belong to his saved people.

Gospel
Before Jesus set out to do the work of the Father, he set out for forty days of fasting and prayer during which he was tempted.

Now we too set out on a forty-day period of prayer and fasting and almsgiving to prepare us to carry out the work God has entrusted to us. But we too will be tempted to abandon it, to see prayer and fasting as silly, and to be selfish and refuse generosity to those in need.

Prayer of the Faithful
President:
Friends, let us give voice to our needs, the needs of those we know, and let us ask for justice and peace for all humanity.
Reader (s):
1. For this church, that during Lent we may grow closer as a community.
2. For this church, that our lenten prayer, fasting, and almsgiving will renew us.
3. For the worldwide church, that we will bear witness to Christ's suffering, death, and resurrection.
4. For the worldwide church, that we may grow in faithfulness as disciples.
5. For all political leaders, that they may promote justice, peace, and development for poor countries.
6. For all who exercise power, that they may grow in respect for humanity and the environment as God's handiwork.
7. For all in need, that the lonely will find companionship, the distressed will find assistance with their problems, the worried will find peace of mind, and the sick will find healing.
8. For all who are being tried or tempted, that they will receive strength.
President:
Father, as we begin this time of learning to be disciples afresh, hear our needs and grant them in Christ Jesus, our Lord, Amen.

Eucharistic Prayer
The preface for this Sunday (P12) although more directly related to Matthew's temptation narrative, also works well with today's gospel.

Invitation to the Our Father
Let us pray that we will be strengthened as disciples to with-
stand temptation as we say:

Sign of Peace
If we wish to be disciples, we must be people who are peacemakers in our families, community, and society. If you are ready
to take on this commitment, then offer a sign of peace to those
around you.

Invitation to Communion
Behold, the Bread of Heaven is broken for the life of the world,
happy are we who are called to share it and eat it as our food.

Communion Reflection
To highlight the fact that Lent should be a time of community
renewal, instead of a verbal reflection today, invest more effort
ensuring that someone can take a particle of the broken loaf to
every member of the community who is sick or housebound.
These ministers to the sick could then be more formally set out
on their mission from the assembly, with words like these: 'As
we have shared in the one loaf and have been united at this
table, so now take these particles of our loaf to those who could
not be here, so that they can be linked with us and united with
Christ through your ministry.'

Dismissal
Prayer over the People n 12 (Missal, p. 381).

COMMENTARY

First Reading: Deut 26:4-10
This passage provides an 'historical' origin point within the life
of Moses for a piece of narrative that was already established
within Jewish liturgy. Within today's liturgy, however, this
deuteronomistic context is irrelevant and what is important is
the content of the liturgical prayer itself. It is a thanksgiving

prayer – and so fits into the larger category to which our eucharistic prayers belong – for making a sacrifice using the first
fruits of the land in the autumn time. These were placed by the
priest on the altar who then invoked an historical narrative of
what God had done for his people as the expression of thanksgiving – again there are parallels with our eucharistic prayers in
the way they use historical narratives, e.g. the narrative of the
Last Supper – not only for the fruits of the harvest, but all his sal-
vivic works in the people's history.

   While the basic structure (invoking God's past actions as the
basis of thanksgiving) has continued in Christian eucharistic
prayers, one must be careful in drawing any direct parallels between this account in Deuteronomy of a sacrifice and the preparation of the gifts at the Eucharist. The Eucharist communicates
with us primarily as a meal which does what sacrifice does,
namely establish connection and harmony with God; in Deuteronomy the notion of sacrifice is communicated primarily
through the symbol of putting something beyond human usage,
i.e. offering it on an altar. The Eucharist therefore takes place at a
table (which is then interpreted as an altar in so far as the
Christian meal is the Christian sacrifice), and the placing of the
bread and wine on the table is an act of preparation, not an 'of-
fertory' (hence the abolition of this term in the present Missal,
although it has survived in common usage). Our placing the
gifts of bread and wine on the table is not to put them beyond
human use, but so they can become the bread of life and the
spiritual drink of the community which placed them there.

Second Reading: Rom 10:8-13

This passage forms part of a longer section (Rom 9:1-11:36) on
the place of Israel in the plan of salvation. Israel, so Paul argues
in Rom 10:1ff, has failed to recognise that it is God who makes us
holy, for the law has come to an end with the coming of the
Christ (10:4). Now people are to find righteousness (being 'at-
rights' with God) through Jesus (10:8-13). Then Paul invokes an
early liturgical formula ('Jesus is Lord') and wraps it within his

own theology of what it means to adhere to Jesus: believing from the heart that you are made righteous, and confessing you are saved. Because of the nature of this righteousness (a gift) and of this adherence, it is available to all, both Jews and gentiles alike.

Paul's presentation of what constitutes adherence to the Christ, especially in this section of Romans, is so limited (because he approaches it in terms of righteousness), it is probably best to ignore this reading, as any detailed comment cannot avoid the fruitless old discussions of what constitutes that faith that is righteousness. These old sores are best not picked!

Gospel: Lk 4:1-13
The Lukan temptation account is very similar in content and language to that in Matthew (4:1-11), but differs from it in two respects. First, in Matthew, Jesus is led by the Spirit into the wilderness in order to be tested by the devil. In Luke the Spirit leads him as a preparation for his ministry, and then while there the devil sees his opportunity and seizes it. Second, in Matthew the devil leaves and Jesus is looked after by angels; here the note of angelic consolation is absent, and the devil is presented as only going away for a while: the devil will hover on the edges seeking another opportunity to strike.

The presence of these temptation stories at the beginning of Matthew and Luke reflects communities where – as we see in the *Didache* – at the outset of any important act (e.g. baptism) a period of preparation by fasting and prayer was essential. Jesus embarking on the ministry must, therefore, prepare in a similar way by fasting for what is the biblically ideal period of forty days. In Luke's world the devil is hovering quite low down and close to humanity, just off the edges of everyday existence waiting for a chance to pounce in any moment of weakness, so it seems natural to him that any period of fasting is a time when he might strike; and even when rejected he still hangs around watching for a weak moment.

HOMILY NOTES

1. Lent has three themes intertwined within it as we celebrate it. (1) It is a time of preparation for Easter, especially for those who are to be baptised. (2) It is a time of repentance and reparation for wrongs done to others around us, the larger community, and the creation. (3) It is a time of stocktaking and renewal in discipleship, the skills needed to be a disciple, and in the commitment to the work and activities of being a Christian.

2. The homily today could take the form of a 'checklist' or examination of conscience on these aspects.

3. Preparing for Easter.

    • What plans has the community to make Easter the central moment of the year? We should recall that today in many places this is the time when many people think of going for a 'spring break' and a time when many who are involved in the liturgy during the school-term times are going to be away.

    • If people are going away for Easter, how do they view it as their community's central celebration: will they miss the community, will they be missed?

    • What opportunities are going to be provided, and by whom, for preparation and reflection; and do people see this as important?

    • Are there candidates preparing for baptism; how is the community involved in this; are there people designated to pray for the candidates?

    • Can particular talents be harnessed for all this lenten preparation? If so, what are they and who has them?

4. Repentance and reparation.

    • How does the community plan to celebrate reconciliation with God in Christ this Lent?

    • How will people be helped to experience this reconciliation?

    • What help do members of the community want to help them overcome bad memories of the confessional?

    • Will the community want to celebrate healing during this time?

•What plans have the community to make reparation to poorer peoples across the globe this Lent?

• How will lenten preparation take concrete forms in working for justice, peace, and reconciliation in our world?

5. Stock-taking of discipleship.

•What plans have the community to renew itself in prayer?

•What plans are there for fasting to give physical form to prayer?

• What plans have the community for generosity that will enhance the world, aid the poor, and provide resources for building the kingdom of justice, love, and peace?

• How will the community support these plans with special liturgies, groups, or inputs form other Christians?

• How can the community's liturgy be enhanced during this time?

6. Many clergy think that these are only questions for them, but it is the whole community that needs the time of renewal; and if any lenten activity is to have more support than just 'the usual suspects,' then the whole lenten agenda has to be owned by the community. The community can only own it if it has been offered to them as an option.

Prayers of the Faithful:
Some Notes on their Theology and Form

This prayer has become for many just a series of petitions without any form: it is just a place where people can make their own needs and intentions known, and has even been seen as the place where 'Novena Prayers' can be 'stuck into' the liturgy. In many places it is seen as the 'informal bit' of the liturgy where 'ordinary prayers' can be inserted amidst the formalities of the liturgy itself. This state of affairs has arisen partly because there is a genuine place for such informal spontaneity in this part of the liturgy, and partly since it is an element that can be omitted (as at a weekday Eucharist). The problem with any part of the liturgy that can be omitted is that in people's minds it is then silently transformed into something that is an 'optional extra' – and hence anything will do.

However, this is not the way the church has seen this prayer down the centuries (see the solemn intercessions in the Good Friday Liturgy), nor how it is to be understood today. The theology of the prayer (n 45), the structure it is to have (n 46), and the directions for its celebration (n 47) are all given in the *General Instruction on the Missal* (Missal, pp. xxix-xxx).

These can be summarised as follows:

It is not just the prayers of individuals or of a collection of individuals. This prayer is the prayer of the whole People – a single entity – which make up a church, and who as the People of God exercise a priesthood: they can stand before God and intercede for themselves, the universal church, and all humanity. The Christian people can do this because it acts in union with the great High Priest. So as in the Jerusalem temple the High Priest entered the Holy of Holies and interceded for all, so now we with Christ can come before the Father directly and express our needs. Therefore this is a priestly function of the whole assembly (not just the celebrant), which is made in Christ. Each Sunday this part of the Liturgy is a practical expression of the theology of the Letter to the Hebrews.

From this certain things follow: (1) since this prayer is made in Christ, its intentions can never be addressed to Jesus Christ; (2) since it is the priestly action of Christ, head and members, the petitions are addressed to the Father; and (3) since we are standing before the Father in the new temple which is the Son, no prayers to any other being – angel or saint – can be included without tacitly negating the basic belief of the church about its liturgy – therefore, the inclusion of a petition addressed to Mary or the recitation of the 'Hail Mary' is wholly out of place. If Mary or another saint is to be mentioned, it must be in the form of asking that we might imitate her or another saint in a particular way: e.g. 'Remembering that Mary's soul was pierced with sorrow, let us ask the Father to strengthen all who are suffering for their belief,' or 'Recalling today that St Joseph was a workman, let us pray that all who work may find in their labour a way to glorify the creator.'

Since it is a priestly act of intercession, it should be made standing: this posture can already be found in the liturgy of the earliest Christians when they were conscious that they were acting in the liturgy of the New Temple (see Mk 11:27 and 1 Tim 2:8).

Its structure 'as a rule' is petitions for (1) 'the needs of the church' – which can be seen as referring to the universal church, particular churches, and the church gathered on that occasion; (2) 'for public authorities and the salvation of the world'; (3) 'for those oppressed by any need'; and (4) 'for the local community'. Since the whole church includes the faithful departed, there is space in the prayer for a petition for the dead, and this is in line with the theology of the prayer, for Christ intercedes for the faithful departed as part of his/our priestly work (see Eph 5:14; and the second reading in the Office of Readings for Holy Saturday, Breviary, vol 2, pp. 320-322).

Since it is the whole people, as a priestly people, that make this intercession, the Missal says that 'it is desirable that the intentions be announced by the deacon, cantor, or other person.' If the intentions are announced by someone in presbyteral orders, then the general priestly character of the prayer is obscured and this prayer can seem to belong to those who are ordained priests through the Sacrament of Holy Orders. The role of the presiding presbyter of the eucharistic Assembly is to introduce the prayer – a statement addressed to the Gathering – and to conclude it with a collect addressed to the Father in which he acts as the president of the Assembly.

The actual statement of our needs ('let us pray for ... ') is not the actual prayer, but the address to the Father at the end of each intention: the 'Lord hear us.' On this, the actual petition, the Missal states: 'the congregation makes its petition either by a common response after each intention or by silent prayer.'

There are a series of sample Prayers of the Faithful given in the Missal on pp. 995-1004.

Second Sunday of Lent Year A

Note

In all three years, the gospel today is that of the Transfiguration (Matthew in A; Mark in B; Luke in C), and there are three themes running through the readings: (1) that God has established a covenant with his people which is realised in his making known to his people the Christ through a 'voice from heaven'; (2) that the disciples of the Beloved are 'to listen to his voice', and listening to the Word is presented as a key theme of Lent; and (3) that just as the Transfiguration strengthened the first disciples for the coming passion of their Lord (Matthew)/ Rabbi (Mark)/ Master (Luke), so our hearing about it today should strengthen us and make us more responsive to the whole Paschal Mystery which we are preparing to celebrate.

Introduction to the Celebration

As we continue our Lenten journey towards Easter, we recall today the experience of the first disciples on their journey to the first Easter in Jerusalem. On a high mountain they beheld for a moment the glory of Jesus and heard the Father's voice saying, 'This is my Son, the Beloved, he enjoys my favour, listen to him.' Let us now reflect that, forgiven our sins, we may behold Christ's glory in this celebration, and let us ask the Spirit to help us hear Christ's voice in our lives.

Rite of Penance

Option c iv (Missal, p. 393) is appropriate.

Opening Prayer

The alternative opening prayer fits more closely with the gospel.

Headings for Readings
First Reading
Abram – later to be called Abraham – whom we call 'our father in faith' listened to the word of God and obeyed it. His obedience to God's word was for him the key to holiness.

Second Reading
The Good News, the word of God, comes through Jesus Christ who has abolished death and proclaimed life and immortality to the world.

Gospel
As the disciples of Jesus we acknowledge him as the Beloved of the Father, and also declare that discipleship becomes a reality in our lives when we listen to him.

Prayer of the Faithful
Use the Sample Prayer of the Faithful n 5 (Lent 1), (Missal, pp. 998-999).

Eucharistic Prayer
Note that the Preface for the Second Sunday of Lent (P 13, Missal, p. 416) is a reflection on the significance of the gospel within the larger perspective of the Paschal Mystery – in order to make the preface stand out it is best to use Eucharistic Prayer II.

Invitation to the Our Father
We have heard the Father's voice identifying Jesus as his beloved Son. Now in communion with Jesus let us address the Father:

Sign of Peace
Jesus tells his disciples not to be afraid, and so standing here we can bridge the barriers that fear creates, and offer one another a sign of peace.

Invitation to Communion
This is the Son, the Beloved who enjoys the Father's favour, happy are we who now share his Supper.

Communion Reflection
The Preface of the Transfiguration (P50, Missal, p. 453) can be adapted to become a reflection for today:

The Father revealed his Son's glory to the disciples,
To strengthen them for the scandal of the cross.
His glory shone from a body like our own,
To show that the church,
Which is the body of Christ,
Would one day share his glory. Amen.

Dismissal
Prayer over the People n 15 (Missal, p. 382).

COMMENTARY

First Reading: Gen 12:1-4
This is the beginning of the stories of Abraham in Genesis. In the preceding verses Abraham has been linked by a genealogy into the second period of primeval history after Noah, then his family have set out for Canaan but settle in Haran. Now Abram enters the scene and will be the father of the nation and will be told to stake out the nation's land. Within the schematic history of Genesis this passage serves three purposes: first, there is a single nation as it has a single progenitor; second, that progenitor is linked to the crucial territory not by accident but by divine choice to which he was obedient; and three, there is a blessing on this nation so that however bad the present seems, it will be eventually victorious in that all the nations will eventually bless themselves by Abram.

Christians have, down the centuries, taken these stories as 'real' history and been interested in them from the perspective of 'Abraham our father in faith' (cf Rom 4:12). This became one perspective for viewing how non-Jews could become Christians, and later was used by missionaries to argue that other 'nations' were part of God's great plan in Abraham. This use of the Abrahamic motif is not jeopardised by the fact that Abraham is the mythic *pater patriae*, for the crucial point is that within the stories was the recognition that God is not a tribal deity but the creator of all. It is this perspective of the Genesis Redactor that testifies to the consistency of belief, not the story which he used to give it visible form.

Second Reading: 2 Tim 1:8-10
This text invites Timothy – who is presented as the ideal bishop – to be willing to endure suffering for the faith, conscious that God will give him strength. Then vv. 9-10 present a summary version of Pauline theology.

Gospel: Mt 17:1-9
Found in all three Synoptics (and possibly referred to in 2 Pet 1:16-18) the story of the Transfiguration was an important element in the early preaching by the Christians about the identity of Jesus: it forms a distinctive christology that would have resonated deeply with Jews as it incorporates so many motifs and memories from the Old Testament. While the details vary between the gospel writers, in each case the clear purpose of the event is to show links with the great persons of the existing covenant, and with the tradition of prophecy. Both Moses and Elijah are prophets and lawgivers, both suffer, both had a vision of the glory of God on a mountain (Ex 24:15 and 1 Kgs 19:9), and most significantly neither had a natural death and neither had a tomb.

Jesus is now the fulfilment of all this history and the similarities with the events on Mount Sinai show this as Jesus being the New Moses establishing the New Law. As the Mosaic epoch was inaugurated on Sinai, so now the Christian epoch was being inaugurated here, but would only be fully recognised after the resurrection.

HOMILY NOTES

1. This gospel challenges all the easy reductions that we make about Jesus: Jesus the inspiring teacher, Jesus the compassionate preacher, Jesus the friend of the poor. He is all these, but he is also the One who comes from the Father, the One who, we believe, was prepared for by the prophets, the One who stands at the centre of history. The transfiguration calls us to expand our religious horizons.

2. But the story has a curious comic element: the Lord of history is transfigured with these earlier prophets each side of him, and Peter wants to set up a campsite! This shows the intimacy with which the human and the divine are present in Jesus: he is with his friends and interacts with them; he is present in the glory of God. All handy distinctions such as 'high christology' versus 'low', or 'immanence' versus 'transcendence' are seen as too tied down to the limits of our understanding by this scene: God is always greater, and what we can say about God is what we can see in Jesus.

3. Preaching must not try to 'explain' this scene, nor even to 'expand' upon it. Rather the scene calls for our minds and imaginations to dwell on it and seek to make its 'picture' of the advent of God our own. So give a bit of the background that the first audience would have known, and then let imagination seek greater depths.

Second Sunday of Lent Year B

Note
See Year A.

Introduction to the Celebration
As we continue our Lenten journey towards Easter, we recall today the experience of the first disciples on their journey to the first Easter in Jerusalem. On a high mountain they beheld for a moment the glory of Jesus and heard the Father's voice saying, 'This is my Son, the Beloved, listen to him.' Let us now reflect that, forgiven our sins, we may behold Christ's glory in this celebration, and let us ask the Spirit to help us hear Christ's voice in our lives.

Rite of Penance
Option c ii (Missal, p. 392) is appropriate.

Opening Prayer
The alternative opening prayer fits more closely with the gospel.

Headings for Readings
First Reading
Abraham's obedience to God leads him to be willing to kill his son. It is this willingness to obey the voice of God that constitutes true sacrifice.

Second Reading
We follow Jesus who died for us, rose from the dead, and who now stands at the Father's right hand pleading for us.

Gospel
To follow Jesus is to know that he is the Son of the Father, to desire to listen to him in our lives, and to look forward to rising from the dead.

Prayer of the Faithful
President:
Fellow disciples, the Beloved is not visible to us as he was to Peter, James, and John; but we are in his presence, and he has given us access to the Father, so let us pray:
Reader (s):
1. For ourselves, that we will hear the word of the Beloved for our lives and listen to him.
2. For all Christians, that we may make known the presence of the Father's Beloved in the creation.
3. For all in public office, that they will recognise our duties to the creation – human, animal, vegetable, mineral – and respect it as the Father's handiwork.
4. For all who seek to hear the voice of God, that he will reveal his presence to them.
5. For those preparing for baptism at Easter, that they may encounter the Beloved in a new way.
6. For this community, that this Lent's discipline will renew us.
President:
Father, you identified Jesus our Rabbi as your Son, the Beloved, to the first disciples, so now hear us who are also his disciples, and grant us what we ask, for we ask for our needs through that same beloved Son, Christ our Lord. Amen.

Eucharistic Prayer
Note that the Preface for the Second Sunday of Lent (P13, Missal, p. 416) is a reflection on the significance of the gospel within the larger perspective of the Paschal Mystery – in order to make the preface stand out it is best to use Eucharistic Prayer II.

Invitation to the Our Father
Following the teaching of the beloved Son, let us pray to the Father:

Sign of Peace
In Jesus the beloved Son, we are made daughters and sons of the Father, so let us express this familiarity with one another by the sign of peace.

Invitation to Communion
The Beloved bids us to share in his supper, happy are we who hear that invitation.

Communion Reflection
See Year A.

Dismissal
Prayer over the People n 2 (Missal, p. 380).

COMMENTARY

First Reading: Gen 22:1-2, 9-13, 15-18
This story, in all likelihood, first appeared as a way of showing divine disapproval of human sacrifice, and in particular the sacrifice of youths, or indeed of children, by their parents. The prohibition of child-sacrifice might seem worlds away from the world of Genesis as traditionally understood, and indeed our world, but such sacrifice as a way of placating the divinities was common in many ancient societies as a 'supreme way' of gaining access to the divine and to cosmic power; and we should not forget that there are muti-killings of African boys still today, and indeed one has been recorded in the first years of the twenty-first century in London among African immigrants! This cautionary tale is a direct statement by God that he does not want such acts as child killing to be used as part of religious ritual. The story was then incorporated by the Redactor into the main Genesis narrative.

The reading is used in the lectionary as this has been one of the ways of presenting the death of Jesus: Abraham sacrificed (or was deemed to have sacrificed) his son; so too the Father sacrifices his Son. However, this whole approach depends on a patristic system of typological exegesis which is no longer part of our worldview and, moreover, in this case it was always flawed and tended to produce a picture of God the Father as someone who could only be placated with blood. Those who used this style of christology, e.g. St Anselm, always needed to hedge it round with so many qualifications that one wonders was the work worth the candle. It is best to ignore this reading in terms of saying anything about Christ – but it is still a valuable reading in showing that God does not want rituals of death and destruction.

Second Reading: Rom 8:31-34
This is one of the crisp summaries of his teaching that Paul provides from time to time. Those in Christ are acquitted and chosen.

Gospel: Mk 9:2-10
See Year A.

HOMILY NOTES

1. Each year at the beginning of Lent Christian agencies devoted to the relief of poverty or for the promotion of justice and peace invest a great deal of effort and resources to produce information packs on how relatively affluent communities in the developed world can assist in their work. This information is often treated as if it belonged to a parallel universe when it comes to announcing the lenten call to repentance. However, such a separation between doing good in the world and personal penitence and renewal is based on a distinction that is foreign to the Good News. If God offers us the possibility of new life through his forgiveness, then we on the earthly plane have to be offering new life to all who are deprived. One cannot wish to belong to the new creation brought about by Christ's death and resurrection without being concerned about those for whom this creation is full of suffering. Likewise, one cannot be sorry for personal sins without recognising that we may live within systems in soci-

ety or the economic world which are as much at odds with God's plan for the universe as a life of personal debauchery.

2. There is, of course, a strong lobby that believes that Christian faith is a purely personal matter, either on a purely 'spiritual' plane, or that its morality only has application at a personal level. Thus 'religion should stay out of politics' or 'church people should not meddle in economics' or Voltaire's desire that religion be confined to his wife, his servants, and his tradesmen so that there would be a suitable fear to keep them in check. However, Christian faith cannot accept these reductions, for our faith is that God is creator of all, of every single scrap of matter, and the whole creation is reconciled in Christ, and we are a people who must act morally at every level. Hence, the social teachings of the church, and the constant stream of teachings from the magisterium on social justice and development – summed up succinctly by Paul VI as 'development is another word for peace'.

3. In order to link these endeavours from agencies working for justice and development with the liturgy of the church as church – i.e. at the Eucharist – you could replace the homily today by going through whatever pack has been given out in your congregation this Lent. Noting the statistics it gives, noting how it is seeking to alleviate suffering, and repeating what it sees as the help it needs from people in the developed world.

Second Sunday of Lent Year C

Note
See Year A.

Introduction to the Celebration
As we continue our Lenten journey towards Easter, we recall today the experience of the first disciples on their journey to the first Easter in Jerusalem. On a high mountain they beheld for a moment the glory of Jesus and heard the Father's voice saying 'This is my Son, the Chosen One, listen to him.' Let us now reflect that, forgiven our sins, we may behold Christ's glory in this celebration, and let us ask the Spirit to help us hear Christ's voice in our lives.

Rite of Penance
Option c i (Missal, p. 391-2) is appropriate.

Opening Prayer
The alternative opening prayer fits more closely with the gospel.

Headings for Readings
First Reading
This is an account of a ritual for establishing a covenant – a deed of mutual trust. Now this ritual is being used to symbolise the relationship being set up by Abraham, our father in faith, with God: to enter into a covenant with God – as we have done at our baptism – is to invite God into our lives, listen to him, and to be willing to build his kingdom.

Second Reading
The longer form is preferable as there is little gained, save a minute of time, from reading the shorter version.
As Christians we must have a sense of perspective about the

value in our lives of material things: our homeland is in heaven. It is from God, not from our possessions, that happiness comes.

Gospel

Jesus, who is one of us as a human being, is also the one who is the beloved Son, reflecting the Father's glory: Jesus is one with us and Jesus is one with God the Father.

Prayer of the Faithful

President:

Sisters and brothers, Jesus took his disciples up a mountain to pray to the Father. He now gathers us here to pray to the Father, so with him let us make our needs known.

Reader (s):

1. That the whole church will listen to the words of the Chosen One of the Father.

2. That each Christian will have a deeper appreciation of the identity of the Christ after whom each of us is named, and a renewed energy to follow the Chosen One.

3. That all who seek the truth and all who seek for justice will be inspired and strengthened by God, that he will support them in their trials, and give them the reward of their labours.

4. That those seeking to join this community at Easter will be renewed by the Lord, and that we be given the strength to support them by prayer and fasting.

5. That as a community we will be united in following a way of life, that we will not make gods of food or wealth or power.

6. *Local needs.*

7. That the dead may be transfigured into copies of the glorious body of our Lord, Jesus Christ.

President:

Father, seeking to be disciples of your Son, the Chosen One, we now pray to you. Hear us, for we make these prayers as did the disciples Peter and James and John in union with Jesus Christ, our Lord. Amen.

Eucharistic Prayer
Note that the Preface for the Second Sunday of Lent (P13, Missal, p. 416) is a reflection on the significance of the gospel within the larger perspective of the Paschal Mystery – in order to make the preface stand out it is best to use Eucharistic Prayer II.

Invitation to the Our Father
The Father spoke from heaven to identify his Son. Now let us speak to the Father in heaven as taught us by the Son:

Sign of Peace
The Chosen One of the Father bids us to build the kingdom of peace. Let us offer each other a public pledge that we shall work for peace.

Invitation to Communion
Behold the Lamb of God, the Chosen One of the Father, happy are we who are called to his supper.

Communion Reflection
See Year A.

Dismissal
Prayer over the People n 6 (Missal, p. 380).

COMMENTARY

First Reading: Gen 15:5-12, 17-18
This is the account of the establishment of the basic covenant of Israel. The key point is that it is the divine guarantee of the Land and its extent, an extent which reaches from Wadi el-Arish in the north of Sinai to the Euphrates – an area greater than that ever ruled by any Israelite king.

All these earlier covenants have been read by Christians as serving as a way to highlight the 'new covenant' in Christ: Abraham obtained a land for his people, Christ obtained a dwelling in heaven for his people.

Second Reading: Phil 3:17-4:1

This is the conclusion of Paul's warning against false teachers (3:1-4:1) and the audience is to take Paul and the other Christians who follow the rule of life of the Christians as their model. If they do this they will be heirs to Christ and obtain their true homeland.

Gospel: Lk 9:28-36
See Year A.

HOMILY NOTES

1. Given that all the years use the Transfiguration story on this day, see the Homily Notes for Year A.

Third Sunday of Lent Year A

Note

The assumption of these resources is that the community is not celebrating the Rite of Christian Initiation of Adults process; if it is, then its liturgy will differ from that in the Missal (pp. 96-7) and have its own specific requirements.

Introduction to the Celebration

During Lent we reflect on God's loving mercy: he comes to us as sinners with the offer of new life, he puts no limit on those to whom he offers his love and forgiveness, and he bids us to do the will of the Father. Christ is offering us now his love and forgiveness. Let us recall that we are in his presence, let us recall our need, let us ask him to give us new life and pour into our hearts the Holy Spirit.

Rite of Penance

Option c ii (Missal, p. 392) is appropriate.

Headings for Readings
First Reading

This is a story of the Lord's care: in a hostile parched environment he provides his people with water: the Lord is caring, interested when he hears his people's pleas, and compassionate.

Second Reading

This is St Paul's great proclamation: Christ so loved us that he died for us while sinners – what greater love could there be – and he has poured into our hearts the Holy Spirit.

Gospel

It is best to read the longer form slowly and let people hear the whole story – which has a unified character in John – rather than the shorter form. If time is an issue, then use the longer form slowly and shorten the homily, because the shortened form leaves out several points that John wants to make.

This is the account of another event involving water when Jesus begins speaking with a Samaritan woman 'with a past' and who promises that anyone who worships the Father in spirit and truth with have the water that springs up to eternal life.

Prayer of the Faithful
President:

Sisters and brothers, we have listened to Christ's words and we desire to make them the pattern of our lives. Now let us ask the Father in Christ's name for all we need to be true disciples.

Reader (s):

1. That our worship of the Father, and that of the whole church, may be in spirit and in truth.

2. That those who are marginalised, despised, or down trodden may receive the help, support, and recognition that is due to every human being.

3. That this community may be cleansed of all that inhibits it in making Christ present in this area.

4. That all who thirst for righteousness may be satisfied.

5. That all who thirst for the truth may hear the Good News of the risen Christ.

6. *Local needs.*

7. That the dead who have worked in the field of this world, may reap the harvest of eternal life.

President:

Father, we seek to worship you in spirit and in truth, hear our needs and answer them in Christ our Lord, Amen.

Eucharistic Prayer
Preface of the Third Sunday of lent (P 14, Missal, p. 417).

Invitation to the Our Father
Trying to be the kind of worshippers that the Father wants, who worship the Father in spirit and in truth, let us now say:

Sign of Peace
Jesus has given us an example of overcoming the barriers that set people apart from one another. Let us show a similar desire to be at peace with others by offering each other a sign of peace.

Invitation to Communion
The Christ offered living water to the Samaritan woman; he now offers us living food and living drink. Happy are we who share this supper.

Communion Reflection
Although traditionally used as an individual's preparation for receiving communion, the 'Prayer of St Ambrose' (Missal, p. 1017) makes a suitable reflection after communion during Lent.

Dismissal
Prayer over the People n 24 (Missal, p. 383).

COMMENTARY

First Reading: Ex 17:3-7
Although this incident is usually read though the lens of its recollection in Ps 94 where it is the people testing God, in Exodus this is one of three tests which the Lord sets for his people to see will they trust in him, his care, and his rule. All three tests involve food or drink: water in the first test at Ex 15:22-7; food – quails and manna – in the second test at Ex 16:1-36; and water again here in the third test. The people must learn to trust in the Lord that he will provide, and that even in a hostile environment he will show his love to them. There is no hint of a divine rebuke for having complained and made their needs known, and in answer to their prayers, mediated by Moses, he feeds them with bread from heaven and water from a rock.

(Such water was prized for the fact that it was pure – literally mineral water – rather than water that was stale or stagnant in pools: the Lord's people are provided with the best when they turn to him and rely upon him).

Psalm: 94
This Psalm's perception of the same story is very different in approach to that of the author of Exodus. In Exodus the people do the right thing in calling on the Lord and being bold in the pain of their petitions; in the Psalm the argument in reversed: the very act of crying out is some sort of carping / complaining which a suitably trusting people would not even contemplate. In these two presentations of the same basic story we find illustrated the two enduring schools of theology on the nature of petitionary prayer and two long-standing styles in Christian ritual. That of Exodus is 'Lord, why me, hasten to help,' while that of the Psalm is 'let us accept the will of God in patience for he knows our needs already.' There is no answer to this tension in Christian prayer, but the neat juxtaposition of the first reading and psalm today illustrates that it is something worth thinking about and exploring.

Second Reading: Rom 5:1-2; 5-8
This is a fine piece of cutting and pasting together of six verses from the most problematic text on justification in Paul, the verses omitted are the ones that have caused the great difficulties since the theology of grace in the sixteenth century (a debate that seems to have ended) and on the source of original sin (a debate that is still lives on): since the problematic verses have been removed, it is best not to bring up the subject as this produces invariably more heat than light. However, as the lection stands it cannot be commented upon from a position of its possible meaning in Paul as several links in his argument have been removed. So it is best to read it as a statement by Paul that Christ so loved us that he died for us while sinners – what greater love could there be – and that he has poured into our hearts the Holy Spirit.

Gospel: Jn 4:5-42

By locating the story in Samaria John presents Jesus as the Saviour of the World: his mission is not restricted to the world that looks to the Jerusalem temple – a marked shift from the presentation of Jesus both in his focus and in the Samaritan reaction that we find in Lk 9:52-6. Three boundaries are broken in the dialogue: first, between Jews and Samaritans (the archetypal 'us and our sort' and 'them and their sort') so there are no structural limits on God's mercy; second, the dialogue is not even with a man but with a woman – even basic human divisions do not limit salvation – Christ's message even up-turns the most accepted customs of a society; and third, the boundary between the 'pure' and the 'impure' – the nice / not nice people in society – for we are to infer that this woman whom Jesus knowingly chooses to speak with is someone whom the text invites us to see as somewhat less than 'prim and proper'. All these boundaries are set aside, and then to complete this, even the old ritual and cult are transcended. For John's community there is no need for a specific cultic site – wherever the disciples assemble as a church there they can have access to the Father through Christ.

HOMILY NOTES

1. Lent is a time for the whole community to prepare to celebrate new life that arises from water: water which cleanses, renews, and enlivens. It is a preparation for a renewal by the whole community of its allegiance when we declare that 'we know that Jesus really is the saviour of the world' in the renewal of baptismal promises at the Easter Vigil.

2. It is also a time when we reflect on our trust and hope in God: the people were tested by God to see would they call to him as the saviour. How would we fare in that test, or is our trust and hope elsewhere?

Third Sunday of Lent Year B

Introduction to the Celebration

Lent is a time when we renew our minds and hearts by reflecting on what is revealed to us in Jesus Christ. Jesus is the one who came to do the Father's will, to establish the new covenant, and who shares his conquest over death with us all.

Rite of Penance

Option c i (Missal, p. 391-2) is appropriate.

Headings for Readings

First Reading

To be a daughter or son of God is to belong to a community with a way of life. Today we read one of the famous summary guides for the life of God's people which we often simply think of as a set of rules, 'the ten commandments'. This text has become famous as it is so old: it represents the rules needed to create a community in a small desert shepherding village, and reminds us that if we are in a covenant with God we need a suitable way of life to reflect that relationship.

Second Reading

For many people, the Christian Way – what the first disciples called simply 'the Way' or 'the Way of Life' – is stupidity, laughable, or impossible. Paul's reply is that God's foolishness is wiser than human wisdom.

Gospel

Jesus is the one devoured with zeal for the Father's house, whose risen body is our new temple: we exist within it, and so can know the Father.

Prayer of the Faithful

President:

My friends, gathered in Jesus Christ, our Temple, we have access to the Father. So as the people of the new and eternal High Priest, let us make our needs known.

Reader (s):

1. For the whole Christian people, that we may be a temple dedicated to God.

2. For all who trade and all involved with banking, that they may be conscious of the need for a just distribution of the earth's resources among the whole human family.

3. For us in this community, that this Lent may be a time of reconciliation and renewal.

4. For all who find faith difficult, that they may receive enlightenment.

5. *Local needs*.

6. For all who have died, that they may rise in Christ.

President:

Father, your Son was devoured with zeal for your house. Hear now the prayers of your household – for they are made in union with that same Christ, our Lord, Amen.

Eucharistic Prayer

Since the Preface for today is tied to the gospel for Year A, this Sunday provides an opportunity to use one of the Eucharistic Prayers for Reconciliation.

Invitation to the Our Father

Christ our Lord burned with zeal for his Father's house. Now let us address the Father as he taught us:

Sign of Peace

In Jesus, our High Priest, we are reconciled to the Father and one another. Let us celebrate that reconciliation.

Invitation to Communion
Behold the body of the Lord who died and rose from the dead, happy are we who gather with him at this supper.

Communion Reflection
Robert Herrick's poem, 'To keep a true Lent.' The text is in the Breviary, vol 2, pp. 612*-613* (Poem n 77).

Dismissal
Prayer over the People n 6 (Missal, p. 380).

COMMENTARY

First Reading: Ex 20:1-17
This is the famous set of commandments that had already received the name 'the ten commandments' or the 'the ten words' by the time of the composition of Deuteronomy (see 4:13). The list survives in two slightly variant forms in the Pentateuch: here and in Deut 5:6-21. (However, note that the way they are counted varies, and this variation has continued in Christianity with different churches having different ordinal numbers for the same 'commandment.')

What is important to note is that they are not presented as an abstract code of behaviour, but as the characteristic patterns of behaviour that identify the human side of a covenant with God. If God commits his love to his people, then this must provoke a response that enjoins certain ways of acting and which rejects others. Whenever the commandments are separated from this covenant context (as if they were a summary code of moral behaviour), then their actual content does not amount to a basic moral code or set of ethical guidelines. This, however, is the way they are usually seen – and the shorter form of today's reading invites such an approach – but that hardly shows them up as part of the divine plan and covenant; indeed it separates them from their religious context and reduces religion into being simply – as it is often perceived by non-believers –a morality conveyor for those who are incapable of ethical reasoning without a supernatural storyline.

The focus of the reading is that the Lord has established a relationship with a people, he has given them his name, he has
made them a nation, he has delivered them; in response, they
must have a way of living that is worthy of who and what God
has made them through his covenant.

Psalm: 18:8-11 (19:7-10)
This is a key psalm text on how Israel viewed the commandments: they are held up as a blessing for their perfection, clarity,
and truthfulness. In v. 9, where the JB reads 'the command', a
better translation would be 'the commandment' which brings
out more clearly the link with the first reading (see the NRSV),
and which shows how this psalm provides a lens through which
to view the whole notion of the Ten Commandments, which is
very much at odds with the perception of them as a 'Highest
Common Factor' for a religion-based morality. Living in the
way of the commandments is a way of living in the presence of
God.

Second Reading: 1 Cor 1:22-25
Within the context of the letter, this passage is an appeal to
recognise that something totally new has occurred in Jesus
Christ and that his people must place their trust in him. Paul
presents the desire for 'signs' (JB: 'miracles') as a refusal to trust
on the part of the Jews, while the gentile quest for 'wisdom' is a
desire for a religious system which guarantees everything to its
adherents. For Paul something far more radical is needed in
trusting the God of Jesus Christ, the crucified one.

Gospel: Jn 2:13-25
This is one of those few incidents which are found in all four
gospels: see the much shorter references to this event in Mk
11:15-17; Mt 21:12-13; and Lk 19:45-46 – and in the synoptics
there is no explicit theological interpretation as in John. Here lies
part of the problem of reading the text in the book, John, and
reading it in the liturgy during Lent. In the synoptics there is

only one journey to Jerusalem – when Jesus arrives for the sequence of events that culminate in his crucifixion – and this cleansing of the Temple is in the days just before the end. In John there are several journeys to Jerusalem and this event happens during the first of them, at the beginning of his ministry just after the Cana event. So although we read John, we read it in a synoptic time context for that fits our own liturgical time context.

In John this cleansing is presented as a first sign of the resurrection and shows Jesus responding directly to a command from God, rather than simply fulfilling an earlier oracle in the scriptures. Moreover, John wants to present this event in the life of Jesus (who is living in the Spirit) as parallel to the life of the church (which is living a new life in the Spirit as a result of the resurrection. From this context (the similarity between the life in the Spirit of Christ and the church), he can supply a prophesy which interprets the event: 'Zeal for your house will consume me' (Ps 69:10). This process of ecclesial interpretation – so clearly expressed in this passage – not only gives us an insight into the author's pneumatology, but shows us how his community viewed the relationship between 'the scriptures' (i.e. what we commonly refer to as the 'Old Testament') and their Christian identity: they as believers can now understand what was formerly obscure, and those earlier prophesies allow them to understand new depths in the Christ.

HOMILY NOTES

1. Today we see the value of having a lectionary with fixed readings: this gospel presents so many difficulties – and seems to have always done so – that if we were not required to read it, it is a passage that would be skipped and forgotten. So how can we approach this reading and then elucidate it so that a contemporary community is helped to draw nourishment from it?

   One way is to ask the community today to try to imagine what a small Christian community around 100 AD gathered at the Eucharist – shortly after John was written – would have made of it. (Incidentally, in all likelihood this was the ideal setting that the writer had in mind as the location when his text would be voiced and heard.)

2. By that time there was already a clear distinction between Christians and Jews. The two religions had become separate and there was a widening gulf between them. In this reading 'the temple' stands for the Jews, and Jesus represents the new group, the Christians. Yet there is both continuity and discontinuity between the temple and Jesus in this reading, and John knows that his audience must acknowledge this continuity, even if his community have already reached a position when they want to distinguish themselves from the Jews as clearly as possible.

    Jesus is the one who is in continuity with the temple. The temple is not something alien, different from him, his work, his message. The temple is not something belonging to some 'Old Testament God' (to use an expression often heard on the lips of Christians when they think the religious history of Israel is irrelevant to them), but his Father's house. Moreover, John wants to stress that all the work of Jesus is to be understood in terms of 'the scriptures' – a term that refers to what we call the Old Testament. From this perspective, Jesus is the one who purifies and perfects all that has been done in Israel. Jesus is the continuation of what has been revealed by the God of Israel.

3. Jesus is also the one who, from the perspective of his followers, transcends the temple, and so is in discontinuity with it. The new meeting place between humanity and God is not a building made by human hands with stones, metal, wood, but the living body of Jesus Christ who relates to us in his being a human being and who relates to the Father in his being the Son. Because his living body is the link that reconciles us to the Father, Jesus is the new temple and the final High Priest who connects us, God's people, with God. His risen body is at once with us when we gather in his name, and radiant in the Father's house.

4. Jesus inherits, perfects, and transforms the whole history of
    Israel, he endorses the covenant made by God in 'the law and
    the prophets', yet at the same time he stands in judgement
    over them and establishes in his death and resurrection the
    new covenant. It is this paradox of continuity and disconti-
    nuity that stands behind many phrases used in modern stud-
    ies of Jesus, such as 'Jesus – a marginal Jew.' This paradox of
    continuity/discontinuity would have been felt more deeply
    by an early community than it is felt by us today.

5. John stresses that the disciples only understood the events in
    the temple after the events of Easter, when they knew in faith
    that Jesus was risen, but he was no longer with them. Thus
    his congregation – or we today for that matter – are not in
    'second position' compared with those who saw Jesus in the
    flesh: Jesus is only really known by those who celebrate his
    death and resurrection. This activity of celebrating the death
    and resurrection, whether for the community in AD 100 or
    today, is the sharing of his body as real food and his blood as
    real drink (see Jn 6:55) in the Eucharist.

6. Christ, then, is the one who when on earth could know peo-
    ple 'through and through'. So now, with the Father, how
    much more does he know of what each of us is made?

Third Sunday of Lent Year C

Introduction to the Celebration
In today's gospel we will hear again the urgent call of the Christ to change our way of life, to repent, to begin a new relationship with God our Father. This repentance is part of his Good News as it begins the process of being his ministers building the New Creation. As we begin our Eucharist, let us recall our need to renew our lives and ask that this Eucharist will strengthen our resolve to lead renewed lives.

Rite of Penance
Option c iv (Missal, p. 393) is appropriate.

Headings for Readings
First Reading
In this reading we hear of the call of Moses: God saw his people's distress and sent them a liberator. We Christians see this a shadow of what has happened in Jesus Christ: God has seen our need for reconciliation and sent the Christ as our liberator and the reconciler of all creation.

Second Reading
In this reading Paul makes a comparison between Moses and Christ: the Israelites were baptised into Moses and thus were delivered from slavery in Egypt; we are baptised into Christ and delivered from slavery to sin.

Gospel
All are called to repentance: to begin a new life.

Prayer of the Faithful
Use the Sample Prayer of the Faithful n 5 (Lent 1), (Missal, pp. 998-9).

Eucharistic Prayer
Since the Preface for today is tied to the gospel for Year A, this Sunday provides an opportunity to use one of the Eucharistic Prayers for Reconciliation.

Invitation to the Our Father
Option C, Missal, p. 508.

Sign of Peace
Each of us needs the forgiveness and mercy of God; each of us needs to be merciful and forgiving to those we meet. Let us offer each other a token of mercy and forgiveness.

Invitation to Communion
Behold the Lamb of God who in his mercy takes away the sins of the world. Happy are we who stand around his table.

Communion Reflection
Although traditionally used as an individual's preparation for receiving communion, the 'Prayer of St Thomas Aquinas' (Missal, p. 1018) makes a suitable reflection after communion in Lent.

Dismissal
Prayer over the People n 4 (Missal, p. 380).

COMMENTARY

First Reading: Ex 3:1-8, 13-15
This is the immediate preliminary – the call of Moses -- to the deliverance of Israel from Egypt, the exodus, which was the central event in the memory of Israel, and forms for Christians the background to one of the central ways for understanding the Christ-event (the Paschal Mystery).

Over the centuries there has been great attention to the divine name revealed in this passage: YHWH interpreted as 'I am who am' (*Ego sum qui sum*) particularly by Christians who have treated it as a proposition in ontology. However, the importance within the text is that the people do not only know there is a God, but have been given by him his name: therefore they can call him by name. Although in practice, reverence meant that the practice grew up of not sounding out those four consonants (Y-H-W-H) but rather using 'Lord' as the address.

Second Reading: 1 Cor 10:1-6, 10-12
This reading is two snippets from a section of the letter (10:1-13) where Paul makes a comparison between the Israelites during the Exodus and the church in Corinth: the church in Corinth must not be over-confident or the same fate will befall them as befell many of the Israelites. As the text is edited in the lectionary it hardly can be given any meaningful interpretation, and so it is best not to draw attention to it.

There is no agreement as to what Paul was referring to by his reference to 'the Destroyer' in v. 10. It is probably a reference to the special exterminating angel sent by God to those houses in Egypt that did not have the lamb's blood on their lintel (see Ex 12:23).

Gospel: Lk 13:1-9
This passage is found only in Luke and the incidents (those killed by Pilate and the fall of the tower) are mentioned in no other ancient source. The passage shows the compassion of Jesus, but this compassion does not exclude the need for repentance. The message is that we humans do not know when the hour of judgement will come and must be ready – it appears to restate the words 'you do not know the day nor the hour' found in the other synoptics (Mk 13:32; Mt 24:36 and 25:13). The parable is then a parable of crisis: repentance is urgent and there is no time for procrastination.

HOMILY NOTES

1. During Lent the themes of repentance and reconciliation are very much part of the liturgy. These two themes are intimately intertwined: repentance is possible because God is offering us reconciliation, and being reconciled with God involves the commitment to a new style of life and building the new creation made available in Christ. The call to repent is the call to turn over a new leaf, to begin afresh; reconciliation is the fruit of this turning around and links the personal new beginning with the work of the whole body of Christ to establish the kingdom of peace and love.

2. What is brought out in today's gospel is that the possibility of repentance is continually offered to us. But the actual act of turning is a painful process of evaluating our lifestyle, actions, and attitudes – a process far more painful that just the trip to the confessional.

3. In preaching today, the task is to locate the personal act of turning within the whole process of reconciliation inaugurated by Christ who reconciled the world to God through his suffering and death. Carrying on this process is the task of the whole body of Christians, our 'ministry of reconciliation' (cf 2 Cor 5:18). Reconciliation, at this level, is the establishment of new creation – and it links evangelisation, and work for peace and justice in the world. Thus, almsgiving has always been seen as a key element in personal penance. This larger process of reconciliation must also find a parallel at the individual level: a search for a greater personal integrity, a willingness to forgive wrongs done to us, and a willingness to renew our relationships with those around us. Neither the larger process nor the individual process can be carried out alone: the Christian message is not one of individual salvation independent of the other humans and the community, nor is the church simply a movement for a better world.

4. These two themes have to be preached together, and equally both have to be present in communal celebrations of reconciliation during Lent.

Fourth Sunday of Lent Year A

Note

This Sunday is traditionally known as 'Laetare Sunday' from the opening word of the introit: *Laetare Ierusalem* ... (Be joyful O Jerusalem ...) (Is 66:10-11), which has been retained as the entrance antiphon in the current Missal (p. 104). And, on account of these opening words, it is often asserted that this Sunday has a special tone of joyfulness which distinguishes it from the rest of Lent. This is not really the case, but simply a whole approach being built on one word, the 'laetare' of the old introit. One way that this supposed special 'joyfulness' was, and in some places still is, manifested was in the choice of vestment colour: the violet of Lent was replaced by 'rose' vestments. The value of this was that it contributed to making this Sunday stand out in a special way and added another note of variety. So if they are available there is no reason why they should not be used. It is all these little variations within the themes of the liturgy that adds texture to liturgical time. However, do not set too much store on this particular variation, for while subtle changes in vestments / uniforms and their colours are always meaningful to the structures that wear them (be they clerics or military officers), and a few dilettantes who are experts in these matters, for most people they have little or no effect. Indeed, in a liturgy which does not give any prominence to the opening antiphon, in contrast to the pre-1962 introit, it is doubtful whether making any comment on this day as 'Laetare Sunday' or its antiphon is of anything but antiquarian value.

A far more important aspect of today is that it is Mothers' Day – or as it was formerly known 'Mothering Sunday' – which is one of those days that is in the ritual calendar of our society in a way that most liturgical days are no longer. Mothers' Day – with much help from the greeting card industry – is one of the fixed days for many people which has that special stressed and exceptional character which is the essence of ritual time. If you ask the average urban congregation whether they spend more time and effort thinking about Mothers' Day or Good Friday, I suspect that the former will easily outstrip the latter in significance in their ritual year. This situation presents us with an opportunity and a challenge. The opportunity is to re-possess this theme of Mothers' Day by showing that it originates because this is the Fourth Sunday of Lent, and to make it part of today's celebration – this is one day when people are expecting the liturgy to be special, and that 'specialness' is that the liturgy is linked to a feast they are actually celebrating outside of the context of the liturgy. The challenge is that today must be celebrated as a Sunday of Lent, and not simply made the religious aspect of Mothers' Day. We should note that there is no agreement as to how this day originated as Mothers' Day. The most commonly given reason was that there was a custom in some parts of England for people to visit their mothers on this day, or that servants were given a day off to visit home on this day, but that still does not answer the question of why this day was chosen for this practice. The other theory as to its origins is that on this day there was a visit to the cathedral or mother church, or that it refers to the old epistle for this day (found in the pre-1970 missal and in the Book of Common Prayer) which was Gal 4:22-31 (a reading not used in any year in today's lectionary) which has a reference to Jerusalem as 'our mother' at v. 26. In all likelihood it was this reference, when picked out in preaching, that gave rise to the practice of people visiting their mothers, and this, in turn, became the origin of our Mothers' Day.

Introduction to the Celebration

Today we reflect on our belief that Jesus is the chosen one of God, he is the anointed one, he is the Christ. He is the one who gives sight to our blindness, the one who restores our health, the one who reconciles us to the Father. Today, because it is the Fourth Sunday of Lent, is also Mothers' Day when we give thanks to God for our mothers, we make a special fuss of them, and think of how much we owe to them for their care and love. So let us begin by thinking of all of God's blessings to us: for giving us loving mothers, for giving us his love and forgiveness, and for sending us Jesus the Christ.

Rite of Penance
For the times we have not fasted, Lord hear us.
For the times we have not prayed, Christ hear us.
For the times we have not given to the poor, Lord hear us.

Headings for Readings
First Reading
This is the story of the selection and anointing by Samuel of David as the future king of God's people. For us Christians that was only a shadow of things to come: Jesus is the one anointed by the Father as our king and saviour.

Second Reading
We are the people who now live in the light, for Christ is the one who calls us from the sleep of death and shines his light upon us.

Gospel
Today the shorter form of the gospel is to be preferred as it gives the story of the blind man in a more succinct form.
Christ miraculously gave sight to a man born blind; that man stands for each of us, for Christ has given us all eyes to see the world as God's creation, to see the way to our heavenly home, and eyes that can one day see God face to face.

Prayer of the Faithful
Use the Sample Prayer of the Faithful n 6 (Lent 2), (Missal, pp. 999-1000).
Or for intercessions with a Mothers' Day theme, see Year B.

Eucharistic Prayer
Preface of the Fourth Sunday of Lent (P 15), (Missal, p. 418).

Invitation to the Our Father
The Christ has given us eyes to see the glory of the Father and words with which to address him, so let us pray:

Sign of Peace
On Mothers' Day let us pray that all families may enjoy peace and happiness, and let us offer this prayer by showing our desire for peace with one another.

Invitation to Communion
This is the Lamb of God, the chosen one of the Father, he who gives us sight, he who reconciles us. Happy are we who share in his supper.

Communion Reflection
Use the central section of today's preface as a reflection. Begin 'Jesus Christ came among us as a man' and continue to 'we are reborn as your adopted children.'

Dismissal
Prayer over the People, n 10 (Missal, p. 381).

COMMENTARY

First Reading: 1 Sam 16:1, 6-7, 10-13
This text forms within 1 Sam the 'authority'/'mandate' and background for all that will be said about King David: he is the anointed one, and whether what he did later was in accordance with God's law or not, those events have to be seen against his vocation as the chosen leader of the people.

Within today's liturgy the key message of this reading is that God had sent his anointed to Israel in David (chosen over all the more obvious candidates); so too has God chosen Jesus as the one who will lead his new people.

Second Reading: Eph 5:8-14

The author locates the drama of humanity using the duality of light and darkness: each represents a particular way of living, and the baptised are those who have chosen the way of light and with it obedience to the Father's will. This message is then reinforced by the quotation from an early baptismal hymn: 'Wake from your sleep [i.e. come out of darkness], rise from the dead, and Christ will shine on you.'

Today is one of those exceptional Sundays in the liturgy where the imagery and theme of both the Second Reading and the Gospel come into (within the liturgy's interpretation of the texts) perfect alignment.

Gospel: Jn 9:1-41 (shorter form: Jn 9:1, 6-9, 13-17, 34-38)

The shorter text focuses the listeners on one of John's great 'signs' that reveal the Christ is the light of the world. The blind man encounters Jesus and thereby received his sight. The blind man is to be interpreted as standing for every human being, for each person is in need of having her/his blindness healed. However, the blindness is not fully removed, nor faith complete, until the second encounter with Jesus when the healed blind man returns to him and confesses that he is willing to believe in him. Then Jesus reveals another aspect of his mystery: he is the Son of Man, the one sent to restore creation to God's plan.

HOMILY NOTES

1. Light and darkness together form one of the great images by which human beings seek to describe both the universe and the mystery beyond the universe. The contrast of light/dark is basic to our existence as day and night, and with light is the association of life, goodness, understanding, and hope; while with darkness there is fear, evil, and confusion. We are beings who live and learn in the light and through sight. Here too lies the sorrow of blindness and the horror that it instills in many: a horror so great that in Jesus's time the fact that God could let someone be born blind was thought of in terms

of God deliberately punishing the blind person (see the longer form of the gospel). Likewise, it is only when we think of how we crave light and sight and vision, that we can see the force of calling Christ the 'Light of the World'.

2. Because the dark and the light alternate with one another in the physical world, many people think of moral light and darkness similarly changing places, as if light and darkness are in a continual struggle. We glibly hear lines such as 'the eternal struggle of good over evil' or speak about 'the ups and downs in human affairs'. But Christians see Christ as having won a victory over the powers of darkness once for all – we are called to be children of the light. But this victory can now only be seen in our hope: in glimpses, in a glass darkly, in shadows, in images. We will only see the fullness of the light in the life to come.

3. As we approach Good Friday we should recall that this is our victory celebration for Christ's expensive victory over all that is dark, wicked, evil, and life-destroying in the universe. Today we read John's sign that Christ is the Light; next week we shall read in John that Christ is Lord of life, and on Good Friday we shall read John's passion when he declares that his work is accomplished – and in John's image of Good Friday there is no darkness: Christ conquers the powers of darkness and scatters them in clear daylight. This celebration of Christ as light will reach its climax in the liturgy in the opening moments of the Easter Vigil when we shall gather around the light in the midst of darkness, and then sing the praises of the risen Christ as our light.

4. But the victory of light demands that all who belong to the light be themselves lights, enlighten other areas of a darkened world, and oppose all that takes place in the dark or which darkens the lives of people. One cannot belong to the light and be indifferent to human suffering. One cannot simply shrug shoulders when one hears of policies that oppress people in the developing world. One cannot ignore falsehoods or dishonest dealings in any organisation, be it one's

workplace or community or in the church. One cannot rejoice that the light of the creation is but a shadow of the true Light of the universe, and then happily ignore the destruction of the created environment.

5. The desire for Light is great and universal, and the call of Christ the Light of the world is the call to come into the Light. But in a world where there is still much darkness, to be a child of the light is to take on the burdens and crosses of discipleship.

Fourth Sunday of Lent Year B

Note
See Year A.

Introduction to the Celebration
We have gathered here as God's holy people, and we are God's work of art, created in Jesus Christ to live the good life as from the beginning he intended us to live it. So we have to be both thankful for his mercy, and sorry for our failures to live life in that way. Since this is the Fourth Sunday of Lent, today is Mothers' Day – the day when we thank our mothers for all they have done for us, and also express our sorrow for any way we may have hurt them.

Rite of Penance
Option c vii (Missal, p. 394-5) is appropriate.

Headings for Readings
First Reading
This is the story of the people of God being scattered from Jerusalem and exiled for their infidelity, but even after that God still renewed his covenant and moved the heart of a pagan king to rebuild their temple and let them return. No matter how far we feel exiled from God, he is seeking us out.

Second Reading
Who are we as the Christian community? This reading's answer is: we are God's work of art created in Jesus Christ to live the good life as from the beginning he intended us to live it.

Gospel
The human mind thinks of God primarily in terms of almighty power and so fears God as 'punishment' and 'vengeance'. We

Christians must take our image of God from Jesus – what we say about God is what we see in Jesus – and Jesus says: 'God sent his Son into the world not to condemn the world, but so that the world could be saved through him.'

Prayer of the Faithful
If Prayers that do not focus on mothers are appropriate in your assembly, then see Year A or Year C.

President:
Today we make our prayers to the Father, conscious that this Sunday of Lent is also Mothers' Day when we show our thanks and love to them through a series of special actions and celebrations. But we should recall that many people who do not take part in the life of the church are also celebrating their mothers as one of the gifts in their lives (although they may not think of their mothers as gifts from God) and for them this is just a secular feast day – so let us also keep these people who are celebrating today in mind as we pray.
Reader (s):
1. For all the mothers in this gathering, that God will grant them health, happiness, and long-life.
2. For all the mothers in our society, that they may be given joy through this day of celebrations.
3. For all the mothers who cannot care for their children, that the Lord will give them strength and comfort.
4. For all mothers who live in poverty and cannot feed their children, that our hearts will be moved to help them this Lent.
5. For all mothers who are estranged from their children, that they may find reconciliation.
6. For all mothers who see their children suffer though lack of medicine, education, or from prejudice, that we might be inspired to work for justice and peace.
7. That all who celebrate this day may have their eyes opened to see the mystery that is beyond all the goodness in this world, and that they may be inspired to come to worship our creator.

President:

Father, we are your work of art and we have gathered here to thank you for all our gifts, and especially today for your gift of our mothers. But we also stand in need of your continuing love and help, so hear our prayers and grant them through Christ our Lord, Amen.

Eucharistic Prayer

Preface of Lent II (P9, Missal, p. 412) is appropriate along with Eucharistic Prayer III which recalls the prophesy of the perfect sacrifice which links with the gospel.

Invitation to the Our Father

As God's work of art, created in Jesus Christ to live the good life as from the beginning he intended us to live it, let us pray now to God our Father:

Sign of Peace

The Father has established peace with us through sending us his only Son. Let us celebrate that peace and reconciliation now with one another.

Invitation to Communion

Behold the Lamb of God, he who is lifted up so that everyone who believes may have eternal life in him. Happy are we who believe and gather at his table.

Communion Reflection

The thanksgiving prayer of St Thomas Aquinas (Missal, p. 1020) picks up many Lenten themes.

Dismissal

Prayer over the People n 4 (Missal, p. 380).

COMMENTARY

First Reading: 2 Chron 36:14-16, 19-23

One event seared itself into the memory of the Jewish people and left its mark of every bit of their religious writings that has come down to us: the destruction of Jerusalem, the destruction of the Temple, and the deportation to Babylon at the time of Nebuchadnezzar. In their later memory, and so in the way they wrote their history, that was the defining moment: everything could be located as either before or after that event (see for example Mt 1:11-12, and 17). And it is this perspective that lies behind this part of 2 Chronicles. Part of the reason why this was shocking was the fact that it resulted in the people being without a temple, and this is something that we today find great difficulty in appreciating. We use the word glibly and very often as a metaphor or as a theological shorthand: but having a temple was central to the religious imagination of many people in the ancient near east. Think of it like this: when some early Christians wanted to say how important to them Jesus was, the way they expressed it was that he was their temple. We miss the force of this for we think of a temple just as a big church or the Jewish equivalent of St Peter's basilica. But the temple was much more: it was the place where God was present among his people, there they could encounter him, there they could experience his protection, and because the temple was there the whole land was ordered, filled with God and fruitfulness, and things were as they should be.

If the temple were destroyed this was far more than a calamity such as a great building being destroyed, it was tantamount to God moving away from his people, abandoning them. Why? It must be on account of their sins. Here we meet a basic human response to tragedy: it is God punishing and so we must have deserved it. It is the response here, it was the response down the centuries when plague struck Christian communities, and we hear it still today from fundamentalists who speak about AIDS. This is a view of God, and of the freedom that he gives the universe (i.e. bad things can happen to good people), that Christian faith – despite frequent lapses – has always challenged; and it is a major weakness not only of 2 Chronicles but of much of the historical writings in the Old Testament. However, there is something else happening in this passage: even if God punished, then their was still hope in the words of the prophets (prophesy is now being interpreted as one of the presences of God), and that after a period of purification God would restore the people. Indeed, God is in such overall control of history that he could even use the will of a pagan king to effect his will. Needless to remark, this notion of God as the 'almighty puppet master' has appeal to many fundamentalists today, but it is clearly alien to the tradition of Christian belief. So in any comment on this reading, more attention needs to be paid to what is defective in the author's theology than to its strengths.

Psalm: 136
This is the classic psalm expressing the centrality of the deportation and loss of the temple in later generations' memory. The psalm helps us appreciate the importance of the temple and its place at the centre of the whole of society.

Second Reading: Eph 2:4-10
This passage sets out what the author (someone writing in the theological footsteps of Paul) sees as God's grand scheme for the universe: you who were once dead, are now alive again in the Christ. The author sees the work of Christ as being at the very centre of the whole of history, his work is to bring the whole of creation to its divinely intended destiny.

Gospel: Jn 13:14-21
This reading combines two strands of John. First, vv. 14-15 related to John's use of the Son of Man theme: when the Son of Man is exalted it will mark a turning point for Israel, for it will be at that point that they will be called to return to the Law and start afresh a life with God. Second, vv. 16-21, this reading focuses on the significance of God sending his only Son to give life (that Jesus is the only Son is only found here and in the prologue to

John). This life is explained in terms of the ethical imagery of light/darkness. Christ is the Light of the World (see Jn 1:9; 3:19; 8:12; 9:5; 11:9; and 12:46) while darkness represented human evil deeds. Anyone who 'lives by the truth' is someone who lives a righteous life and thereby shares in the life of the Christ. 'Doing the truth' is an ethical life following the law of God, not simply an intellectual activity of believing.

HOMILY NOTES

1. As Lent progresses the focus of preaching has to shift from the discipline of Lent itself to that for which it is a preparation: the event of Holy Week and Easter. Therefore, part of the role of preaching in Lent is that it should be a catechesis for the events of the forthcoming festival, so that people can appreciate their significance within the whole Christian year, and can take part in those liturgies with greater understanding. Of all the reforms of the liturgy that took place in the twentieth century, the reform of Holy Week (beginning in 1955 and being progressively reformed until 1970) has probably had the greatest impact on Catholic theology, yet these reforms have had probably the least impact at community level. While the building may be filled for midnight Mass at Christmas, the Easter Vigil usually only attracts a moderate number and has often been relegated in status to that of an ordinary vigil Mass for Sundays with a few extra readings; while on Good Friday many people see little difference between attending the Stations of the Cross and taking part in the Liturgy of the Passion.

2. That being the case, one way to catechise the whole community is to focus now on the days of Holy Week and examine the liturgy of one of the days in detail using the question 'what will we be celebrating on Holy Thursday?' as the focus of your explanation.

3. If you choose to go down this route, then today you could begin by 'going through' the liturgy of the Mass of the Lord's Supper on Holy Thursday. See the notes for that day for some pointers.

Fourth Sunday of Lent Year C

Note
See Year A.

Introduction to the Celebration
Today we recall that we are the beloved children of the Father and we will read the parable of the 'Prodigal Son': he left his father, squandered his inheritance, and yet was welcomed back with open arms: this is the welcome that our heavenly Father offers each of us when we turn to him. For most people the basic experience of this kind of love is the love that they receive from their parents – and this is a thought that is present in the minds of many today since we are also celebrating Mothers' Day. The origins of this custom of remembering mothers on the Fourth Sunday of Lent are obscure, but it touches a basic theme of our humanity and it is a celebration that is now far wider than the church. So as we begin our Eucharist let us reflect on the love we have received and continue to receive from God our Father and from our mothers, and let us thank God.

Rite of Penance
For the times this Lent when we have not fasted, Lord hear us.
For the times this Lent when we have not prayed, Christ hear us.
For the times this Lent we have not given to the poor, Lord hear us.
(These may seem inappropriate on 'joy-filled' Mothers' Day, but we have to keep in mind that we are celebrating the lenten season, not 'The Eucharist for Mothers' Day'.)

Headings for Readings
First Reading
This is the story of the first Passover of the people in the land of Canaan and it was remembered as the first act of thanksgiving

of the people on reaching freedom in their own land. It is established a covenant: they were in the land as they were his people. This first Passover in Canaan formed part of the memory of all, including Jesus and his disciples, who kept the Passover.

Second Reading
Here Paul tells us that to be a Christian, that is someone who is baptised, is to be a new creation, and that we Christians are Christ's ambassadors.

Gospel
Today we read the parable of the prodigal son – a name derived from the fact that the son who left his father's house was 'prodigal' or 'generous' with his inheritance with those he met in a 'distant country' spending 'his money on a life of debauchery'. However, the lesson is that the father was prodigal with his love in welcoming home his wandering son. So too the heavenly father is generous with his love towards us when we choose to return to him.

Prayer of the Faithful
Use the Sample Prayer of the Faithful n 6 (Lent 2), (Missal, pp. 999-1000).
Or for intercessions with a Mothers' Day theme, see Year B.

Eucharistic Prayer
Today is a suitable occasion to use one of the Eucharistic Prayers for Reconciliation.

Invitation to the Our Father
Our heavenly Father rejoices in our coming to him, so let us pray:

Sign of Peace
As the prodigal son was welcomed with joy, and as the Father in heaven welcomes us, so let us offer reconciliation and welcome to those around us.

Invitation to Communion
Behold the Lamb of God who was the guest at table of sinners
and tax collectors, now he is our host at this table. Happy are we
to be his guests.

Communion Reflection
The Lord ate at the table of his friends Martha, Mary and
Lazarus,
The Lord ate at the table of Zacchaeus the tax collector,
The Lord ate at the tables of sinners, outcasts, and the unwanted,
The Lord ate with all who welcomed him to their tables,
The Lord ate with his disciples and showed them how to be
thankful as they gathered at his table.

Now we have eaten at the Lord's table,
Now we have thanked the Father in this sacred meal,
Now we are united from sharing one loaf and drinking one cup,
Now we are ministers of reconciliation charged with building
the New Creation,
Now we must be Christ in the world.

Dismissal
Prayer over the People n 4 (Missal, p. 380).

COMMENTARY

First Reading: Jos 5:9-12
When Joshua was written – and it was certainly at least six hun-
dred years after the events it purports to narrate – one of the
book's purposes was to describe an ideal time in the history of
the people in the Land. It was a time of national unity, a time of
good leadership, a time of military success, and a time when the
Law was observed with purity. So the writer imagines that the
people began life there with a perfect Passover: they had now
been delivered from slavery in Egypt, and now were able to
carry out the Lord's command to keep the Passover with produce of their own land.

From the perspective of our liturgy, this reading shows the place of the Passover in Jewish memory: it was the festival that thanked God for his deliverance. This helps us to appreciate its place in the minds of pious Jews such as Jesus and his followers who looked back to these texts as the portrait of an ideal time. That such texts were valued in the milieu in which Jesus grew up is beautifully illustrated by the fact that his parents named him after Joshua (in Greek *Iesous*; and commentators in Greek and Latin have always used the formula Jesus ben Nun for Joshua to distinguish him from the Christ).

Second Reading: 2 Cor 5:17-21
This is part of a larger unit within this rather fragmentary letter. 5:11-6:10 is concerned with bringing together two ways of seeing the Christ-event: firstly, as reconciliation of humanity with God; and secondly, Christ as the new creation, the Last Adam, who draws all who believe in him into this new creation. So here Paul presents his resolution of how reconciliation takes place within the new creation. The old creation is that which needed reconciliation; the new is the fruit of reconciliation and is far more wonderful than simply a restoration to humanity's original position. Moreover, those in Christ have a ministry of reconciliation and it is in this sense that they are 'ambassadors'. 'Ambassadors' is a faulty translation and would be better rendered as 'We have been sent on Christ's peace mission' – in the same way that diplomats are sent to 'peace talks' as a 'mission'. The implication is that we are sent out to establish his peace and reconciliation in creation, and thus usher in the new creation which is Christ.

In this passage Paul uses the phrase: 'the ministry of reconciliation' which reads in the Vulgate: *ministerium reconciliationis* (v. 19). Within the western church, this passage never played any part in the discussions of sin after baptism, the nature of penitence, or after the appearance of the sacrament of penance in the twelfth century in any of the practice or theology connected with it. The dominant theological motifs were those of the powers of decision given to Peter: Mt 16:19 and Jn 20:23. However, in the later 1960s this passage from Paul began to exercise a crucial in-fluence among those theologians who were developing the new theology of penance that finally appeared in the *Ordo Paenitentiae* of 1973. In the Introduction to that rite there is a stress on the image of reconciliation and on this being a ministry of the whole church and not simply a 'power' derived from 'the power of orders'. This has had two important effects: first, the term 'sacrament of reconciliation' has begun to gain currency; and second, the formula of absolution is no longer simply de-claratory but has a prayer-element which highlights the ministry of reconciliation existing within the whole church: 'God the Father of mercies through the death and resurrection of his Son has reconciled the world to himself' – this is a theological per-spective very similar to today's reading; 'and sent the Holy Spirit among us for the forgiveness of sins' – this too is Pauline but from within a very different theological framework to that used in this reading; 'through the ministry of the church' – this is the liturgical acknowledgement within contemporary Cathol-icism of Paul's 'ministry of reconciliation'. However, there are two serious weaknesses within this position at the moment: first, while the theology of the rite has moved towards this notion of a church-wide ministry of reconciliation, this is not reflected in the liturgy where the actual act of reconciliation is still expressed as a judicial act on an individual – this is probably inevitable as it is the legacy of an earlier theology, but it has created an unre-solved dissonance between group celebrations of reconciliation and 'individual confession'. Second, the ministry of reconcilia-tion has been seen principally in terms of the same territory as the former sacrament of penance: a way of dealing with individ-uals' sins after baptism. However, the Pauline ministry of recon-ciliation is far wider than this in scope and involves the whole of creation: so apart from individuals' sins, it involves the structural sins existing within our societies, it involves the whole justice, peace, development agenda, and it involves care for the envir-onment. It is as all embracing as the reconciling work of Christ, which is shared with us as his appointed legates; its scope is nothing short of establishing a new creation. It is within this larger picture, that we must locate the sacramental rituals of reconciliation.

Gospel: Lk 15:1-3, 11-32
This beautiful story has as its intention showing why Jesus is not spending his time with the righteous but sinners – in Luke it is a reply to the initial anger of the Pharisees who are enraged that Jesus welcomes sinners and eats with them. Eating together is a basic way of establishing community.

HOMILY NOTES

1. One of the nastier sides of people who are devoted to religious practice is a certain smugness and a certain elitism: we are the people who have taken all the rules and regulations and duties seriously, and we are superior to those who have ignored them. So we find the Pharisees in that situation, we find the elder son in that mode, and many of us may find ourselves there more often than we would like to think!

2. However, Jesus radically challenges this smugness: he offers table fellowship to all sorts, breaks down the carefully marked out borders of religious purity, and will even take the insults that arise from this. He is the one who will be a guest at every table that make him welcome, and at the table where he is host, all who seek the kingdom are welcome.

3. This new relationship is based on the fact that the Father's coming kingdom is not a judgement for the punishment of those who have ignored the Laws, but one of forgiveness and reconciliation. It is the sick who need the physician; it is the outcasts that need welcome at the Lord's table. This is a fact that raises awkward questions about the canonical practice of excluding people form the eucharistic table because of 'irregularities' in their lives: the more life is irregular the more one may need the spiritual food of the Eucharist – and if someone with an 'irregularity' is seeking to eat at the Lord's table, then who should say they are not welcome to benefit from its food?

4. Moreover, we do not sit at the Lord's table because we deserve it: the Lord's bounty is greater than our deserts – who can claim such a life as to be worthy of a place at his table? The welcome we receive is a product of the Lord's own nature: the father was overjoyed to see his son, and so prepared the feast; so God welcomes us.

5. The elder son seems to have a good point; so do the Pharisees who were zealous for the Law, and many among us will no doubt feel this in our bones. But the Good News is that Jesus has shown us that God's love is greater than our imaginations; and the extent that we still resent God's generosity is a measure of how far we have to grow to have in us the mind of Christ.

Fifth Sunday of Lent Year A

Note

In many Eastern rites the day before Palm Sunday is known as Lazarus Saturday, thereby locating another scene from the gospel in what is its 'historical' location: Jesus arriving near Jerusalem just before the first Holy Week. In the west this episode, only found in John, is used on this day in Year A only. In the gospel, John presents the episode as a 'pattern' which is to alert the audience, just prior to the beginning of the final week (starting in Jn 12), that the Christ is the one for whom tombs are not a barrier. He uses the story in a way somewhat analogous to the way a 'trailer' is used to announce a forthcoming film. So today's liturgy presents the structure of the disciples' perception of the Paschal Mystery prior to the event itself: sadness, becoming consolation, becoming hope, and ending in joy. However, the complex timing (a pattern being shown beforehand so that what happens later will be understood) inherent in John is thereby transferred to the liturgy. Therefore today there is a theme of Paschal joy, even though we are still in Lent.

Introduction to the Celebration

Today we recall how Jesus was told of the death of his friend Lazarus and how he restored him to life. In this we have a 'trailer' of the whole message of Christian life: to believe in Jesus Christ is to be brought out of the tomb of death, freed from what binds us, and offered eternal life. Let us now reflect on our own need to be freed from sin, our own need to have burdens lifted, and our own need to begin life afresh.

Rite of Penance

Option c vii (Missal, p. 394-5) is appropriate.

Headings for Readings
First Reading
The prophet looks forward to when the Lord will give new life and will give his Spirit to enliven the people. We Christians see this new life with the Father coming through the death and resurrection of Jesus and the gift of the Holy Spirit. In baptism we are reborn to a new life and the Holy Spirit comes to dwell within us.

Second Reading
The Spirit raised Jesus from the dead, and he is now within us giving us divine life. To be a baptised people – which is what we are – means that we live in Christ through the Holy Spirit.

Gospel
The shorter form of the text should be avoided as it destroys the narrative sequence that John desires.
We believe that Jesus is the Christ, the Son of God, the one who was to come into the world: he is the resurrection and the life.

Prayer of the Faithful
President:
Fellow disciples, as believers in the resurrection let us make our prayers to the Father.
Reader (s):
1. That we, and the whole People of God, may testify to the resurrection in our life styles and in our hope in the face of adversity.
2. That there may be peace, respect for life, and reconciliation among all peoples.
3. That we may be unbound of our sins during this holy season and begin life anew.
4. That those who are despairing may experience the hope-giving word of life.
5. *Local needs.*
6. That all who have died may know, with Lazarus, the new life to which Christ calls them.

President:
Father, our Saviour thanked you for hearing his prayer for those who stood around him. Hear us now for we too stand in the presence of Jesus, your Son. Amen.

Eucharistic Prayer
Preface of the Fifth Sunday of Lent (P 16, Missal, p. 419).

Invitation to the Our Father
Jesus thanked the Father for hearing his prayer so that those with him would know that the Father would also hear us, therefore with confidence we pray:

Sign of Peace
Christ calls us to a new life. Let us begin the new way of living with a sign of peace to one another.

Invitation to Communion
The Lord calls us to new life and bids us begin it by sharing together in this supper. Happy are we to be here.

Communion Reflection
The central section of the preface for today ('As a man like us ... to lift us up to everlasting life') makes an ideal reflection – its richness is passed over all too quickly when it is prayed at the beginning of the Eucharistic Prayer.

Dismissal
Blessing n 5 [The Passion of our Lord] (Missal, p. 369).

COMMENTARY

First Reading: Ezek 37:12-14
The whole of ch. 37 of Ezek is the vision of the Restoration of Israel that will come about at the close of the age in which the prophet believes Israel is living. The first section of that vision is another vision: that of the dry bones (vv. 1-14). However, focus-

ing on that vision of the dry bones is of little help in interpreting today's reading which only uses the last three verses of that vision. Here we have a good example of a specifically Christian interpretation of 'the scriptures', which is achieved by highlighting the exact verses that are seen to help us interpret the Christ-event. In effect, we have the scissors being used as an instrument of hermeneutics – and this exact piece of editing has a long tradition in our reading of Ezekiel. Within a Christian context, this piece of text about the dead the rising from their graves is to be interpreted as Christ who at his death opens the graves of the righteous who are waiting for him (see, for example, Mt 27:52), and thus 'harrows hell' (see the Second Reading in the Office of Readings for Holy Saturday for how important that theme was for early Christians, or look at an eastern icon of the resurrection which shows the dead being led out from their graves by the risen Christ who has the gates of the underworld under his feet). Likewise the reference to putting 'my spirit in you' is seen as referring to the gift of the Holy Spirit who is given at Pentecost and in baptism (see today's second reading for the significance of this theme to early Christians). These verses of Ezekiel were of major importance in the first decades of Christianity when they provided one focus (as in Mt 27:52) by which the death and resurrection was understood and preached.

Second Reading: Rom 8:8-11

This is part of a larger unit (8:1-39) within the overall plan of Romans. The key point of this unit is that the life of the Christians, both individually and as a body, is not lived apart from God, but in the Spirit – Christians have life because they live in the Spirit – and the destiny of those who live in the Spirit is to live in glory. The reading elaborates that larger message in terms of being dead on account of sin, and being restored to life in Christ in whom the Spirit dwells. Because the Spirit dwells in Christ, and we are united to Christ in faith, the Spirit communicates life to us.

Gospel: Jn 11:1-45

In John there are a series of 'signs' (*semeia*) that reveal the deepest identity of Jesus, and the raising of Lazarus (a narrative only
found in John) is the greatest of these signs. In the sign of healing
the man born blind (last Sunday's gospel), Jesus is portrayed as
the 'light of the world'; now he is shown as the 'life of the world'.
It is worth noting the subtle difference between this Johannine
miracle of raising from the dead and the miracles found in the
synoptic tradition. In Mk 5:22-23 and Lk 7:11-16 Jesus is presented
as being able to give life back to someone who has just died;
John deliberately wants Jesus to be away for some time after the
death of Lazarus: he only arrives when the death has taken place
several days before, the tomb is sealed, and the decay of death is
already well underway. Jesus being able to give life back to
Lazarus in these circumstances is a demonstration that he holds
all life in his hand, he is Lord of life, and his power reaches even
into the tombs. The tomb is not a barrier for him – a theme of
great importance for early Christians for how they presented the
resurrection.

HOMILY NOTES

1. What does believing in the resurrection mean in our lives?
    The temptation is to make an abstract statement about what
    one 'believes' will happen post mortem, but Christian faith is
    much more than this: it requires that we live as people who
    have been raised to new life and for whom death and the
    tomb are not the end. To believe in this sense is not to assent
    to a set of statements beyond what can be proven by some
    sort of empirical observation, but to adopt a lifestyle that em-
    bodies the assumption that God is calling each of us to new
    life. Christian believing is, therefore, something that requires
    constant practice. This means that I cannot believe, in my life
    and living and activity, that God is offering people new life
    while being indifferent to human suffering, pain, poverty, or
    oppression.

2. Many people dwell at length on the 'difficulties of believing'

and wondering whether they can assert as true or false some statement such as 'there is life after death' or 'there is a continuation of personal identity after death' or whether or not there is 'a cycle of reincarnation'. But these speculations are quite irrelevant to the gospel – and its challenge of taking the difficulties of the lifestyle of resurrection do not attract the same attention as the abstract 'difficulties of believing'. The gospel writers all believed that there was a caring and involved God, and an individual identity that survived death, and that there was an 'afterlife' – none of these beliefs are an issue in the gospels, they are simply assumed. What they proclaim as new, and as revealed in Jesus, is that God offers a covenant of forgiveness that cannot be destroyed, and the invitation to follow the way of holiness is to live life after the pattern of that forgiving and constant divine love. As we are loved, so we love; as we are forgiven, so we forgive; as we receive mercy, so we must be merciful, and as our lives are transformed, so we must help to transform the lives of others. What we wish for from God on the heavenly plane, must be that which we transmit to others on our own human plane. So to believe in resurrection, and in the resurrection of Jesus, is to live such a life of hope: if I look forward to mercy and fullness of life from God, how can I not show mercy to someone in need; if I look to the transformed life of heaven, how can I not want to transform the lives of those suffering on earth? Here lies a difficulty: is it easier to engage in disputes over abstract beliefs, or to engage in almsgiving and be really committed to a just world – perhaps one where one has to take a fall in one's own standard of living so that others can have a better life? Believing in resurrection is not 'yippee, I'm saved by Jesus', but something very costly: I believe I am given new life; I must act on that as the fact in my life and convey new life to others.

3. On the other hand, we have to note how we often live within a pattern of attitudes that are equivalent to denying resurrection. The gospel today shows up several of the main forms of

non-belief. First, attitudes of despair in the face of human suffering deny resurrection. Here are some of the standard expressions of despair: 'Why bother when it will make no difference,' or 'There is nothing to be done,' or 'It is too late.' We must act with hope and one only needs hope when one is in the presence of adversity. Second, attitudes of it 'all being too much bother' when faced with wickedness or falsehood or discrimination. There are always difficulties – 'there will now be a smell' – but until we confront them as a community which is strengthened by God's grace, those difficulties will only grow. Not that there is any guarantee that in confronting them we will succeed or that we will not encounter suffering – our symbol is a cross – but that in confronting the difficulties we look forward to the final victory of the Christ. Thirdly, attitudes of fatalism: the assumption that there is really no hope of things changing, and that there is no possibility of conversion. Lazarus is already in the tomb, dead and bound. Such an attitude of fatalism denies the forgiving nature of God, and denies that there can be goodness in his universe.

4. It is in confronting each day the suffering, darkness, and wickedness that can engulf us that we show that we believe that Jesus is the resurrection and the life, the one who has shattered all that oppresses us. Belief in resurrection may seem one of the most abstract aspects of our religion, yet nothing makes such concrete and material demands on us.

Fifth Sunday of Lent Year B

Note

The readings for Year A may be used as an alternative to those given for Year B. If this is done – and the Year A readings are far more accessible: good reason for using them in most settings – then see Year A for the appropriate notes and comments.

Introduction to the Celebration

As we approach Holy Week and our celebration of Christ's mystery, his death and resurrection being our opening to the fullness of life, today we read in the gospel that anyone who loves his life, loses it, any anyone who hates his life in this world will keep it for eternal life. This challenges each of us to recognise just how different a vision of life we must have if we are to serve and follow Jesus Christ.

Rite of Penance

For the times we have not fasted, Lord hear us.
For the times we have not prayed, Christ hear us.
For the times we have not given to the poor, Lord hear us.

Headings for Readings
First Reading

The prophet looks forward to a new covenant between God and his people when the Lord himself will speak and forgive sins. We believe this desire was fulfilled in the coming of the Son of God among us: Jesus the Anointed One.

Second Reading

Jesus is he who established the new covenant through his obedience in suffering, and so can give eternal life to all his people.

Gospel
Jesus is the one who confronts and overthrows 'the prince of this world,' who is glorified by the Father, and who beckons each of us to follow him.

Prayer of the Faithful
Use the Sample Prayer of the Faithful n 6 (Lent 2), (Missal, pp. 999-1000).

Eucharistic Prayer
Preface of the Passion of our Lord II (P 18, Missal, p. 421) is appropriate as it picks up several of the themes in today's gospel.

Invitation to the Our Father
The Father heard the prayer of Jesus and glorified his name, so now let us too pray to the Father:

Sign of Peace
We are called to follow Christ who made peace through his death on the Cross, so we are called to be peacemakers. Let us begin this work afresh now by giving a token of peace to each other.

Invitation to Communion
Behold the Lamb who draws all men and women to himself. Happy are we who gather at his table.

Communion Reflection
The 'Prayer to our Redeemer' (Missal, p. 1020).

Dismissal
Blessing n 5 [The Passion of our Lord] (Missal, p. 369).

COMMENTARY
First Reading: Jer 31:31-34
This oracle belongs to a section of Jeremiah that is a collection of

disconnected oracles (31:23-40) which were originally distinct units and have been gathered together here with the theme that they will console Israel running through them. This particular oracle looks forward to a re-united people (the division into the Kingdoms of Judah and Israel will be no more) and there will be a new law 'written on the hearts'.

This is the only place in the entire Old Testament where there is reference to a 'new covenant' that will supercede the covenant made in the past. As such, it was a central text for the first Christians who picked upon it to express the new relationship established in Jesus between God and his people. So we see it being used by Paul in 1 Cor 11:25, by Luke at 22:20 ('This cup which is poured out for you is the new covenant in my blood' which has, in turn, become one of the central texts of Christians through the use of the phrase 'new covenant' at the Eucharist), and by the author of Hebrews (8:8-12).

As Christians have read this text, the Eucharist now being celebrated is that which Jeremiah looked forward to, and this reading can thereby form a lens through which to view the assembly gathered today for the Eucharist. The assembly are those in whom God has planted his Law, they are identified by their sharing in the new covenant, and they have their iniquity forgiven.

Second Reading: Heb 5:7-9
It was in Christ's perfect obedience to the Father that he learned to be our perfect High Priest, who can intercede for us and present us to the Father. That Jesus learned this through suffering shows that he is the merciful High Priest for just as he shares human suffering, so his fellow humans share his glory.

Gospel: Jn 12:20-30
John presents this discourse as taking place at the 'now' which is the decisive moment in all human history: judgement is being passed on the world and the people of the light are being gathered around the Son of Man. The text is part of John's portrayal of Jesus as the perfect High Priest who defeats humanity's enemy and gathers a scatted people by his death.

HOMILY NOTES

1. Follow the same strategy today as last Sunday (Fourth Sunday of Lent, Year A) and 'go through' the liturgy of the Easter Vigil. See the notes for the vigil for some pointers.

2. If you highlight the significance of the Mass of the Lord's Supper (last week) and of the Vigil today, then the significance of the Liturgy of the Passion on Good Friday may be explored briefly on Palm Sunday.

Fifth Sunday of Lent Year C

Introduction to the Celebration

Today we read one of the most moving passages in the whole of the gospels: a woman, a wife who had been caught committing adultery is brought before Jesus so that he can be tested to see if he will 'do the right thing' and say she should be stoned. Jesus asks for the man who is not a sinner among the accusers to begin the stoning, and the group melts away one by one. Jesus does not condemn the woman for her conduct, but challenges her to begin life afresh. This is the challenge Jesus puts to us each Lent: begin life afresh and let others begin life afresh after they have hurt us. Let us reflect that we are all sinners, we are in need of mercy, and we need to make fresh starts.

Rite of Penance

Lord, you gave us an example of fasting, forgive us our self-indulgence.

Lord, you gave us an example of prayer to the Father, forgive us our neglect of prayer.

Lord, you gave us an example of care for the poor, forgive us our selfishness.

Headings for Readings

First Reading

There is no need to recall the past when we encounter the Lord, he is 'doing something new': there is always the opening to a new life.

Second Reading

Christian life is like a race: we strain ahead to what is to come, for the prize is union with God in Christ Jesus.

Gospel

A wife, guilty of a crime whose punishment is stoning to death, is brought to Jesus: Jesus will not condemn her, for with him the past is dead and we are freed to begin a new life.

Prayer of the Faithful
President:

My friends, the mercy of God knows no bounds, so now in union with Jesus our High Priest let us stand in the presence of the Father and intercede for ourselves and all humanity.

Reader (s):

1. That our teaching of the Way of Christ may be life-giving.

2. That we may avoid self-righteous condemnation of others.

3. That all in public office may pursue justice rather than retribution.

4. That justice systems seek to rehabilitate wrongdoers rather than satisfying lust for vengeance.

5. That the hearts of all in prison, especially those awaiting execution around the world, may be moved towards the good.

6. That everyone in this community may experience the forgiving voice of Christ this Lent.

President:

Father, your Son shows us that mercy is your very nature. Hear us now and grant our petitions through Christ our Lord, Amen.

Eucharistic Prayer

Preface of Lent I (P 8, Missal, p. 411); or one of the Eucharistic Prayers for Reconciliation.

Invitation to the Our Father

Option c (Missal, p. 508).

Sign of Peace

Peace can flourish after we have let the past be past, so let us express our forgiveness to one another, and offer a sign of a new beginning in our relationships.

Invitation to Communion
Behold the Lamb who forgives us and bids us to begin a new life
of holiness. Happy are we who are called to his supper

Communion Reflection
Robert Herrick's poem, 'To keep a true Lent.' The text is in the
Breviary, vol 2, pp. 612*-613* (Poem n 77).

Dismissal
Blessing n 5: The Passion of Our Lord (Missal, p. 369).

COMMENTARY

First Reading: Is 43:16-21
This passage from Second Isaiah, an oracle in the form: 'Thus
says the Lord', is very corrupt and that limits our ability to understand it, and indeed it can even be heard in the English translations when 'rivers in the wild' has been put in brackets.
However, that does not mean that we cannot extract a meaning
from the text which has coherence. The Lord is presented as recalling one great redeeming work which he did for his people,
the exodus from Egypt, and then promising that there will be in
the future an even greater divine act of deliverance. This next act
will be beyond all that the people can imagine. This will be
something completely new and mark a new beginning in history.
This has consistently been interpreted as the Christ-event, bringing about the final age of history, being a new exodus, and being
beyond all the expectations of Israel.

Second Reading: Phil 3:8-14
This passage contains what is, probably, Paul's most concise
statement of his 'doctrine of justification' in verse 9. Being at
rights with God he now recognises as not the result of his own
work in keeping the Law, rather perfection comes from the gift
of Jesus Christ which he has through his relationship with
Christ. The perfection he now has is from God and is based on
his involvement with Christ. When in this passage we hear of

'knowing' the danger is that we think of this as conscious awareness or as intellectual understanding; when Paul uses the word
he thinks of 'knowing' as deep personal involvement that em-
braces every aspect of life. We make jokes as '"knowing" in the
biblical sense'. Well, this is a case where we must understand
knowing in 'the biblical sense' and realise that what is intended
is far more embracing than simply comprehension of some religious detail. Moreover, this 'knowing' entails, according to this
passage, a sharing in Christ's sufferings as well as in his resurrection.

It is worth noting that the word 'rubbish' (*skubala*) is a very
weak translation although it is now found in almost all English
versions. 'Rubbish' is too polite; the word's meaning is 'excrement' (the Vulgate rendered it more robustly as *stercora*). Its key
value here is that it represents all that Paul is definitely finished
with and wants to dispose of absolutely. Excrement is not just
surplus rubbish, one wants to get rid of it and forget is as just so
much 'excrement'. This image of the past being absolutely past
he also addresses in the race image at the end of the passage: the
past is behind, and all his focus is upon what is ahead.

In today's liturgy there is an important common theme between this passage and the gospel: both assume that Jesus
stands between the past and the future, the past is gone totally,
and the future is the only realm of concern. Moreover, while
these two readings present the decisive moment of the entry of
Jesus Christ into individual lives and marking a gulf between
past and future, the first reading explores a similar breach between the 'now' and a definitely different future at the larger
level expressed in terms of the whole people and the cosmos.

Gospel: Jn 8:1-11
This little section of the four gospels has caused so much trouble
to those who produce copies of New Testament (both in manuscript and in print), to exegetes, to theologians, and to preachers
that it has had a special name for more than a millennium: the
pericope de adultera. One thing upon which all modern scholars

are agreed is that it is not part of the original gospel of John. However, if it is not part of John's original text, it has all the signs of a genuine piece of oral tradition that circulated within the memory of the communities, especially in some churches in the West, and which subsequently embedded itself in the canonical text either at this point in John or after Lk 21:38. However, while normally such matters of textual criticism are irrelevant, here they add more complexity. Usually, omissions in manuscripts or silence among commentators indicates simply non-knowledge of the piece of text (e.g. no Greek Father or theologian before the twelfth century comments on the text, while the few Latins who do so usually provide a 'health warning' before doing so), but here we know that there were deliberate omissions of the text and positive refusals to preach on it before women lest they take it as indicative of the non-seriousness of adultery, (note that until the sixth century adultery, along with murder and apostasy, were seen as the greatest sins), or that men might think it subversive of good order in society. So what have we got? We have a genuine piece of early Christian tradition that was not included by any of the four canonical evangelists, but which survived and which became frozen in writing. Even though it was not too much to the liking of many, so convinced were some communities of its expression of genuine Christian tradition that they – after the appearance of the notion that genuine tradition was confined to the four canonical gospels – sought a location for the pericope either here or in Luke. The pericope's message being at once so startling that the communities believed it represented, somehow, a core message of Jesus, yet at the same time being so shocked by it that they were embarrassed by it.

It is worth noting that there is no question in the pericope that the woman was innocent: she is guilty of the crime as charged having being caught *in flagrante*. The notion that Jesus saved an innocent woman is a far more palatable message; and sometimes this notion of 'vindicated innocence' even creeps into scholarly exegesis. Equally, there is no notion that she has to make 'satisfaction' as found in many medieval and modern theologies of the sacrament of penance which employ a processual model of reconciliation (the *processus iustificationis*), i.e. of contrition, confession, satisfaction, and absolution. The woman is not addressed about the past in any way.

HOMILY NOTES

1. The gospel does not invite a narrative, a story, or a single 'message'; rather it demands we reflect on some very common attitudes. The homily could point out some or all of the following 'points'. However, beware of 'watering down' this text as has happened so frequently: it is deeply disturbing of many attitudes common among Christians and non-Christians alike.

2. This is a text that many over the entire history of Christianity have wanted to disappear – quite literally – in that they chose not to copy it in their copies of the gospels. Moreover, when it was included in the gospel text – it is now part of the standard Greek text and has been present in the Latin text since the beginning – it was the incident that preachers and writers commented upon least frequently, at least in the period before AD 1000, and it has only become popular with preachers in the last century or so. The reasons for these objections and hesitancies are usually quite openly stated in the traditions: first, it is socially disruptive as a husband must have leverage over his wife's sexuality – and even if there is no stoning, then there must be some threat and warning; second, what husband could find Christianity an acceptable religion when this gives a wife such licence – there must be a price for adultery or it brings the 'gospel' into disrepute; and thirdly, this seems to present Jesus as 'soft on sin' or on the need for penitence – this hesitation has been to the fore in recent centuries.

3. This text therefore raises the whole issue of what is Christianity about: is it a social control system or the Way to the Father who is forgiveness?

4. This text presents a male-centred universe: it is a wife who is accused, it is men who pass judgement, and it is men to see their rights/property misused. The copyists, writers, and preachers who ignored the text or were hesitant about it, all viewed the text from the standpoint of men and the control of society. It reminds us that Christianity emerged in a male-centred world and has in many ways colluded in that world. Just recall that no man could be stoned for adultery. This is a worldview we see challenged by Jesus – in him there is no male or female (cf Gal 4:4) – yet as our history of hesitance over this text shows, this is a part of Jesus' proclamation that most preachers (men) have been most unwilling to take on board.

5. We have to acknowledge that men and women are not treated equally in the tradition of Christianity.

6. One writer, St Ambrose (c. 339-397), did tackle the text but his concern was with the question of the death penalty: if only one without sin can throw the first stone, then can we inflict the death penalty? He recognised, even then, that the call for the death penalty arose from desires for revenge rather than for rehabilitation. This is still a major issue today where many Christians still support the notion of an eye for an eye and do not see that the Christian vision of morality is based on love, forgiveness, and helping people to start anew rather than on retribution and retaliation. So the text challenges us to see if we really believe in the call to repentance and renewal of Jesus, or whether that is something we only want for ourselves and those with us.

7. There is no mention in the gospel of the notion of penitential reparation – she is not told to do penance but to sin no more. This silence has troubled many Catholic theologians down the centuries, especially since the Council of Trent. Do we reduce the new life that God offers us into a system of 'paying back' and clearing bills: this reduces reconciliation to a set of laundry lists and bills, and makes the divine mercy into a banking system of tabs and repayments.

8. The story exposes a basic message of the Christ: the divine mercy is greater than law.

9. Note the absolute death of the past of the woman before Jesus: 'Go and sin no more.' Much to the annoyance of many Christian writers there is not even a 'stern moral word' for the woman. Needless to say writers do not suggest that Jesus was wrong on this count; they rather suggest that in the copies to which they have access there might be something omitted! The story presents us with a past that is wholly over, and the only thing now is to start afresh. This absolute death of the past is good news.

10. In a world where people are unable to let the past be past but want to continually re-open old wounds and seek retribution and retaliation, then any new vision/life is strangled at birth. This raises many 'points to ponder':
    - are desires for vengeance present in our lives?
    - how present is a desire to moralise?
    - do we see religion as a 'control system'?
    - do we see God as mercy or the final reckoner dealing out retribution?
    - do we project a God-image of a 'dealer of retribution'?
    - how willing are we to let others let go of their past?

The Passion in the Liturgy:
The demands of celebration

Twice each year, on Palm Sunday and Good Friday, the reading of the gospel becomes visibly a liturgical event in its own right. On these occasions the dramatic reading with several voices may replace the solitary tone of the deacon/priest. Yet in most parishes this is not only a missed opportunity to do something which can enhance the whole celebration, but actually becomes something counter productive. At the very least it can become a shambles of voices coming in off-cue, lines-lost, or confused mumbling ('Whose line is it?' 'Whose that voice supposed to represent?'). At worst it can send hidden signals to the congregation about how we view the passion, the Jews, and the ministry of proclamation.

Involvement

The traditional format of using several voices to read the passion has much to recommend it: the unusual style picks out this reading as special; and given that the Passion or Palm Sunday is the longest Sunday reading of the year, the variety of voices makes the story easier to follow and less monotonous. However, some points should be noted about reading it in this way. First, if people are 'following it' in missalettes/booklets, then they are not listening but engaged in a kind of semi-reading/semi-listening that has the disadvantages of both activities, without the particular benefit of either. So we should dispense with the missalettes and let the whole story be listened to: listening to the sacred stories is a primary liturgical action. Being without missalettes has other advantages. First, the periodic rumble as people turn pages is removed; and second, the congregation are not watching out for their 'bits' when they join in as the various 'crowds' and instead of a clear shout 'Crucify him! Crucify him' we get a ragged volley of voices that just makes noise. The 'crowd' parts are best done by a specific chorus who come in on cue in harmony.

This suggestion may seem to fly in the face of the praise-worthy desire to involve people in the liturgy: giving the congregation 'some lines' seems to 'get them doing something'. However, while giving everyone 'something to do' is the correct strategy in running a school concert, when applied to these readings it fails to grasp the essential dynamics of the event. Storytelling is a linear process by which one group reveal the tale to another part of the group who act as the audience: the involvement of the audience is that they listen and provide an audience for the tale. Cultural anthropologists looking at sacred narratives and cycles of mythology make a crucial distinction between the 'active transmitters' (the storytellers) and those who, already knowing the tale ('passive transmitters'), occasion by their presence this recital of the sacred events. A related experience is still part of our culture: the devotees of the soap opera are drawn into the story, but they are there as an audience, not as actors. The closer parallel to our involvement in the liturgy through listening is to be found in observing those who are listening to a radio play: the whole message is carried in the sound of voices – and if you disturb someone who is following such a play or soap you will know they are involved! This involvement of listening may seem too passive, but note the apparent contradiction in the folklore term 'passive transmitters': it is the fact that there are listeners to the gospel that creates the need to recite it.

Three voices?

In liturgical books the Passion is still set out in three voices (N[arrator], J[esus], O[ther]) and a C[rowd]. This is simply a small development of the older three voice model of Christus, Synagoga, and Narrator. That in turn was a product of the tridentine High Mass liturgy of the priest, deacon, and subdeacon as the only lectors. This three voice model is, apart from being a hangover from the legal concerns of a now abandoned rite, quite useless: in a media conscious age, there must be as many voices as characters – imagine a radio play like 'The Archers' with just three voices! However, there is a far more serious problem with just using three voices whereby, unintentionally, a perverse message is sent to the congregation: when the 'other voices' are lumped together (i.e. the synagoga) this is based on a dated theology of the passion as Christ-versus-the Jews (referred to as 'the synagogue'). In this the Christ is represented as the one who suffers because of the Synagogue, while the narrator is the neutral observer. All that is linked to his suffering and death is thereby brought together and laid at the foot of the Jews.

Anti-semitism
We can see part of the thinking beneath the three-voice reading of the passion by noting the significance of naming one of the voices 'synagoga' – 'the synagogue.' The word has a wholly negative connotation in the Latin tradition: in exegesis and preaching throughout the Middle Ages it was used to represent all that was opposed to Christianity and all those who wilfully rejected the truth. In many writers, for example the highly influential Isidore of Seville, any opinion expressed against the teaching of the church is that of the 'synagogue' which is linked to the body of the Devil (*in partem diaboli*) in the same way that the Christian is part of the body of Christ. At a later date the tag 'the synagogue of Satan' became a cliché and its implication was complete: the meetings of the Jews were conventicles of Satan. When this many-voice reading of the passion emerged in the liturgy, the choice of the name synagoga for all the speaking parts was an obvious one. The popular preaching theology of the passion was that Christ was handed over into the hands of his enemies, and thus into the hands of his chief enemy, the Devil. The Devil working through his cohorts – primarily the Jews – now set about his destruction and they buzzed about him like bees (cf Ps 118:12). The image is of a feeding frenzy by mad beasts whose voices we occasionally hear as they cannot bear the words of the Christ and they scream out in blind rage and wilful hate, fully knowing that they are crucifying their king (see especially the Johannine narrative). This binary theology (us-them; Christian-

Jew; Church-Synagogue; God-Devil) may now be rejected theo-
retically, but we have to be aware that we may still perpetuate it
in our operative theology – not least in the manner of reading
the passion. We have removed this anti-semitism from our com-
mentaries and preaching, and the reference to the 'perfidious
Jews' may be gone from the Good Friday prayers, but as long as
we use one other voice alongside that of Christ, then we actually
send the signal that it is that voice versus Christ, and perpetuate
a view of the passion that Vatican II formally rejected. The 'Jews
crucifying Christ' is theologically unacceptable, and we must be
wary of sending-out unconscious signals in the liturgy such as
that the passion is the 'goody against the baddies'.

The Voices of Women

One of the developments in political society that has not yet
found its place into the way many think liturgically is that 'we
choose our own representatives.' In ordinary society we no
longer say – nor would we accept – 'they will speak for you.' We
appreciate that 'each voice must be heard' and must be allowed
to choose its own representatives. What is of interest here is that
we use the metaphor of 'voice': each group must have its 'voice',
each particular 'voice' must be heard, no 'voice' must be smoth-
ered. If this is part of our reality – and it is – then what message
do we send out when the voices of women in the gospels are
then taken by a male voice in this reading? It is one thing when
the story is read by a single voice, then any distinction of voices
is impossible: indeed the single voice becomes that of the narrator and *oratio recta* is presented as quotations. It is quite another
matter when the narrator becomes a separate person and the
text is acted out with distinct voices: now for a woman's voice to
represent a man, or a man's voice to represent a woman, sends
out a message of sexual imperialism. If distinctive voices are
going to be heard in the passion, then each voice must be heard
in a voice of the appropriate sex.

One might deride this idea that the reading voice should be
of the same gender as the person whose words are big read with

a *reductio ad absurdum* like this: if a woman should read a female part, then only a soldier could read a soldier's part, a Galilean that of a Galilean. However, this retort misses the whole point of the liturgical reading of scripture. We read the text that the tradition delivers to us; we do not try to have an historical reconstruction. If we chose to dramatise the passion, or any other text (e.g. *Hamlet*) then we need those who can recreate the text for us in sound: we need a male for Peter and for Polonius; a female for Mary Magdalen and Ophelia. We do not need a Galilean nor a Danish crown prince; but equally we no longer use boys to play the female parts in Shakespeare. When three clergy read the passion, or any male voice reads the parts which belong to women in the text we are suppressing a female voice in the liturgy, and sending out a sub-verbal message: women's voices do not really register in the gospel as we understand it. Or, put literally: 'women have no voice as we read the gospel.'

Dramatis personae
A. Palm Sunday
So how many voices should one use? This depends on the Passion being read that year: Matthew in Year A, Mark in B, and Luke in C.
To read Matthew 26:14-27:66 requires:
    (1) Main narrator (Male [M] or Female [F] voice);
    (2) Second narrator for prophesy embedded in the narration, i.e. Jeremiah at 27:9, (M);
    (3) Jesus (M);
    (4) Peter (M);
    (5) Judas Iscariot (M);
    (6) Accuser before Chief Priests (M);
    (7) High Priest (M);
    (8) Servant girl #1 (F);
    (9) Servant girl #2 (F);
    (10) Pilate (M);
    (11) Pilate's wife (F);
    (12) Centurion (M);

(13) Disciples of Jesus (some mixed voices);

(14) Sanhedrin/Chief Priests/Scribes (some male voices);

(15) Bystanders at High Priest's house (some mixed voices);

(16) Group of soldiers (many male voices);

(17) Crowd outside Pilate's house and at the cross (many mixed voices); and

(18) Mocking passers-by at 27:40 (best if some female voices read this to make a contrast with the male voices of the Chief Priests at 27:42).

Obviously the chorus can combine and recombine for the group voices.

To read Mk 14:1-15:47 requires;

(1) Narrator (M or F);

(2) Jesus (M);

(3) A Disciple (M);

(4) Peter (M);

(5) Judas Iscariot (M);

(6) High Priest (M);

(7) Pilate (M);

(8) Servant girl (F);

(9) Man with sponge of vinegar (M);

(10) Centurion (M);

(11) Disciples of Jesus (some mixed voices);

(12) Sanhedrin/Chief priests/Scribes (some male voices);

(13) Group in Simon the leper's house (some mixed voices);

(14) Accusers before the chief priests (some male voices);

(15) Soldiers (some male voices);

(16) Mocking passers-by at 15:29 (best if some female voices to make a contrast with the male voices of the Chief Priests at 15:31);

(17) Bystanders in the courtyard of the High Priest (some mixed voices); and

(18) Crowd at Pilate's house and at cross (many mixed voices).

To read Lk 22:14-23:56 requires:

(1) Narrator (M or F);

(2) Jesus (M);

(3) Peter (M);

(4) Servant girl (F);

(5) Second accuser of Peter (since there is only one explicitly female voice in Luke, it is best if the role of narrator and of this second accuser of Peter are given to women);

(6) Third accuser of Peter -- a man (M);

(7) Pilate (M);

(8) Thief #1 (M);

(9) Thief #2 (M);

(10) Centurion (M);

(11) Disciples of Jesus (some mixed voices);

(12) Soldiers (some male voices); and

(13) Sanhedrin / Chief Priests / Scribes (some male voices).

B. Good Friday

The passion is from Jn 18:1-19:42. For John the passion is the public exaltation of Christ that completes his work. Throughout this reading Christ is the powerful one (a king before earthly power personified in Pilate) who is powerless; yet his power is manifested when he is raised on the cross. The text proposes to the readers the question: who is your king? Have you no king but Caesar, or, do you recognise him as king and stand by his cross? When done well, the passion read by multiple voices turns this into a liturgical high-point of the year. This style of reading makes the event stand out, involves a wide variety of people, and when properly practised can draw out the story's narrative force. However, it is well to bear in mind that John is the most notably anti-Jewish of the gospels and it is here that we have to be most careful to avoid the older stereotypes of presenting the narrative as the account of treasonable regicide.

The following voices are needed for John:
  (1) Main narrator (M or F);
  (2) Second narrator for prophesy embedded in the narration
  (M or F);
  (3) Jesus (M);
  (4) Peter (M);
  (5) Servant girl (F);
  (6) Second accuser of Peter (M or F);
  (7) Third accuser of Peter (M);
  (8) Guard (M);
  (9) Pilate (M);
  (10) Soldiers (some male voices);
  (11) the Chief priests (some male voices); and
  (12) 'the Jews' (male and female voices).

The Priest's Task

Many priests – allowing that it is very rare to have a deacon – believe that the voice of Jesus is still reserved to them; however,
since 1970 this is not the case. The current rubrics simply state
'that if possible, [it is] reserved to a priest' (Missal, p. 132, rubric
22). This permission should be exploited to the full: let the
passion be read entirely by a group who have practised for this
particular ministry and let the priest – who has already read the
gospel at the entrance on Palm Sunday and figures throughout
the liturgy on Friday – stand aside. When the priest does join in
it sends a signal that he is the 'real' reader with some second-rate
assistants for 'the big day.' Is this message compatible with Lk
22:24-7? Moreover, in the priest being vested while the others
are not, it presents an unevenness in the visual effect of the narrative that is distracting and makes too big a contrast between
his words and the rest of the story. This can invoke the older
image of Jesus and his persecutors.

     In the final analysis, there is a practical reason why the priest
should stand aside: it is simply not possible unless there are
many priests available. Given that more often than not there is
only one 'sacred minister' at any of these liturgies, most priests

find themselves more than busy in Holy Week. The multiplicity of jobs means that liturgy is often poorly prepared with the genuine excuse that there was not enough time to get it all done properly. Preparing the passion to be read well by several voices is time consuming and needs careful practice – thus it is often not possible that the priest should be available for all this plus his other activities. In such cases it is clear that the voice of Jesus cannot be reserved for a priest – and he should hand it over to others who do have the time to prepare it carefully and thus execute this focal point in the whole of the annual narration of the gospel with the care it deserves.

Passion (Palm) Sunday Year A

CELEBRANT'S GUIDE
With the exception of the gospel before the procession and the passion, the Liturgy of the Word today is the same in all three years.

Note

This is not just another Sunday: it is the beginning of a week with Christ that culminates next Sunday. It recalls all the pointers in the gospels (e.g. Mk 10:32-3) to the journey that the Lord must make to Jerusalem to perform his great work. The liturgy of Holy Week is a participation in this work at Jerusalem: today the church building is a symbol of the city (hence we begin outside it, and then enter it), then there are the final days (Monday to Wednesday), then the final meal and the commissioning of the apostles (Thursday), the time in the garden and the passion (Thursday night/Friday until 3 pm), the exaltation on the Cross which is recalled by the church as a victory celebration (the Good Friday liturgy), the tomb (Saturday), the resurrection (the Vigil) and its announcement (Sunday). This is the symbolic week, in the sense that we by participating in the liturgy are not just on-lookers engaged in a pageant, but are uniting ourselves with Christ now in his Great Work. Everything that is said or done in today's liturgy must aim at conveying this sense of a week of participation.

So while the Missal still thinks (compiled in 1970) of a 'principal Mass' and then other Masses, we must be aware that in our pastoral situation few places have this rigid dichotomy of celebration: whatever Mass people are attending is the principal Mass for them. So that whether it is the vigil Mass on Saturday evening, or any Mass on the Sunday, there should be the full entry celebration: the introduction and blessing of palms somewhere other than the main building where the Eucharist will be celebrated; and then the procession into the church/Jerusalem/this week. Unless we set the scene of a week with Christ today, the great liturgies later in the week are held without their proper context. They stand as individual 'bits' (one 'bit' today – a pageant of one episode in the gospels, another 'bit' ('the first Mass') on Thursday, etc.) because the introduction to the whole has been missed. In such a fractured presentation the liturgy cannot convey the message of the Paschal Mystery shared in by the baptised, and becomes a bunch of historical commemorations more akin to anniversaries of ancient events (e.g. the way we recall events like 'the first Dáil,' 'the battle of the Somme,' 'the day Jack met Jill') rather than a week that somehow presents us with the basis of Christian faith and a foretaste of the New Jerusalem (cf Gal 4).

In many parishes there is a feeling that this is just an ordinary Sunday plus a few extras, and that careful planning and arranging special things like extra readers, assembling outside the church, decorations, and so forth, does not have to start until Thursday. The hard fact is this: if you do not start the extra work that 'the Easter Ceremonies' involve today, then by Thursday it is too late, and all the worries about readers, thuribles, and what not, is more a desire to fulfill rubrics than as attempt to adequately create the ritual environment which allows us to grow in our understanding of the mystery of the Christ.

Introduction to the Celebration
The text in the Missal (p. 123: 'Dear friends in Christ ...') cannot be bettered. However, care should be taken to read it as if it were one's own notes so as to stress the notion that we are entering into the Great Week, accompanying Christ in the Paschal Mystery.

Headings for Readings
First Reading
We read Isaiah in the light of Christ the innocent one who suffered insults, mocking, and blows, yet remained faithful to justice, truth, and his Father.

Second Reading
Here we have an ancient Christian hymn presenting Christ as
the one who came among human beings to fight their enemy. He
conquered that enemy and gave them life. Hence we rejoice as
we acclaim him as victorious king.

The Passion
Any verbal introduction destroys the starkness of the opening. Since
the liturgy even removes the greeting ('The Lord be with you') and the
conclusion, to say anything 'introductory' is counter-productive. See
the note on The Passion in the Liturgy: The demands of celebration.

Profession of Faith
Today the 'Apostles' Creed' with its staccato recitation of the moments
of the Paschal Mystery (suffered, crucified, died, buried, descended
[picking up a theme from Phil 2: those under the earth], and rose) is
better than the 'Nicene Creed'.

Prayer of the Faithful
President:
As we enter this week, the Great Week, when we share in
Christ's victory over alienation, separation, suffering, evil and
death, let us pray with him to the Father.
Reader (s):
1. For all our sisters and brothers who will be baptised at Easter.
2. For ourselves, that the coming week may give us a new appreciation of the mystery of Jesus Christ.
3. For those of us in situations of strife or difficulty, that they
may have renewed hope.
5. That those who have died may rise in Christ who on the Cross
conquered death.
President:
Father, as we enter with Jesus into Jerusalem, the place where he
made intercession for us, hear now the petitions we make in this
place, for we ask them through that same Christ, our Lord. Amen.

Eucharistic Prayer

The Preface for today (P19) is very short – presumably as not wishing to lengthen a celebration that is already lengthy due to the passion – but also very trite. Today there is a note of joy and triumph, the messianic king is entering into his capital with the historical acclaims from the psalms that should accompany the event. However, Preface 19 is a variant on the Funeral Prefaces 1-3 (PP77-9). We therefore need a preface that stresses the joy of the king entering his kingdom, stresses his victory over the ancient enemies of humanity, and which forms a noble preparation for our cry of 'hosanna' in the Sanctus. I suggest using the Preface of Christ the King (P51); it too has a stress on Christ the priest, but emphasises the victory of his kingdom, and moves in elegant cadences towards the Sanctus, which today is especially appropriate.

Eucharistic Prayer III, with its echo of the prophesy of Malachi (1:11) that there will be a time when one will come who will offer a new and perfect sacrifice, is appropriate.

Invitation to the Our Father

Beginning this week, in which we accompany Christ in his prayer to the Father in the Upper Room, on the Mount of Olives, and on the Cross, let us pray now with him:

Sign of Peace

Jerusalem was the 'city of peace' and Jesus entered it as the prince who brings peace; let us offer that peace to one another.

Invitation to Communion

Behold the Lamb of God, behold him who went up to Jerusalem to suffer and to die, behold him who rose victorious over death, and who now calls us to his supper.

Communion Reflection
Another verbal element today can overburden the liturgy – it is best to have none.

Dismissal
Solemn Blessing 5 (The Passion of Our Lord), Missal, p. 369.

COMMENTARY

Procession: Mt 21:1-11

This little bit of text has caused either laughter or heartbreak to preachers down the centuries: laughter to those who see it as a case of Matthew being so literalist in his attitude to his version of the Old Testament that he will alter Mark's account (the basic synoptic text) to make an additional theological point – even at the expense of common sense; while to those who are literalist in their view of these early Christian texts, be they the older type that sought 'verbal inerrancy' or the more modern type of fundamentalist ('God said it in the Bible, so it is true'), this text produced headaches: how do you get Jesus to ride both a donkey and a young horse at the same time, especially when Mark and Luke are happy that he just ride the young horse? Since the early third century (Porphyry attacking the Christians) a vast effort has been expended on this problem (Eusebius, Augustine, Aquinas, and almost everyone else writing on Matthew looked at it), and still today when it is read people seem to know that there is something wrong. The general image of Jesus entering Jerusalem is of him sitting on an ass (only mentioned in Matthew; both Mark and Luke have him riding a colt), but as one would expect – and as is written in Mark and Luke – Jesus is riding just that animal. However, here, the disciples are sent to fetch an ass *and* a colt, to untie *them* and bring *them* for *they* are needed. They laid their cloaks on *their backs* and Jesus sat on *them*. There is no simple slip here: Matthew really wants you to imagine this impossible feat. The listener might immediately ask: how do you sit on two animals and ride them? The answer lies in Matthew's desire to quote the prophesy from Zech 9:9 (to which he adds an opening phrase from Is 62:11), but he does this using the Greek translation of the Old Testament (the Septuagint). Now in that translation – of which there was already in Matthew's time a legend among Greek-speaking

Jewish communities that the translation as such was inerrant, and this legend passed on to Christian communities – there was an error in rendering a phrase in Hebrew. Zech 9:9 now reads in the NRSV: 'riding on a donkey, on a colt, the foal of a donkey.' The Septuagint inserted 'and' into the phrase – the possible reasons why this happened are not important – and the Greek text was read as literally inerrant by Matthew: the king would be able to ride two animals, and Jesus must have ridden two animals. Why? Because the inspired text says so! This little conundrum does contain an important challenge to us: there are many people today who imagine Christianity as adherence to a book called 'the Bible' – and those who think 'it's true' call themselves 'believers', while others with the same opinion about what Christians believe state that 'the Bible is not true' and so justify a rejection of the notion of believing. The believing and unbelieving is then about a book and claims about the book, not in the living Christ or the mission of his people. We often cite the scriptures as if they were the almost perfect accounts of faith (e.g. 'Jesus said it, so I believe it!') and can give the impression that there is no difference between the church's use of scripture and that of the fundamentalists. So today's opening gospel reminds us that these books are the products of the memories of the churches for reciting at their gatherings for the Eucharist, not tomes that fell from heaven. And they are the product of theological writers like Matthew, every one of whom has their little hang-ups (like his biblical literalism as here) and makes mistakes! All these early Christian texts, such as the four gospels, are precious not because they are perfect, but because with all their limitations and errors they are the vehicles of our earliest memories as the community which believes itself to be one in Christ, and who through our interaction, study, and questioning of these early memories can discover more about what are the demands of belonging to this community that is at once earthly and heavenly.

So what was Matthew's aim in citing Zech 9:9? In Matthew Jesus only goes to Jerusalem once: the journey was announced at

16:21 with a prediction of suffering. Now Jesus has arrived. He arrives as a prophet, exactly as earlier prophets had foretold he would arrive, and Jesus fulfills the prophecy down to the smallest detail. It is worth noting that Matthew here plays down the shouts of Hosanna from the crowd – he keeps the detail as it is in his source (Mark) but has really no use for it in his interpretation of this event – in both Mark and Luke these shouts are central to the story as they are the acclamations for the Davidic king (Mk) or the king of peace (Lk), but in Matthew the word 'king' has been removed.

Incidentally, it is the Matthaean text of this acclamation that has become the recited form in western Eucharistic Prayers as the second phrase of the Sanctus.

First Reading : Is 50:4-7
This is part of one of the songs of the servant-prophet: he will persevere as a disciple and carry out YHWH's wishes to the end. Here it sets up an echo by which we can situate Christ as the one who does the Father's will even to death on a cross (Phil 2:8-9: the next reading and gospel acclamation).

Second Reading : Phil 2:6-11
This is a hymn of the early Christian community (sometimes called 'The Christ-hymn') which Paul has incorporated into his letter. Its complex structure presents one of the earliest 'high' christologies. Its basic structure is two-fold: part 1 (vv. 6-8) dwells on Christ's original status being 'emptied' and his being made powerless (i.e. from his birth to the moment of death); while part 2 focuses on Christ from the moment of death onwards: his exaltation as sovereign of the universe.

Passion: Mt 26:14-27:66
Exegetical Notes:
1. For those who seeking in the gospels an historical record of the events of Jesus' life, the passion accounts present an awful problem: for the most crucial event in the whole story the early

churches had at least four different pictures. When Christians today think of Jesus's death their picture is invariably a mixture with the people drawn from John and the general scene from the synoptics. Christ is flanked by two other crosses (Jn 19:18; but a detail common to all four), and standing near him are 'his mother, and his mother's sister, Mary the wife of Clopas, and Mary Magdalene' and John (Jn 19:25-26). Nearby also are soldiers casting lots for his clothes (Jn 19:23-25 but with parallels in all four). The scene is one of darkness covering the earth (Mt 27:45; Mk 15:33; Lk 23:44 – a darkness unknown in Jn). Against this conflation, it is worth noting how Luke sets out his scene as it allows us to see his particular perception. The scene of the crucifixion is dark (Lk 23:44) not only in terms of light, but in terms of the courage of his followers: those who knew him, men and women who had followed him from Galilee stood at a distance watching the event unfold (Lk 23:49). Near him there are a crowd of spectacle lovers, scoffing leaders and mocking soldiers (Lk 23:35-36). In Matthew and Mark both criminals also taunt him (they are silent in John), but in Luke (23:39-43) we have the dialogue of the Good Thief whose opening words are a confession that Jesus is suffering as an innocent man (23:41). The centurion's confession is found only in Mark (15:39) and Luke (23:47), but while in Mark this is a christological statement, in Luke it is a declaration of the innocent suffering of Jesus: 'Now when the centurion saw what had taken place, he praised God, and said, "Certainly this man was innocent!".' Luke, uniquely, adds another detail at this point: 'And all ... who assembled to see the sight, when they saw what had taken place, returned home beating their breasts' (23:48).

2. Many of the details of the passion as it is remembered in the tradition come solely from Matthew: e.g. Pilate washing his hands and then the Jews saying that the blood will be on them and their children (27:24-5); the story of Judas's suicide and the use made of his 30 pieces of silver (27:3-10); and the cosmic events that took place under a darkened sky at the moment of Jesus's death: earthquake, rocks splitting, people coming out of their tombs (27:52-3).

3. There is also an underlying contrast in Matthew between the power of God, which is intimately linked with Jesus, and the actual suffering, and powerlessness of the Christ. Challenged as to his power at 26:53-4, Jesus says he can simply appeal to his Father for 'twelve legion of angels' – an image we relate to in its secular modern form: 'calling in an air strike' – but the task of the Christ is not to use the power of God to achieve his wishes, but to act so that the scriptures be fulfilled. This theme is found again, but in reverse form, at the moment of the death: then Jesus is least powerful in the eyes of humanity, but his hidden power is such that the elements react to his death (earthquake, darkness, rocks splitting) as do the dead whose vision is no longer limited to this world (27:52-3). This is a presentation of Jesus that is not too common in preaching today, but it does remind us of the basic conviction of Christians about Jesus Christ, that he is the Lord of History, and the One whom all the creation must obey, even if we express this in a different register than that used by Matthew to show that the death of Jesus is no ordinary event but an event, literally, of earth-shaking importance.

HOMILY NOTES

The Missal (p. 132) says that 'a brief homily may be given.' There is definitely a case today for taking up this permission to omit the homily altogether; not because such an omission might shorten an already long liturgy, but since we have just come through one of the longest verbal elements in the whole of the liturgy (the passion), another verbal event (a homily) does not bring contrast or help the gospel reading to sink in. A better way to highlight what has been read would be a couple of moments of structured silence (e.g. 'Let us now reflect in silence on the passion of our Saviour') before standing for the Creed. On the subject of the length of today's liturgy we should remember that length of time is one of the key non-verbal ritual cues that humans use to indicate special importance: a crucial symbolic event that is over in a moment, or takes just the same length of time as an ordinary event is an anti-climax – do not forget that

Christmas dinner must take longer than an everyday meal. Because this is a special day opening a special week, it should and must take a noticeably longer time than an ordinary Sunday.

If one does preach, then the brief comments should be directed to introducing the week as a whole rather than particular comments on the readings. This could take its starting point from the gospel outside – that Christ has arrived at, and entered Jerusalem, and that 'his hour' has arrived. As Christians we are sharers in this event.

If the situation calls for a meditation rather than a homily, then a suitable meditation is provided in the Christ-hymn (the second reading) as a way of interpreting the events narrated. However, rather than re-reading it directly from the lectionary it can be broken up into its verses and read with pauses. The version used in the Office is better for such use than either the RSV or JB. Better still, have it sung by a soloist and simply introduce it as the earliest Christian meditation we possess on what we have just recalled about the death of Jesus.

Passion (Palm) Sunday Year B

Note
See Year A.

Introduction to the Celebration
See Year A.

Headings for Readings
First Reading
See Year A.

Second Reading
See Year A.

The Passion
Any verbal introduction destroys the starkness of the opening. Since the liturgy even removes the greeting ('The Lord be with you') and the conclusion, to say anything 'introductory' is counter-productive. See the note on The Passion in the Liturgy: The demands of celebration.

Profession of Faith
Today the 'Apostles' Creed', with its staccato recitation of the moments of the Paschal Mystery (suffered, crucified, died, buried, descended [picking up a theme from Phil 2: those under the earth], and rose), is better than the 'Nicene Creed'.

Prayer of the Faithful
See Year A.

Eucharistic Prayer
See Year A.

Invitation to the Our Father

Beginning this week in which we accompany Christ in his prayer to the Father in the Upper Room, on the Mount of Olives, and on the Cross, let us pray now with him:

Sign of Peace
Jerusalem was the 'city of peace' and Jesus entered it as the prince who brings peace; let us offer that peace to one another.

Invitation to Communion
Behold the Lamb of God, behold him who went up to Jerusalem to suffer and to die, behold him who rose victorious over death, and who now calls us to his supper.

Communion Reflection
Another verbal element today can overburden the liturgy – it is best to have none.

Dismissal
Solemn Blessing 5 (The Passion of Our Lord), Missal, p. 369.

COMMENTARY
Procession : Mk 11:1-10 or Jn 12:12-16
1. Mark's account is the oldest account of this event which opens the final chapter in the life of Jesus; Mark's text formed the basis of what we read in Matthew and Luke, although both will interpret the event in ways very different from the way that Mark does. In Mark the trip to Jerusalem is first mentioned in 10:32-45 which ends: 'the Son of Man came not to be served but to serve, and to give his life as a ransom for many.' Then six verses later the group have arrived at Bethphage. But this arrival is for Mark so significant that he presented the whole scene as the arrival of the long-awaited king taking possession of his capital in triumph with the acclamation of the crowds. Mark probably wants this image of the public adulation of the king to be remembered and contrasted with the king's public humiliation on the following Friday. Since both this text and Mark's passion are read in

conjunction in today's liturgy, this is a contrast to which it is well worthwhile to draw attention.

In Mk the whole scene unfolds as a pre-determined drama: Jesus knows what will happen, it is all planned. The disciples are told that they will find a colt, what they will be asked, and what they are to do; then it all happens exactly as Jesus said it would. In the background to the story is Zech 9:9 which imagines a future king coming into Jerusalem on a young donkey and who would swiftly establish his rule: now, for Mark, that moment has arrived.

The JB in 11:3 has translated *kurios* as 'Master' which is a possible meaning, but which is meaningless in the context. In Mark there has already being the petrine confession at 8:29; now Jesus is the promised king coming into his capital and all is prepared for him, so the obvious meaning that Mark's community would have taken from *kurios* here is that it is the full christological title. So the text needs to be changed – as it is in the NRSV -- to 'the Lord needs it.'

2. While it is probably best to use Mark's entry story with Mark's passion, the Lectionary offers the option of the Johannine version of the event which is clearly based on the kind of story that was in use in the churches of which our earliest textual evidence is Mark. The story is now cut down to its simplest element – essentially that Jesus is fulfilling the prophecy of Zech 9:9, but John wishes to make one point of his own: when these things happened, the disciples did not understand. Understanding only came when they recalled the whole event from the standpoint of resurrection faith. This is a point worth making, for the gospels can only be appreciated by us when we recognise that everything that is recorded about Jesus was so recorded from that standpoint, and indeed our retelling of these stories (especially around Easter) only make sense because we believe in the mystery of Christ's victory over death.

First Reading: Is 50:4-7

See Year A.

Second Reading: Phil 2:6-11
See Year A.

Passion: Mk 14:1-15:47
Exegetical Notes:
1. See note 1 on the passion narratives in Year A.
2. Mark's passion is the single largest section of his gospel, and it is the text that provided the structure, and much of the content, of the passion accounts of Matthew and Luke. It seems to move more swiftly to the end than the others and so the final scene stands out more starkly than in them. In reading the text today it is noteworthy that the Lectionary begins with the meal in Bethany that is most fully recounted in this gospel (it is shortened by Matthew and omitted by Luke). This meal has the character of a pre-last supper: the anointing is presented as recognition of Jesus's real identity as the anointed ('the christ') and an anticipation of his passion. It is significant that Mark places this event in a meal context and it is assumed that it will be remembered in a meal context. However, despite the fact that popular memory of this scene identified the woman as Mary Magdalene, this woman, whose act is recalled in the whole world wherever this gospel is preached, remains un-named. It is a reminder of the fact that there were a great many women in the support network of Jesus's ministry who have been all but forgotten in our concentration on the named male 'disciples'/'the twelve'/'the apostles'. She is told that she did a beautiful thing to the Lord, she is to be recalled for her lovely gesture, but so male-centred was the memory-making tradition in the early generations of Christians that her name was not worth noting or inventing!

HOMILY NOTES

See Year A.

Passion (Palm) Sunday Year C

Note
See Year A.

Introduction to the Celebration
See Year A.

Headings for Readings
First Reading
See Year A.

Second Reading
See Year A.

The Passion
Any verbal introduction destroys the starkness of the opening. Since the liturgy even removes the greeting ('The Lord be with you') and the conclusion, to say anything 'introductory' is counter-productive. See the note on The Passion in the Liturgy: The demands of celebration.

Profession of Faith
Today the 'Apostles' Creed', with its staccato recitation of the moments of the Paschal Mystery (suffered, crucified, died, buried, descended [picking up a theme from Phil 2: those under the earth], and rose), is better than the 'Nicene Creed'.

Prayer of the Faithful
See Year A.

Eucharistic Prayer
See Year A.

Invitation to the Our Father
Beginning this week in which we accompany Christ in his prayer to the Father in the Upper Room, on the Mount of Olives, and on the Cross, let us pray now with him:

Sign of Peace
Jerusalem was the 'city of peace' and Jesus entered it as the prince who brings peace; let us offer that peace to one another.

Invitation to Communion
Behold the Lamb of God, behold him who went up to Jerusalem to suffer and to die, behold him who rose victorious over death, and who now calls us to his supper.

Communion Reflection
Another verbal element today can overburden the liturgy – it is best to have none.

Dismissal
Solemn Blessing 5 (The Passion of Our Lord), Missal, p. 369.

COMMENTARY

Procession: Lk 19:28-40
Entering a city with a group of followers is not a neutral action in the ancient world: to bring your group through the city's gates is to take it captive and to declare that you are its ruler. Everyone who originally heard this story would have spotted that immediately – as indeed would our grandparents who would have seen photographs of General Allenby walking into Jerusalem at the head of his troops in December 1917 – and that realpolitik is echoed in the Pharisee's cry in v. 40. The contradiction is that Jesus does not use a symbol of power – a horse or chariot – but a colt, which could be interpreted as incompetence or that he has a different vision of kingship. This tale, derived from Mark, is developed differently by Matthew and Luke; Luke expresses it as Jesus as the king of peace. The message of

the text in today's liturgy is that Jesus has now entered the Holy City, he is the One sent by God, and he is the Prince of Peace.

First Reading: Is 50:4-7
See Year A.

Second Reading: Phil 2:6-11
See Year A.

Passion: Lk 22:14-23:56
Exegetical Notes:
1. See note 1 on the passion narratives in Year A.
2. A convenient way to see how Luke's passion differs from the other is to note those items which are proper to him. These present Christ as the righteous one who is faithful to the end alone. Luke presents Jesus as alone from all those whom he had spent time with, eaten with, and been with in the good times; yet in the dark hour his goodness still shone out and transformed people. While his long-term followers were lying low, Jesus was gathering new witnesses to his truth amidst the moral chaos which was his crucifixion. The sense of finality is heightened at the beginning of the passage when Christ states his longing to eat the meal (the final meal in a whole series of meals in Luke) and that he shall not drink wine again until the kingdom comes (22:15-20). It is also seen in his instructions for the church after his departure (22:35-7) and his warning to Jerusalem (23:27-32). His aloneness is pointed out in the prophesy that the disciples will desert him (22:21-3 and 33-4), and this is fulfilled in the detailed story of the triple denial of Peter (22:54-62). By this time Luke presents all the disciples as having fled. By the time of the crucifixion – in stark contrast to John from whence comes our familiar picture of John, Mary, and the other women standing beneath the Cross – there is not a single friendly face nearby: his acquaintances (*hoi gnóstoi*) and the women stand watching at a distance (23:49). In the end the only ones who acknowledge him are outsiders who at least recognise him as a good and righteous man:

Pilate, a criminal, and Roman soldier. Luke alone has Pilate recognise him as one without fault (23:5; 14-5; and 22); similarly he alone has 'the good thief' incident who states that this man has done nothing wrong (23:39-43); and finally the centurion, but while in Mark 15:39 and Matthew 27:54 he states, 'Truly this was the Son of God!', here Luke has him state simply: 'Certainly this man was righteous (*dikaios*).'

For Luke Christ in his passion is utterly abandoned, and he in turn abandons himself to the Father to do the Father's will (22:22, 29, 37, 42-3). This abandonment reaches its climax in the final cry from the Cross (23:46).

HOMILY NOTES

See Year A.

Holy Thursday (Years A, B, C)

Note

On these great days there is a tendency to bog the liturgy down with words and commentary, so that the liturgy drags and people become conscious of time. Then corners are cut to get things finished. It is far better to cut the words to a minimum and make the liturgy's actions fulsome rather than tokens performed before the rest of the congregation. If plenty of time is given to the foot-washing and then to the eating and drinking of the Eucharist, it will communicate this day's message far more than commentary.

Introduction to the Celebration

This meal brings us together as the church, Christ's people on earth, and holds out to us our destiny of sharing in the heavenly banquet. We are called to be a people who rejoice together, serve one another, and will be prepared to suffer for one another.

This evening we gather with Christ for the meal he desired to eat with us before he suffered. Using an already ancient meal recalling the whole history of God delivering his people, and the people reaffirming their commitment to be his people (the older covenant), Christ established a new relationship. This meal would bring his disciples together as his people on earth, and teaches us that in his covenant we must love and serve one another.

This meal tonight brings us together as the church, his people on earth, and holds out to us our destiny of sharing in the heavenly banquet.

Invitation to repentance

We have failed to serve one another, Lord have mercy.
We have failed to support to one another, Christ have mercy.
We have failed to love one another, Lord have mercy.

Headings for Readings
Two forms are given here, the brief form could be used by the reader if a word of introduction is needed; the longer headings could be used in newsletters and in preparing for the liturgy.

Brief form
First Reading
Tonight recalls the night of the first Passover. This is the great night of deliverance when a people in slavery ate a meal in haste before a journey that would take them into a new life.

Second Reading
It was in continuing to gather for the Lord's meal, and imitating the way he broke one loaf and blessed one cup for his disciples, that the earliest Christians established their identity. Gathering at this table tonight, we are making ourselves one with one another and with Christ.

Gospel
To be part of Christ's table family means accepting the call to serve one another.

Longer form
First Reading
Each reading highlights one aspect of what we are celebrating this evening. This reading recalls that this is the night of the Passover: the great night of deliverance when a people in slavery ate a meal in haste before a journey which would take them into a new life. The command to celebrate it annually was both a reminder of what God had done and a token of what he would still do for his people. The Passover meal was the people's acknowledgement of God's alliance with them. It was to fulfill that command that Jesus gathered in the Upper Room with his disciples. We read it as the background to Jesus's supper, and as a reminder of the constancy of God in loving his people. Liturgically it makes us a community now recalling what Christ recalled.

Second Reading

'Do this in memory' – the Last Supper recalled the earlier meal, now this meal tonight recalls the Last Supper. From the beginning of the covenant, and on into the new covenant right to this very day the Lord shows us his mercy. And we, in the constancy of our recollections, praise his goodness and proclaim him until he comes again.

On this night seated with his disciples, Jesus transformed the Passover into the new alliance in himself between God and his people. This new meal is the Eucharist and from the earliest times it has been handed on as the way in which we share in Christ's life, death, and resurrection. Here we hear what this gathering meant to the first generation of Christians.

Gospel

So many of the world's woes are caused by the divorce of 'leadership' from 'service': to be a 'leader' is to be an owner, a controller, one who is served, a 'taker' not a 'giver'. This human situation is acknowledged here in that the disciples are surprised that a lord and master would serve them. But following Jesus is a basic challenge to how we arrange our affairs with each other. If we want Jesus as Lord, then we must see service to one another as basic to our relationships.

In the middle of the meal Jesus gave us an example of love and service. If we are to know him in the Eucharist, the rest of our lives must strive to follow this example.

Prayer of the Faithful
President:
On this holy evening gathered here with Christ at his supper, let us make our prayers to the Father.
Reader (s):
1. For us all, that we follow Christ's example of service to one another.
2. For all who are suffering, that they may find rest and strength.

3. For Christians, that we may fulfill the Lord's new command-ment by working for justice.

4. For all those who will be baptised, confirmed, or ordained with the chrism consecrated this morning, that they may put on Christ.

5. For all the sick who will be anointed with the oil blessed this morning, that they may know healing and peace.

President:

Father, you have called us to be servants of one another and of you. Help us to carry our this ministry and grant our requests through that same Christ, our Lord. Amen.

Collection/Preparation of the Gifts

The Missal (n. 9, p. 151) suggests that there be a 'procession of the faithful with gifts for the poor' – this expresses in real action what is a basic aspect of the theology of the Eucharist: if we are here feasting on the bounty of God, then we should be seeking to imitate God by sharing our bounty with those less fortunate. Just as we must forgive to be forgiven, we must share with others from our wealth if we wish to share in this precious supper. This care for the poor as an activity at eucharistic gatherings goes back to the earliest days of the church and is commented upon by Justin c. 150 AD (see Breviary, vol 2, pp. 530-1). When this collection is for the poor it is a true liturgical activity, and it bonds what we are doing in our ritual to the rest of our lives in a very perceptibly real manner. If the proceeds of the collection are then presented in the procession, it is good if it is not only cash that is presented, as this does not have the visual impact of some items of food which create an image that if we are fed here with celestial food, then we must be thinking of those who need ordinary food in a world of hunger and poverty. One way of getting people to bring to real foodstuffs is to point this out to the daily congregation in the first three days of Holy Week.

In the procession of gifts many communities also present the new holy oils, while, in general, the presentation of items which are not for the eucharistic meal nor for the poor can obscure understanding of the Eucharist, on an occasion such as this it expresses the larger community of the diocese and links the celebration of the Paschal Mystery over these days with its celebration in various ways over the coming year.

Eucharistic Prayer
Preface of the Holy Eucharist I (P 47) with Eucharistic Prayer I as it has several special variations. These are sometimes quite small (e.g. in the institution narrative the addition of 'that is today'), but of great significance for our understanding of the liturgy. However, it is best to mark the Missal on p. 486 at n 82 with some sticky labels so that you or a concelebrant just cannot forget and read on, but must turn to the proper on pp. 152-3. Note the deficiency of the present missal in that this text is not rubricated to indicate the different concelebrants' parts – so these too need to be marked.

Invitation to the Our Father
Jesus came from the Father, and returned to the Father, and through him and with him and in him we can pray:

Sign of Peace
Christ's charge to the disciples around him at this meal was to love and serve one another. Let us express our desire to follow that example by giving each other the sign of peace.

Invitation to Communion
This is our Passover Lamb, happy are we whom he calls his friend's and invites now to his banquet.
Or
This is our Passover Lamb, who takes away the sin of the world, happy are those who are called to his supper.

Communion Reflection
There should be none.

COMMENTARY

First Reading: Ex 12:1-8, 11-14

1. Groups, peoples, are constituted by what they remember together. Indeed, if you have no common memories with some one or some group, it would be very hard to say that you have anything, humanity apart, in common with them. This story of deliverance and its ritual expression was and is one of the great common memories of Israel: we are one people because we have been through this, we are a holy people because the Lord has done this for us. But common memories need common and periodic rehearsals so that we are conscious of them: anniversaries, annual meetings, annual memorial events, and the like – these are the regular moments when the past is remembered and used to establish the present and explain it. Such common regular rehearsals are the very stuff of human culture, and we see this recognised at the end of the reading with the divine command to keep the festival forever.

2. Today we recall this as part of our heritage. We have adopted it as our past – all pasts are adopted to some extent; but we also continue the pattern: this very meal is our rehearsal of our common memory that Jesus gathered his people about a table and united them in himself in his offering to the Father.

3. This passage reflects the developed ritual theology of the Priestly source. A variety of early cultic practices that had fused together over time are given a formal shape and an historical justification with an origin at the very beginning of the great myth of Israelite identity: the Exodus journey. It is seen as a 'last supper': ending one period and beginning another in the people's history. What is most interesting about it is not the text's content but the liturgical theology in which it played the role of being the fundamental narrative element.

4. The people asserted their allegiance to their religion by steadfastly repeating their distinctive rituals in an annual cycle of

liturgy, which retold the stories of their origins as a distinct group with a distinct understanding of God. The relationship with God was forged and maintained by this loyalty to a tradition of ritual, and its meaning was explicated by the stories told during these rituals. Through repeated use each ritual developed new aspects, each of which expressed a more elaborate theological perspective. By the time of Jesus, this meal was one that celebrated deliverance, being a specially chosen people, being a people of the covenant, and being a people looking forward to deliverance. And it was with such an understanding that the disciples gathered. Reflection on how the tradition of this communal ritual united the people, sustained them, and enabled them to hand on their religious identity can teach us a great deal about how history-based religions, such as Christianity, can perpetuate themselves over time and ensure that each new generation is aware of the tradition and identity in which they live.

5. Inserted just before the climax of the plagues (the killing of the first-born), these ancient spring rituals are presented as the immediate preparation for the Exodus journey. It is seen as a 'last supper': ending one period and beginning another in the people's history. This spring ritual is a combination of two rites. First, a rural herders' sacrifice, a lamb, which is eaten so that the participants can share in the sacrifice's power; in spring it marks the end of lambing and the move from winter to summer pastures. The second rite, unleavened bread, belongs to a settled farming community engaged in a cycle of planting and harvesting, and this celebrates the spring new year. These came together; and within the religious tradition became the means for each new generation to participate in the 'first-time': the formation of the people by escaping from Egyptian control.

6. The whole passage belongs to the Priestly source and reflects their developed ritual theology: taking part in the memorial is the means of transcending time and being part, now, of the original great event.

Second Reading: 1 Cor 11:23-6

1. Paul's view on what Christians were doing each week at the Eucharistic meal: sharing the loaf was a sharing in the Lord's body; sharing the one cup was establishing the new relationship (covenant) with God.

2. Paul assumed that transmission of 'the tradition of the Lord' would take place among his disciples in Corinth in much the same way that 'the traditions of the elders' were transmitted among the Jews. That is, that loyalty to the community's rituals which reinforce their sense of being the people who make up Christ's body and who, at their assemblies, would realise their identity by sharing in the Lord's meal and recalling his teaching. The challenge for us of this reading is to know whether, when we meet for the Eucharist, we can really say that this is 'the community's ritual'. Do our gatherings for Mass really convey the sense that we are collectively asserting our bonds with one another by sharing in a meal together, and so reinforcing our solidarity with one another as the church whose life-blood is Christ?

3. This is probably our earliest documentary evidence for the Eucharist, roughly contemporary with the *Didache* (although the Pauline churches and that of the *Didache* have very different theologies of the Eucharist) and predating Mark by perhaps two decades (whose theology of the Eucharist is also different to Paul's). What is important to note is that a theology of the Eucharist is already part of Christian teaching, and that this teaching includes the notion that this is 'the tradition of the Lord'.

Gospel: Jn 13:1-15

1. The 'Last Supper' is a key 'event' in John, portraying Christ as the great priest who at his 'hour' makes intercession with his Father. It is the 'event' upon which John builds his largest theological edifice: no less than 155 of the gospel's 878 verses (18%; chs 13-17) are concerned with the meal before the passion, when

the Hour had come. This is the opening verses of this section that is concerned with the Lord revealing his 'glory' (cf 17:22-4) to his friends (cf 15:15: 'I call you friends, for all that I have heard from my Father I have made known to you).

2. And the first step in this revelation of glory is that he is among them as a servant, and this shows perfect love; so, the section's opening scene is this washing of the disciples' feet. The reader is expected to know that this is the last gathering of the master with the disciples before his death and, knowing this, to be aware that it is an especially significant event – a fact reinforced by the reference to Judas and the note of impending action: already the die is cast for Jesus's arrest later that night. It is with this note of finality in the air that Jesus begins to teach and this lesson is to be treated with the solemnity of 'last words' before he leaves them; it is his testamentary teaching.

3. At Greco-Roman formal evening meals, rich households showed care for visitors by providing a slave-girl to wash the guests' feet. Against that background, we should view Jesus' action and his statement at vv. 14-15. John spells this out in the final verse of the pericope: if he served them, they must serve one another; and the lesson is further pushed home by contrast: he is the master serving the disciples – an act of condescension; while they are disciples serving their own like.

HOMILY NOTES

Preaching the homily on this evening is probably the most difficult piece of communication in the entire year. The reason is simple: there are so many memories and so many events being recalled: the Last Supper, the command to love and serve one another, the night of the arrest, institution of the Eucharist, the Passover meal, Christ's intercession as High Priest, and on and on. The Missal directs that 'the homily should explain the principal mysteries which are commemorated in this Mass: the institution of the Eucharist, the institution of the priesthood, and

Christ's commandment of brotherly love' (p. 149). This, however, hardly takes account of attention spans, and invites a 15 minute lecture (i.e. 5 minutes to each topic). This idea should not be dismissed; there are some teachers who can communicate effectively in the homily setting, but unless you are a proven performer on the podium, another strategy is probably wiser. So what follows are some basic points about the Last Supper, and some options for communication.

1. Background notes.
Today's keynote is that Jesus gathered his people for a meal – something he did often, enjoyed, and was criticised for (cf Mt 11:19). This was an intimate affair of his own people, hence the added horror about Judas one senses in v. 2. A meal has a grammar all its own. (1) It is around one table (which means we are truly equal in his sight and 'friends' – there is no 'top-table' and then places for the rest. (2) There is a sharing of food. This had been transformed in Jesus' table ritual to being a central moment in his whole vision for the Father's new people: a single loaf was broken and anyone who had a share in it was accepting a place among that new people. Uniquely, Jesus asked his table companions to share one cup over which he said a blessing. This established them, through an intimate ritual, as sharing in a common vision and destiny. (This basic table ritual of Jesus, from which our Eucharist derives, was not a Passover ritual – hence we celebrate Eucharist weekly not annually – and this is probably why John omits an 'institution narrative' from his account of the meal on the night of betrayal). (3) At any common meal there is an element of showing one's desire to be of service and to offer of one's best: one way of doing this in Jesus' time was to offer the service of foot-washing. Jesus's action transforms this into making service the basis of community; and this action was so striking that it became a part of many Christian liturgies – now only surviving vestigially.

2. *Strategy A – deeds not words*

Instead of a homily, finding some way to express in actions that are more than tokens, this basic meal grammar and this new vision of sharing and service is the challenge for today. Perhaps it means having the awkwardness of much foot-washing, of people milling around the table (it was for this reason that the tables were taken from the back walls in the 1960s!), a very slow fraction and all the complications with sharing one cup. But all this might make it a ritual that impresses the common memory within the group, and so re-constitutes the gathering as who they are.

Washing Feet

The most effective homily on the command to love one another – the phrase 'brotherly love' is dated – is to perform the ceremony of washing of feet properly. No ceremony is more likely to get cut down, tokenised, or abandoned altogether than this; but if this ceremony – ritual at its most real – is not really done, then preaching about Christ's example is mere words. Do the ceremony well, which means men and women, young and old (and will probably involve more than twelve people if different strands and groups in the community are represented), take off the chasuble (cf Jn 13:4), have the awkwardness of donning a towel (cf Jn 13:4), then get down, have the splashing water, and the rest of it. The shock and communicative power of this ritual is immense. Yes, it all very embarrassing – it is meant to be.

A place at table

The central Eucharistic symbols are one loaf, one cup, and one table. Being at table with Jesus is a key theme in the gospels: he eats at table with those whom others shun, he uses table metaphors to make his points, he teaches while he sits at table. In most church building the table is not gathered around: it is observed. People do not experience being at the table, they have to imagine it – yet the rationale of sacraments is that we experience an earthly reality (being at table) and relate to a heavenly reality (we are sharers in the divine banquet). So the experience of actually gathering around the table is something that is most worthwhile. Instead of looking at one person at a table 'over there' – invite the people to stand around the table and on this special night, not just to look at the table or be 'virtually' at it, but actual share a single table. It is interesting to note that the oldest western eucharistic prayer, what we call Eucharistic Prayer I and which should be used tonight, contains the phrase *Memento, Domine, famulorum famularumque tuarum et omnium circumstantium*, which literally means: 'Recall, Lord, [the prayers] of your servants (male) and your servants (female) and of all those who are standing around ...' This part of the prayer – meaningless in practical terms for more than a millennium – reminds us of a time in the church in Rome when around the table alongside the celebrant stood many women and men. The official translation we use today is a little more reticent: 'Remember, Lord your people ... Remember all of us gathered here before you.'

We constantly use the image of the table, the one table, and gathering at the table: give it sacramental expression by actually gathering people around at the table tonight.

A real fraction

The basic symbolism of the Eucharist is that there is one body, one loaf, and one cup ('The cup of blessing which we bless, is it not a participation in the blood of Christ? The loaf which we break, is it not a participation in the body of Christ? Because there is one loaf, we who are many are one body, for we all partake of the one loaf' – 1 Cor 10:16-17). This was, for most of the first millennium, the most obvious, and a time consuming part of the liturgy was the actual breaking up of a single large loaf by the deacons and the drinking from a single large chalice. When the emphasis in eucharistic theology shifted from sharing in the Lord's meal to what is there in the species which you could receive as a wondrous visitation from God – a process that began with Isidore of Seville (c. 560-636) – we began to think of the sacrifice of the Mass as one activity, and receiving communion as a separate activity. Now, 'receiving communion' was 'an extra' and reservation became a primary part of our theology. Reservation was made simpler when unleavened bread was used (introduced in the late ninth century), and the only loaf that was needed was one big enough for the priest – any other person could be accommodated with smaller individual loaves. Since the Second Vatican Council these trends have been balanced in the west by a greater emphasis on the Eucharist as the action of the whole People of God, in contrast to the notion of a priest saying Mass with a congregation. However, we still, on the whole, use precut round individual mini-loaves: these do not reflect a rich theology of the Eucharist tuned into the basic symbolism of which we read in the scriptures. A similar shift took place with the cup: when communion became infrequent, and then communion under one species became the norm for Catholics, the cup had only to be big enough for one. So tonight why not get the large breads used in many religious communities, so that each person get a broken part, a fraction, and thus part-takes of a loaf with others. Then use only one large chalice. In this way a basic theology of the Eucharist is imparted under the original sacramental signs. This takes time, but we are celebrating a mystery, not running a religious 'fast-food' joint!

3. Strategy B – a reflection on what we are doing
The liturgy is so full this evening that the homily can be a pause for little reflection by inviting those celebrating with you to imagine a series of meals.

Some of the best times in life are marked by assembling with those you are related to by family, friendships, or common interests: the wedding meal, the birthday party, the meal of the team, the class re-union, the Christmas dinner. We all know them, we all have our likes and dislikes about them, but we would not be without them.

Such need for gatherings is embedded deep within us as human beings. Such meals are part of every culture. They are times of celebrating the present, they remind us of our bonds to one another, they proclaim our identity and the group to which we belong.

Such meals are part of virtually every religion – chances to tell the sacred stories and re-establish links. So it was for the Jews for centuries before Christ and the Passover meal. They gathered in houses in cities like Jerusalem, in little villages in the countryside. The houses of merchants, the houses of people who grew vines, others who cared for sheep, others who tilled the ground, others who were fishermen. Sometimes they did it when Israel was free, sometimes they did it when they were controlled by foreigners who did not share or understand their religion or meals like the Passover. They did it when in captivity in Babylon, 'there they wept,' but they kept up the practice of the meal. By the time of Jesus, there were Jews living across the Mediterranean world from Persia, to Egypt, to Rome, to Spain – and one of the things that bound them was that in each house they gathered for this meal. Later across Europe, and later still in Russia, and now across the globe they gather for this meal. They gathered for it in times of persecution by us, Christians, in ghettos, and in camps – but gathering for this meal was essential to identity.

Gathering for this meal as transformed by Jesus is part of Christian identity. It was for this meal, the Eucharist, that Christians in Corinth gathered. Later, Christians would gather for it in houses across the Mediterranean; sometimes in good times, sometimes in bad times as when they met in the catacombs. Later, they would gather for it in churches and chapels and great cathedrals. Sometimes they almost forgot it was a meal at all, and used names like 'Mass' which ignored that its key element was thanksgiving ('eucharist'). But they kept gathering.

So here we are tonight – another gathering for this meal. It brings us together as a group with a common identity as those made children of the Father, and brothers and sisters to one another. It gathers a lot of memories from all the times this meal has been celebrated back to the time of Jesus and long before that again. Being here is also a declaration that we want to keep faith and state again that we trust in God's mercy and will endeavour afresh to be disciples.

4. Strategy C – A short reflection

Most of today's liturgy is in the upper register of ceremony: the bells of the Gloria, thuribles that have been dug out of cupboards, the splendour of the final procession, and the choir dusting-off snippets from the *Missa de Angelis*. So perhaps the homily should adopt a reflective tone, a quieter time to just let the sense of what is being celebrated sink in. For centuries the Jewish people had gathered for a meal to recall their deliverance. Jesus and the disciples were part of that tradition. For nearly two millennia, we have continued to gather in memory of the new act of deliverance by Christ. The mystery is that this meal is not just 'going through the motions,' a piece of historical drama; but rather as parts of the risen and ever-living Christ we are sharing now in his supper, sharing now in his thanksgiving to the Father. We are seeking to mingle our lives with Christ; he is sharing his divine life with us. The reflection could conclude by slowly reading the central portion of this evening's preface: 'He is the true and eternal priest ... we are washed clean.'

Good Friday Years A, B, C

The Tone of Today's Liturgy

This liturgy has two qualities in succession. The first is reflective intercession focused on the death of the Lord's Anointed, in whose death and life we share. This is best introduced without words, by the ministers prostrating and waiting long enough until the silence/non-movement are perceptible in the assembly. The Missal's 'soft option' of simply kneeling is not a strong enough gesture to mark the beginning of so solemn a celebration. The second quality is that of recognising that Christ's death is his conquest over the powers of darkness and so this is a victory celebration, focused on his weapon of victory: the Holy Cross. The quality of joy at a victory is seen at the end where the liturgy assumes that the Cross – not a crucifix – is enthroned with lights and given the full ritual salute, normally reserved for the Blessed Sacrament, of a genuflection. The first quality is disrupted if the celebrant interjects with an introduction or comments on readings in the early part of the liturgy. The second quality becomes invisible if, during the Veneration and Communion, the hymns concentrate on a sentimental interest in the sufferings of the Passion, e.g. *On a hill far away stood an old rugged cross* or *Were you there*.

Introduction to the Celebration

There should be none. The liturgy begins without even 'Let us pray'. If this starkness makes it all feel strange, then the liturgy is working!

This starkness suggests that we are not beginning a new celebration, but simply picking up the next moment in the annual celebration of the Paschal Mystery from where we left off last evening. Many celebrants feel uncomfortable with this starkness and imagine that the liturgy 'needs' some *ex tempore* words of welcome, such as are part of almost every other celebration. But it is this familiarity that the liturgy does not need on this day: this gathering is different to every other liturgical assembly, and an essential part of this is its starkness. There should be no words of welcome, nor explanatory comment, nor even directions such as 'we now sit down'.

Liturgy of the Word
Headings for Readings
First Reading: none. Comment on the readings destroys the essential starkness of the day.

Second Reading: none.

The Passion: none.

The General Intercessions
Note:
These are very carefully structured and are not easily improved upon. Likewise, they are inclusive of the range of our concerns as God's people so the temptation to 'drop one or two' indicates a serious ecclesiological confusion.

The Veneration of the Cross
Note:
The Missal refers consistently to a 'cross' and to its wood – the practice of using a crucifix confuses the focus of the liturgy by moving from a gesture of veneration for the emblem of the victory to a gesture of sympathy / sadness for the mangled body of Jesus.

The use of several little crosses turns this collective act of veneration into individualistic acts of personal devotion (akin to 'getting the ashes'). If the gestures of the liturgy are actually propagating an individualistic false notion of the passion (e.g. 'I love my personal saviour') then one has to question whether anything is gained by 'saving time'. Have you 'saved time' when the message of the action is not only lost but overlaid with another misleading one. Either do it properly with one cross, within the ceremony, or not at all.

Liturgy of Holy Communion
Invitation to the Our Father
Lifted high on the Cross, Christ draws us all to himself; and with him we pray:

Invitation to Communion
This is our sacrificed Passover Lamb who takes away the sins of the world. Happy are those united in him.

Communion Reflection
None.

Note:
After the distribution of communion do not use the main tabernacle to hold the particles not distributed until afterwards. The Sacrament, held at the Altar of Repose until this celebration, should be taken out of the assembly immediately the distribution of communion is finished. When this celebration concludes the only object of veneration in the sanctuary should be the cross with candles. Just before the last prayer ('Lord send down your abundant blessing ... ') someone should point out that as people leave, the custom is to genuflect to the Victorious Cross.

COMMENTARY
First Reading : Is 52:13-53:12
This is one of the servant-songs of Deutero-Isaiah. There are several voices: God, the repentant people, and the voice of the writer/prophet. In this context it should be noted that it begins by God announcing the future victory of his servant (52:13), but this victory over the sins of the people is not enjoyed during his lifetime: the fruits of the servant's victory are only after his death, and the beneficiaries are the people for whom he died (53:10-13).

Second Reading : Heb 4:14-16; 5:7-9

Two snippets from a section of Hebrews concerned with Jesus as
the Merciful High Priest (4:14-5:10). They are combined here as
an interpretation of Christ's death as that which establishes him
as the new High Priest who gains for the people access to the
throne of God. It is this access that constitutes salvation.

Acclamation : Phil 2:8-9

Part of the Christ-hymn (see Palm Sunday notes): note that these
verses link the moment of death with the moment of exaltation.

Passion: Jn 18:1-19:42
Exegetical Note:

For John the passion is the public exaltation of Christ that completes his work. Throughout this reading Christ is the powerful
one (a king before earthly power personified in Pilate) who is
powerless; his power is manifested when he is raised on the Cross
and from whose side flows life (blood) and forgiveness (water).

In John the notion of the king runs right through the passion.
He is the leader and the promised one, the helper, the saviour,
but also the one whom we look upon pierced, whose life and energy (blood and water) he has made available to all who want to
share in it. But there is the challenge of faithful discipleship:
have you no king but Caesar, or, do you recognise him as king
and stand by his cross? There is the uncomfortable question
lurking in the last part of the text dealing with Joseph of
Arimathaea: am I prepared to share my life and energy with
those who look upon me for help.

Practical Point: The Passion should be read using multiple
voices, but remember that this requires care, practice, and many
individual voices. (See the note on *The Passion in the Liturgy*.)

HOMILY NOTES

1. There is a starkness in this liturgy that captures the basic
   paradox at the heart of the gospel. We are a victorious people
   because Christ has conquered. On the one hand we rejoice

and venerate the Cross as his victory standard still standing among us as the memorial of the victory over evil, sin, and death. Today we rejoice in Christ the Victor. But, on the other hand, we recall also the horror of how the sinless One was slain.

We are victorious through his suffering. He is the powerful One who has battered in the gates of the bastion of the ancient enemy, but did it not with a show of divine force, but with the powerlessness that saw him handed over to Pilate's troops. Within this liturgy the central point is the dialogue between Jesus and Pilate about kingship (18:33-19:15) which throws up the questions what sort of king do we serve – and the notion that we are free from serving rulers of some sort, external or internal, is an illusion hiding a slavery – and who is that king. The 'style' of Christ's kingship comes out in the central exchange in 18:36-7. Before this paradox the liturgy's starkness is our response to a victory won by Jesus' powerlessness.

2. However, there is a fundamental problem of interpretation in today's liturgy. We, despite continuing to call it 'Good Friday,' view this day and its liturgy as one of suffering and gloom (as if it really were Bad Friday); thus we emphasise the awful death of Christ, the pain, and the Cross as the instrument of torture and execution. This is then picked up in hymns that emphasise the suffering and the darkness of the day. We see it in Bach's *O sacred head ill-used*, or the truly (theologically) awful *Were you there when they crucified my Lord*. The reflection on the tortuous death of Christ becomes an occasion of mawkish sentimentality. This is a theme that first arose in the late-thirteenth and early-fourteenth centuries, was cast in concrete by the disputes of the sixteenth century, and perpetuated by goulish altar-pieces and the (pre-1955) practice of the Good Friday ceremonies being carried out in darkened churches on the Catholic side, and by hymns like Bach's on the Protestant side. On the other hand,

the liturgy itself was immune from this trend and preserved
a much earlier theology – indeed today's liturgy preserves
some of the most ancient bits of the Latin rite, even bits of
Greek – where this day was seen as a celebration of the lonely
victory of Christ over the whole power of the enemy. So we
have to decide at the out-set if the homily will try to tune into
the theology of the liturgy (which comes with the whole authority of the tradition) or the more recent strata of popular
imagination developed for the most part in the light of the
Black Death, and the Reformation's emphasis on the
wretchedness of humanity without grace.

3.   The homily should point out that the consistent theme of our
     prayer today is that of Christ's victory: by dying he has de-
     stroyed our death. The scene of the Cross is that of the Noble
     Tree, it is the symbol of our victory through the Christ over
     the dismal battlefield of human misery. It is the symbol of the
     Lord lifted up, 'and as Moses lifted up the serpent in the
     wilderness, so must the Son of man be lifted up' (Jn 3:14),
     'and I, when I am lifted up from the earth, will draw all men
     to myself' (Jn 12:32). The liturgy is one of victory, and its
     starkness points out that it was won by the suffering of the
     Holy One. This theme is found in each of the readings, and
     then in the passion. It is continued in the prayers of interces-
     sion: now our High Priest has gained access to the throne of
     God and so we can bring our needs for ourselves and all hu-
     manity to him. The theme reaches it climax in the adoration
     of the elevated Cross: this is not a reflection on the horror of
     the Cross, but a glorying in the Cross as the sign of the con-
     quest of sin and death. It is unveiled as a victory standard.
     We see this in the hymns that the Missal itself proposes to ac-
     company this adoration. First, the ancient Reproaches: 'we
     venerate the Cross ... through it you brought joy to the
     world'; and then the most perfect expression of the earlier
     theology of the Cross, the *Pange lingua* of Venantius
     Fortunatus (c. 530-609) (see Missal pp. 180-1). Its opening
     words capture this vision of today's liturgy:

'Sing, my tongue , the glorious battle, / sing the last, the
dread affray; / o'er the Cross, the victor's trophy, / sound
the high triumphal lay; / how, the pains of death enduring, /
earth's redeemer won the day.' (ET: J.M. Neale).

4. Pointing out this theme of victory removes dissonance from
today's ceremony between what we read and do in the rite
and the interpretation we lay upon it. However, pointing to
Christ's victory, and the Cross as a sign of the Good News of
his triumph, can be set at zero if, first, in addition to the great
sign of victory, a multitude of little crucifixes are used for the
adoration. The Missal directs that there be only one (rubric
19, p. 174). If someone 'for convenience' uses more, what is
achieved: is it convenient if 'in getting it done' the whole
symbolism of doing it is lost? We gather to celebrate the one
victory, it is through one Cross we are delivered: many crucifixes turn it into an individualistic sorrow for what has happened, rather than an act of homage and love for the Victor
who has delivered us all.

HYMNODY

The theme of victory central to today is most often betrayed in
practice through the use of hymns that seek an emotional response to the actual suffering of Jesus rather than reflecting our
faith in the victory of the Christ. Note the themes set out in the
hymns that the Missal proposes to accompany the adoration of
the Cross. First, the ancient Reproaches; and then that most perfect expression of today's theme, the *Pange lingua* of Venantius
Fortunatus.

Avoid hymns which fail to see the Cross as the victory that
makes this Good Friday, e.g.: *All ye who seek a comfort sure; At the
cross her station keeping* (suitable only for paraliturgies such as
the Stations of the Cross); *By the blood that flowed from thee; Dust,
dust and ashes; God of mercy and compassion; I looked up and saw my
Lord a-coming; My song is love unknown; On a hill far away stood an
old rugged cross; O sacred head ill-used; O sacred head surrounded;*

There is a green hill far away; They hung him on a cross; and *Were you there.*

After the Reproaches and the Pange lingua, go for the hymns that stress the Cross's victory, e.g. : *Battle is o'er, hell's armies flee; Crown him with many crowns; How lovely on the mountains; In him we knew a fulness; Lord Jesus think on me; Praise to the Holiest in the height; The royal banner forward go;* or *When I survey the wondrous cross.*

Easter Vigil Years A, B, C

CELEBRANT'S GUIDE

Only one element of this liturgy, the gospel reading, varies over the three-year cycle.

Note

This vigil is the centre of the liturgical year. The fact that it is peripheral to many normally active in the liturgy indicates how little the renewal of theology and liturgy begun in the 1960s has sunk into our consciousness. The Missal describes it as 'the mother of all vigils' (n 20, p. 202) and sees the readings as its core: 'it must always be borne in mind that the reading of the word of God is the fundamental element of the Easter Vigil' (n 21). In practice, it is almost the exact reverse. The readings get squeezed (almost squeezed out) between the opening drama of the paschal fire, and the excitement of the baptism liturgy.

The assumption of the liturgy is that all nine readings are used: they are not offered as options from which to make a selection. An individual community can reduce the number 'for special reasons' (Lectionary, vol 1, p. 399) to five; and 'more serious reasons' are needed if only four are used (Missal, n 21). However, if the reason for dropping any reading is the time factor, then the question must be asked as to why bother with the vigil at all? If any of the readings are dropped, then the purpose of the whole sequence becomes invisible: the idea is that there is a long sequence of texts and that we 'listen ... to the word of God, recalling how he saved his people throughout history, and in the fullness of time sent his Son to be our Redeemer' (Missal). The notion of a long sequence of steps, 'again and again you offered covenant to us,' cannot be conveyed with just two or three readings as that number is simply not large enough to give a sense of God's continual steadfast love.

Given that people have come out specially and on this night are more closely attuned to the liturgy than usual, it is worth taking the extra time (it takes 10-15 minutes max.) to read all nine passages. Doing this well, with a variety of readers, and styles of music for the psalms, can let the vigil's message sink home better that any homily.

Unlike Christmas Midnight Mass, after almost fifty years this vigil has failed to capture the Christian imagination. Indeed, the introduction of the Saturday vigil Mass has often meant that this night has just become an ordinary vigil Mass with 'bits' tacked on. The liturgy tonight uses four great signs in succession (fire, word, water, and food) to convey the message that we have been remade as a people through the resurrection.

Fire breaks out in darkness – so it useless to begin before nightfall – and becomes 'our light our joy.' The great candle is the beacon of the risen Christ.

'Unless one is born of water and the Spirit, he cannot enter the kingdom of God' (Jn 3:5); we rise in Christ through being buried with him in baptism (Col 2:12) so water and baptisms are central to this night. This is the ideal time for the community to welcome new members and, in doing so, to remember that we are there because we are the baptised.

Lastly, there is the Lord's banquet. We encounter the Lord in food and we thank the Father through a food ritual. Christ our Passover has been sacrificed and, therefore, we now celebrate the feast (cf 1 Cor 5:7f) and 'the cup of blessing which we bless is ... a participation in the blood of Christ, the bread we break is ... a participation in the body of Christ' -- we are made into a new people through this sharing (1 Cor 10:16f).

Giving real ritual significance – the opposite of tokenism – to the various parts of this liturgy may be the key to establishing this as 'the night' with all its associations, as listed in the Exultet.

Introductions
The Missal has introductions to the whole vigil, the liturgy of the word, and the liturgy of baptism.

Headings for Readings

The sequence of readings is to be seen as seven steps toward the fullness of God's revelation in Christ. The Christian confession of faith is the narrative of this history of God's dealing with the creation, his repeated acts of mercy and love, until the climax of his love is shown in the coming of Christ – symbolically presented in the fanfare, bells and lighting of candles at the Gloria. The challenge is to enable people to have a sense of history as steps moving towards Christ. Each reading is seen as one such step, and the collection is an opportunity for artistic creativity to express to the senses this understanding of God as Lord of History. The ears are affected directly by the texts proclaimed; as is the voice through the periodic pauses for reflection, thanksgiving, and praise given by the psalms. But the notion of gradation can also involve the amount of light, the locations of the readers, and the use of drama. The vigil can be the occasion for communities to experiment with even more varied ways to suggest the providential movement of God's love from the beginning to the Lord's coming.

First Reading: Gen 1:1-2:2

If time is a problem, there is a shorter form. Ps 103 is better because it reflects on God's orderly care of the creation, making it a home for us. Note that language in the optional collect is exclusive.

Second Reading: Gen 22:1-18

The shorter form is better because it omits distracting details.

Third Reading : Ex 14:15-15:6; 17-18

This, with the Canticle of Moses, is obligatory as it is the type of the Passover and the antetype of the Paschal Mystery. Each collect given for this reading reflects the underlying theology of this night and can be used as keys to it.

Fourth Reading: Is 54:5-14
The Missal's rubric relates this to the notion of the new
Jerusalem (making a link between description of the city in vv.
11-12 and Apoc 21); however, the dominant theme is the Lord's
faithfulness.

Fifth Reading: Is 55:1-11
Most people assume a reading has a 'message' which is somehow a unity, either as a story or coherent as a 'lesson'; then when
they hear a passage such as this they just give up on Old
Testament readings as having any value. The notion that it is a
series of oracles has to be announced: (1) the joy of being the
Lord's followers (vv. 1-3); (2) your mission to witness to the
world (vv. 4-5; change the 'see' of the JB to 'behold'); (3) our vocation to seek God (vv. 6-9); and (4) that God's plan is not thwarted (vv. 10-11).

Sixth Reading: Bar 3:9-15; 3:32-4:4
This passage makes little sense – indeed is full of confusion – as
found in the 1982 Lectionary (1, pp. 410-11) because it uses the
Jerusalem Bible. Read the passage from the RSV or NRSV where
it is a praise of God's Wisdom personified as female (this is the
'she' and 'her' referred to in the lectionary but where 'wisdom'
is rendered sometimes by 'knowledge' and the poetic tone obscured) and the sense and beauty of the passage appear at once.

Seventh Reading
Ps 50 as the responsorial is to be preferred even if there is no
baptism.

Epistle: Rom 6:3-11
This is the classic text linking the various expressions of the
Paschal Mystery. It is a text that does not admit of rational
explanation, but calls on us to recognise that being made parts of
Christ changes our relationship to life, to death, and to one an-
other. When we try to decode this passage into a systematics

(e.g. as a theory of sacramental causality or a doctrine of election / grace) we tie ourselves up in knots; Paul was expressing his belief that the character of his own life and death was transformed by that of Christ in which he had a share.

The Alleluia

As laid out in the lectionary (p. 414) this is only noted as the 'response to the psalm'; but if it is only introduced in this way its impact after its Lenten absence is lost. Note rubric 34 (Missal, p. 207), and that this first use of 'alleluia' needs to be specially marked with some kind of fanfare.

Gospel

Year A: Mt 28:1-10

In this account it is still dark when the women arrive at the tomb. The message of the resurrection is only heard by those who are the Lord's disciples with both joy and fear – the guards are simply held by fear – but they must seek the Lord among the living and so run to be with the other disciples. It is while they are seeking the disciples that they encounter Jesus.

Year B: Mk 16:1-7

In this gospel it is the element of surprise that is its message. We, like those expecting to find the body, see death as a finality; but Jesus is the Conqueror of death. Thus the reading of this gospel is the concluding moment in the liturgy that began on Palm Sunday: Christ is the victorious one who has broken into the kingdom of death and freed all those who wait in bondage.

Year C: Lk 24:1-12

Jesus is not among the dead, but among the living – hence our liturgy is participation, not simply a pageant of reverie.

Prayer of the Faithful

Note: The Missal, n. 49, makes this point: 'the priest directs the general intercessions, in which the newly baptised take part for the first time.' Once someone is baptised s/he has become one of the priestly people and can join in this prayer interceding with the Father. Therefore, a good way of ritually making this point is to have an adult or adults, who have just been baptised, as the reader/s and lead this prayer tonight. If only infants have been baptised, then their parents or godparents would be suitable leaders tonight.

President:
On this night of Christ's resurrection let us tell the Father of our needs.
Reader (s):
Omit material in [ ] as appropriate.
1. For all baptised this night, [here and elsewhere], now our sisters and brothers, may they grow in peace and happiness. Lord hear us.
[2. For the parents and godparents of those baptised here tonight, that they may be examples of faith to inspire these children. Lord hear us.]
3. For all Christians that, as we brought the light of Christ into this darkened building tonight, so may we bring that light into our world in the months to come. Lord hear us.
4. For those who work for peace in the world, whether they call on God or not, or by whatever name they call on the divine, that they may have courage. Lord hear us.
5. For those who have died, may they enjoy the resurrection into the peace of God. Lord hear us.
President:
Father, on this holy night hear and grant our needs for we ask for them through our risen Saviour, your Son, our Lord. Amen

Eucharistic Prayer
Preface I of Easter, with Eucharistic Prayer I which has special variations for tonight

Invitation to the Our Father
Born anew in the risen Christ, we pray:
Or
Born again in the risen Christ as children of the Father, we pray:

Sign of Peace
The risen Lord's greeting is 'Peace be with you': let us exchange that greeting now.

Invitation to Communion
The risen Christ stands among us, happy are we who gather at his banquet.

Dismissal
Solemn Blessing 6 (Easter Vigil), Missal, p. 370.

COMMENTARY

The significance of the Old Testament readings at the vigil lies in their being seen as items in a connected sequence within a view of the Old Testament as a divinely inspired unity where every part speaks in some way of the coming Christ. Thus their meaning in this liturgy is more than the sum of them as individual snippets; and exegetical comments on the passages, examining each contextually, adds little to our appreciation of the scripture as used tonight. It is more useful to try to build a pattern that can form a chain of meaning between the texts. Here is one that I have found useful:

Reading 1: God is the creator – we should have concern for our environment.

Reading 2: God has chosen a people – we have links to all humanity.

Reading 3: God is the liberator of his people – we must work for justice in the world.

Reading 4: God is steadfast love – we must be faithful disciples.

Reading 5: God is generosity – we must seek and praise him.

Reading 6: God is the fount of wisdom – we must pursue wisdom in our lives.

Reading 7: God is forgiveness – we must be forgiving.

Epistle
This passage comes in a section dealing with the experience of being a Christian. The Christian is 'co-buried' with Christ and so 'co-rises' with him through the action of the Father's creative power which fills the universe (the Father's 'glory').

Gospel
In each of the three years we read a variant of the story of the women going to the empty tomb, and there being told that Jesus is not there, but risen. As a piece of text we can see Mark's account as the basic story, and then Matthew and Luke as variants on that story. But while this might explain the synoptic relationships between the accounts, it misses a fundamental point about the primitive kerygma. There are so many varying details between the three accounts, that this story must have been part of the earliest preaching, which became elaborated with slightly different nuances and theologies in the various churches. And, what we have is three of those variants. Thus the position of the story in Mark, which was presumably the form of the story he knew in his church, prompted the location in Matthew and Luke, but each of these used the variant they were familiar with rather than following Mark.

The story has six elements:

1. It is about a discovery by women (who these are and their number varies in each story) who were going to anoint the body of Jesus. It has been commented upon since the earliest times that normally the testimony of women was inferior to that of men. So this insistence on women indicates both how early the story entered the tradition, and would have heightened its surprise element for the audiences. Incidentally, when medieval canon law broke with western legal tradition and admitted equal validity to the testimony of women and men, it was this story that was cited as the precedent.

2. The discovery takes place on the 'first day of the week'. Even

by Mark's time – our earliest witness to the story – Sunday was the day of the weekly gathering for the Eucharist. So locating the story on Sunday indicates that it was a resurrection story for recitation at the Eucharist (long before there were any of the written gospels for reading at the gathering). It is quite possible that the story was recited at each Eucharist as a explanation tale of why it was on that day the church was meeting to encounter its Lord.

3. Someone (an angel in Matthew; a man in Mark; two men in dazzling clothes in Luke) tell them that Jesus is not among the dead but the living – this is the kernel of the story and the kerygma; and has to be understood in its audience's *Sitz-im-Leben*: the liturgical assembly hearing the story. Hence, to seek the Lord among the living, is to seek him in the eucharistic Assembly.

4. 'He will go before you into Galilee' – whatever this meant originally, it was already obscure by the time of Mark, and neither Matthew nor Luke understood it either. Although Matthew tried to make sense of it by repeating it at v. 10, and having the concluding scene of his gospel located there (28:16-20).

5. The women experience a mixture of fear, joy, astonishment, and perplexity at what happens to them.

6. They have to tell or they go to tell the disciples of what has happened at the tomb. In all four gospels it is women who are the first preachers of the resurrection.

Year A

In Matthew's story there are two significant variants. First, the cosmic event (the earthquake, the angel descending from heaven, the rolling back of the stone) only takes place when the faithful women arrive at the tomb – it is not just an empty tomb that they happen upon. The tomb is revealed to them by the angel as empty. Fear is something that only happens to the guards – they become like dead men, but the angel speaks only to the women and tells them not to be afraid. In Matthew the resurrection is something that only makes sense and gives joy to the disciples – to the outsiders, the guards, it is all just a cosmic *mysterium tremendum*. Second, the final verse in tonight's gospel (v. 9) is only found in Matthew: the women met the risen Jesus *en route* to the disciples, and they fell down, grasped his feet and adored him. Note this last point: 'they adored him' was omitted by the JB (the NJB tied to correct this by adding 'and did him homage'; it is in the Greek text (and the Vulgate: *et adoraverunt eum*), and so in the RSV and NRSV which both render it as 'and worshipped him' – so it should be added to the text when read. It is a lovely little detail showing that devotion to Christ was already a standard part of Christian prayer by the time Matthew wrote.

Year B

In the original form of Mark, this passage (with v. 8 which has been omitted as jarring with the liturgy's theme of surprise-joy while Mark has surprise-fear) was the gospel's concluding scene and the sole reference to the risen Jesus. Its force is that a sealed tomb has been opened, a tomb that should contain someone waiting for the resurrection at the end is already empty. Mark's stark ending has troubled readers down the centuries – hence the addition of other endings such as the one commonly found in our editions (vv. 9-20) – but it is the dramatic riposte to the long passion narrative. All that intrigue and wickedness to inflict death, destroy Jesus, his message, and his movement has ended in failure: only hours later the tomb is empty, his promises are being fulfilled.

Year C

This is Luke's variant on the empty tomb presentation of the resurrection. Here the grave symbolises the defeat and captivity that could not bind the Christ. This is a complex symbolism that has become opaque to most Christians through the now standard confusion of the Christian notion of resurrection with the common belief in the soul's immortality. It can be interpreted generically as Christ having died has passed beyond all limitations and so is not in one place, a tomb, but available to all who call on him.

If the liturgy is done well and the Old Testament readings have been introduced, then there has been enough comment. If comment is needed, then it could reflect on the words of the Exultet or blessing of the baptismal water, or just a note on tonight's gospel's place in the early churches.

Easter Sunday

The Liturgy does not vary between Years A, B, and C; but does contain several important options.

Note

There is a fundamental liturgical problem with Easter Sunday: after all the ceremony and symbolism of the Easter Vigil, this day-time Eucharist *looks* very much like every other Sunday. The addition of the Alleluia and the Sequence, the content of the readings and prayers may all point out its unique character within the liturgical year, but such things do not grab the senses and impact on the average member of the congregation, much less those who only come occasionally, and say 'this is special,' 'this idea of celebrating the resurrection is a central idea in Christianity.' Celebrants contribute to this by the fact that liturgically it feels like an ordinary Sunday and most ministers are tired after the ceremonies of the Triduum. So the challenge is to find ways to make this day stand out.

We must remember that the cycle of the year, in the liturgy and every way, is a cycle of 'stressed' and 'unstressed time,' each setting the other off. A birthday or an anniversary is a 'stressed' time, but that stands out because other days are 'just normal', humdrum, unstressed. Easter Sunday is the stressed Sunday in the whole year – and we need ways of ritually displaying this.

An obvious way is to have a more elaborate procession and use incense throughout the liturgy. In a lower register there can be a blessing of 'Easter Eggs' for children before the dismissal, or it might be just the use of the Rite of Blessing and Sprinkling water at the beginning: but the liturgy must convey our joy and that this Sunday is special above every other.

Introduction to the Celebration

Every Sunday we gather to recall that Christ rose from the dead and has given us new life, but today is special as it recalls the original Sunday. This is our great annual feast proclaiming that death has been conquered and our sins forgiven. This is the great day of Christian joy: Christ is risen.

Use the rite of blessing and sprinkling holy water using, after the introduction, formula 'c' (Missal, p. 388).

Headings for Readings
First Reading

This speech put into the mouth of Peter is an expression of the basic Christian proclamation: the ministry of Jesus seemed to end in his death, but God raised him to new life – this is the Christian confession of faith.

Second Reading
1 Cor 5:6-8
This alternative reading is to be preferred as it is easier for people to see its relationship with the feast than is the case with Col 3:1-4.

We are celebrating the feast of our Paschal Lamb. Paul wrote assuming that his audience knew that at the Passover all old yeast was removed from the house and that a new, fresh dough was needed to start a new year. Our Passover, Easter, is also a new beginning in our lives, and the new start we make must be to lives of sincerity and truth.

Col 3:1-4

Today we celebrate not only that Christ is risen, but that we have risen with him, and since we have risen, we must have the lifestyle of new life.

The Sequence: Victimae paschali laudes

Sequences are so uncommon in the liturgy that congregations do not know how to respond to them: should they be read? sung? or what? Sequences were produced in the middle ages as extensions of the alleluia and gradually grew into a musical element of their own. Written in rhyming verse they have a playful elegance in Latin, but this cannot be rendered in translation without seemingly meaningless combinations of ideas – and today's sequence is a good example. However, the sheer difference the sequence makes to the 'ordinary run' of the liturgy, make it a good element to show that this is 'stressed' time.

Since it is a piece of Latin verse for singing, then this may be the time to get the choir to sing it in the original – the use of former liturgical languages has been a means of showing special time in the Roman rite for more than a millennium (e.g. the Greek phrases in the Good Friday liturgy). The counter argument would be everything must be comprehensible – but that would mean that we abandon all talk of God and all liturgy in favour of an arid rationalism.

Gospel
The lectionary allows replacing Jn 20:1-9 with one of the vigil gospels. This is worth doing for three reasons: 1. Mk 16:1-7 has a stark simplicity in its message that the grave is not the end of Jesus; 2. that text fits better with the sequence (which is based on the synoptics rather than John); and 3. John has so many details that it presents a stronger mental image of one apostle running faster than another, than of the fact that the tomb was empty. See Easter Vigil, Year B for an introductory heading for Mk 16:1-7.

If you chose Jn 20:1-9, then here is a heading:
Every time we recall the empty tomb of Jesus, we recall that the grave is not the destiny for those reborn in the risen Christ.

At evening Mass, the Lectionary offers the option of using Lk 24:13-35 – the Emmaus story – which, at that time today, has the advantage of the liturgy following the time sequence of the Easter narrative. Heading:
On this evening of Easter Sunday gathered for 'the breaking of the bread,' we now read the account of the evening of the first Easter Sunday and how the disciples discovered that the Lord had risen and was with them 'in the breaking of the bread'.
The Renewal of Baptismal Promises

This replaces the creed today. This can be far more effective if, as at the vigil, the congregation hold candles lighted from the Paschal Candle. The time taken to do this can serve to focus attention of the Paschal Candle which, while it received much attention at the Vigil, during Easter Sunday can be missed as just one more item of liturgical furniture.

Prayer of the Faithful
President:
On this Sunday of Sundays, when we recall that Christ has broken the chains of death, and made us children of the Father, let us pray for ourselves, all Christians, and all humanity.
Reader (s):
1. For all baptised this Easter, that the risen Christ may become manifest in them.
2. For all of us who have renewed our baptismal commitment, that we may bear witness to our hope in the way we live.
3. For those who work for peace, reconciliation, and justice, that the risen Christ may give them new strength.
4. For all for whom faith is a struggle, that they may be helped by the joy of Christians.
5. For all in difficult situations at home or at work, that this may be a time of hope.
6. For those who have died, may they share in Christ's resurrection.
President:
Father, you raised Jesus from the dead, and your glory raises us to new life today. Grant us our petitions through that same Christ, our Lord. Amen

Eucharistic Prayer
Preface I of Easter; and Eucharistic Prayer I has special variations.

Invitation to the Our Father
The risen Christ stands among us. With him we pray:

Sign of Peace
'Peace be with you' was Christ's greeting when he appeared to
his disciples. Let us use his words to greet one another.

Invitation to Communion
This is the Lamb of God, the conqueror of sin and death, happy
are those who are called to his supper.

Communion Reflection
Edmund Spenser's poem 'Easter' (Poem 71, Breviary, vol 2, p.
608*).

Dismissal
Solemn Blessing 6 (Easter Sunday), Missal, p. 370.

COMMENTARY

First Reading: Acts 10:34, 37-40
This is one of the carefully crafted speeches put into the mouth
of Peter in the early part of Acts and intended to summarise the
earliest Christian message (compare this one with that in 2:14-
36). What is most significant about them is that they take the
form of a history of salvation: the events leading up to Jesus, the
events of his life and death, with the event of the resurrection as
the culmination which leads directly to the offer of salvation
now being made by the apostles.

Second Reading:
1 Cor 5:6-80
This passage, so apposite for Easter, is part of an exhortation to
Christians to live morally up-right lives and is directed in parti-
cular to a case of incest in the community in Corinth of which
Paul has heard (5:1-8).

Col 3:1-4
Paul points out that Christians do not just believe in the resurrection of Christ, but in their own resurrection now through baptism. It is this new life that is the basis of all Christian morality. However, the meaning of Christ's rising and our rising is not some material fact, it belongs to the heavenly realms, it is a mystery in which we share, and we will only 'know' it when it is fully revealed in the future. So 'we walk by faith, not by sight' (2 Cor 5:7).

Gospel
If you use one of the gospels set out for the Easter Vigil, see the comment offered there.

If you use Jn 20:1-9:
One of the features of John's use of the empty tomb narrative is that it was only at this moment that the disciples could understand the message of the scriptures about the Christ. In this narrative being located 'on the first day of the week' we see the practice of the early church to gather on Sunday to celebrate the Eucharist and encounter the risen Christ there.

At evening Mass, use Lk 24:13-35, and see Third Sunday of Easter Year A for comment.

HOMILY NOTES

1. The resurrection is the source of Christian hope: our lives are not circumscribed by life as we know it now, but can open onto a new life in the presence of God. This is the mystery beyond words, yet somehow today it has to be the subject of our preaching. However, there are two widely held misconceptions which prevent people hearing what the liturgy says about the resurrection today in its symbols, prayers, and readings. A useful task in the homily is to draw attention to these mistaken ideas. The first is that it was some sort of resuscitation, a trick to prove that Jesus was right, an event which you either believe happened or did not happen back then. This misconception distracts from a hope in our resur-

rection in the future. The resurrection is not about resuscitation, but our future transformation. The second, and far more widespread notion, is that resurrection is just a fancy terms for a belief in an afterlife of some sort or other – the number of practising Christians who think that re-incarnation can be squared with Christian faith is an indication of this confusion's prevalence. Our faith is not about some kind of post mortem survival, but in God's gift of the fullness of life.

2. So, the first point is to avoid 'explaining ' the mystery as if it were a series of 'facts' that can just be acknowledged as having happened so-and-so many years ago. In earlier times each item in the resurrection accounts was studied like the clues in a detective story with the aim of building an apologetic that would explain the 'how' of the resurrection and the 'what' of the risen body of Jesus. But the kerygma of the resurrection lies not in the details of 'the first Easter,' but in the reality that those who join their lives with the Christ shall share a fuller, glorious, transformed life as the gift of the Father. We can inherit the Father's gift of glory as the final fulfilment of human life. It is worth pointing out that the disciple today must not be distracted by the 'how' and 'what' questions of 'the first Easter' from remembering that Christian faith strains onward to the future: the cost of discipleship now and tomorrow is worth it for the path of righteousness does not end with a grave. Many wonder whether or not they 'can believe' in the empty tomb, but this misses the point. Belief in the resurrection is seen when someone, even in the face of death, still follows the path of love with the confidence that the Father will 'not abandon my soul to Hades, nor let his Holy One see corruption' (Acts 2:27 [Ps 16:10]).

3. Second, belief in the resurrection is not some christianised version of a belief in the immortality of the soul. A belief in immortality is a human sense that a bit, some sort of spiritual

residue, can survive without a body. The belief in the resurrection is that we are each creatures willed by God, in whose histories God is interested as the loving Father, and into whose history he has sent his Son sharing our humanity, and therefore whose whole existence 'spirit, soul, and body' can be transformed to become part of his Son's glorious body. Easter is not a celebration of a 'survival factor' in humanity, but of the Father's love so that nothing good shall perish, but be given even fuller life.

4. To believe in the message of Easter is not a matter of tombs long ago in Palestine, but having the conviction that it is worthwhile to seek to bring light in darkness, to oppose lies with truth, to work for justice in the face of human corruption, and to say that death does not have the last word.

5. When we profess our faith in the resurrection of Jesus we are not setting out something with the intention that our understandings should grasp it and comprehend it. Jesus has been transformed to a new kind of existence by the Father beyond our understanding and we can only express it in symbols such as that of the empty tomb – tombs, after all, are designed to hold their remains indefinitely. By contrast, the proclamation 'Jesus is Risen' is an invitation to share in a new way of seeing God and the universe, and it is only from within this new vision (faith) that it makes sense. Hence, the ancient theological dictum, based in Isaiah 7:9, 'unless you believe, you will not understand.' The message of Acts and the gospel is that we are invited to live, to live in a new way, to live in Christ – and that in living in this way we discover in the midst of suffering and death that the Father will raise us as he raised the Christ.

6. If we join with those who accept the invitation to new life in Christ, which is what we say we are doing in accepting baptism and renewing our baptismal promises, we become part of a new people. The Christian 'thing' is about being part of a people, not about individualist survival or a privately-defined relationship with 'the Wholly Other', and as such it

commits us to a way of living. The early followers were referred to as being on 'The Way' (see Acts 9:2; 18:26; 19:9 and
23; 22:4,14 and 22) and our oldest extant teaching manual
(The *Didache*) begins by contrasting 'The Way of Life' (to be
followed by disciples) with 'The Way of Death.'

7. The thought of resurrection may fill us with joy, but the life-
    demands that accepting it makes on us can be great: we must
    do as we would be done to (cf *Didache* 1:2; Mt 7:12; Lk 6:31),
    we must practice the forgiveness we desire from the Father
    (cf the 'Our Father'), and we must act with gentleness. Only
    in constant effort to live life in this way can we glimpse the
    truth of the empty tomb.

8. To live this life demands patience, a waiting for the good
    things to be revealed – the practice of the virtue of hope: we
    must always be of good courage ... for we walk by faith, not
    by sight (cf 2 Cor 5:6f). Today is our day for rejoicing in the
    risen Christ, for thanking the Father for his love, and for re-
    minding ourselves of that to which we have committed our-
    selves: The Way. Death has contended with Life, yet despite
    tombs and symbols of death all around us, we proceed to
    commit ourselves to life, confident that as the Father trans-
    formed the existence of Jesus, so he will transform the whole
    creation.

Preaching on Sundays in Eastertide

Every time we preach at the Eucharist there is some, at least incidental, element of self-reference in the homily. We preach of the encounter between the risen Lord and the people with whom he shares his resurrection – otherwise either (a) we would not be preaching to baptised brothers and sisters, or (b) our statement would not be a homily but a religious lecture intruding into the Eucharist – and we make this statement as an integral part of an event that celebrates the central moment of that encounter within our lives. In effect, we always say something in a Eucharistic homily that pertains to the Eucharist we are celebrating. This reaches a high-point during Eastertide when each Sunday – not just as on Sunday 3A when we read the Emmaus story (Lk 24:13-35) – the theme of encountering the risen Christ is in every gospel text, and so consequently is the eucharistic theme. But this raises some fundamental theological and historical problems. Is this eucharistic interpretation a development – albeit a legitimate one – from the gospel texts (i.e. the gospel writers were primarily interested in preaching the risen Jesus and the possibility of encounter with him, but we now link this with the sacramental encounter); or is it something inherent in the texts (i.e. that the gospel writers were already thinking in terms of the regular Eucharistic encounter when they wrote)? Many writers slip unconsciously into the first position for we think of the events in the narratives' time (a few days after the crucifixion) rather than in their historical setting which is their authors' time (many decades later). Moreover, there is a tendency to imagine that the book came first and then came the church (as when Christians adopt the title 'people of the book' for themselves) forgetting that the book was produced by the church for its needs and reflects the church, and not vice versa. Lastly, there is a tendency to forget that ritual was a central part of Christianity from the outset and not some later sign of degeneration – as the eighteenth-century Rationalists and nineteenth-century Liberal Protestants imagined – and so it is within the framework of their formative rituals (such as Baptism, the Eucharist, fixed times for prayer and fasting) that we should read their literary products. For example, if we think of John's gospel in terms of the Johannine community, then we must remember that that community was celebrating the Eucharist each week long before it heard the stories in Jn 6, and it is in the light of their community experience that they would have heard them.

For the earliest generations of Christians the weekly Eucharist was not only the main occasion of the kerygma (cf Acts 20:7) whereby they re-affirmed their identity by retelling their 'narrative' of the Christ-event (cf Lk 1:1), but it was the moment of their sacramental encounter with the risen Christ through their fellowship (*koinónia*) in 'the Lord's table' (cf 1 Cor 10:21) which Luke refers to as 'the breaking of the loaf' (Lk 24:35, and Acts 2:42 and 46).

A case in point is the Emmaus story (Lk 24) which today we read on Sunday 3A (and on the evening of Easter Sunday). The living practice in the churches in Luke's time – and an increasing number of scholars think he wrote last, possibly in the second decade of the second century – lies behind that story, and so offers an obviously rich field for the homilist to explore the text in the light of the community's own experience of the Eucharist, for the text has always been heard by people with such eucharistic experience. In effect, that story presents us with two groups. One is in the building around you the reader, the other is implied in the texts of Luke and Acts. Both are groups of Christians gathered for Word and Table, but separated by nineteen centuries, languages, and cultures – they are quite literally worlds apart. Yet both groups see this weekly gathering as an encounter with the risen Christ. Let us assume that we, the various people who make up the assembly, know why we have gathered, then it is interesting to see what reasons drew the earlier group to this meal – or, more pointedly, what reasons Luke (as their preacher) believes should be attracting them to this liturgy.

The structure of Luke's text is based upon the ritual of his community. Firstly, the whole event takes place on a Sunday (v. 13 referring back to 24:1). We do not know when Sunday became the day of Christian assembly, but it was so prior to the traditions recorded in the *Didache* and so was, in all probability, well established by 50 AD. It is worth noting that John – see Sunday 2A – assumes Sunday is the day of gathering, for he structures his resurrection narrative around it. In any case it was long-established custom by Luke's time (Acts 20:7), and already Easter day was seen as the paradigm for each Sunday. Luke reverses the logic, so that if each Sunday has a Eucharist, and Easter day is the paradigm for each Sunday, then the first Christian day must have had a Eucharist – hence the Emmaus story. Secondly, once the trio mentioned as walking towards Emmaus have got together, we are told of their recounting the events surrounding Jesus and then the exegesis of the scriptures (vv. 19-27) which corresponds to the reading and preaching section of his communities' ritual – the equivalent in our liturgical terminology to 'the Liturgy of the Word.' Thirdly, there follows the gathering at table when 'he took a loaf and blessed and broke and give it to them' (v. 30) – the rite Luke calls 'the breaking of the loaf' (v. 35) and we 'the Liturgy of the Eucharist'.

It is worth noting that the verbal similarity between v. 30 and surviving eucharistic prayers (e.g. our EP I) is more probably explained as parallel developments from the earliest usage of the church, rather than a case where an anaphora borrowed phrases in an attempt to deliberately echo a gospel text. Luke's text is redolent of ritually established prose (compare v. 30 with 22:19 and 1 Cor 11:23-4 [the earliest extant witness to the phrase]; Mk 14:22 and Mt 26:26). We have, in essence, a single formula ('took bread ... blessed ... broke ... gave') with slight variations in the five texts (no two are identical); this indicates a phrase shaped by repetitive oral usage being independently committed to writing from memory.

For Luke, it is in this ritual of breaking and sharing the loaf that the community experience the risen Christ, and so it is at this point that the two disciples recognise him – and he vanishes from sight (v. 31). This is significant in that Luke does not want to make the sacramental experience of his own community to appear any less real than that of these prototypical disciples, i.e. both his community and the first disciples can only glimpse the risen Jesus when they reflect from their standpoint of knowing the whole plan of revelation – which the community believed it had – upon what happens in their weekly Eucharist (v. 32).

So how does Luke imagine that the disciples in his story could suddenly recognise Jesus 'in the breaking of the loaf' (v. 35)? The answer probably lies in his community having a particular ritual form of breaking which distinguished this sacramental action from the practical breaking that took place at ordinary meals. Thus, within the narrative, when someone on that first Easter day can both explain the scriptures and knows their specific way of breaking the loaf, that person must be their eucharistic leader who had shown them that way of breaking earlier (Lk 22:19)! Within Luke's understanding of the connection of the church's life with the risen Christ (seen more in Acts than in his gospel), Emmaus is both a paradigm and the archetype of the weekly Eucharist. We must never forget as we read the Emmaus story that the written texts we call the gospels are the products of a church gathering to celebrate the liturgy (the sequence is: Jesus > community liturgy > texts > [our] gospels), and not vice versa. It is all too easy to revert to the false historical sequence (Jesus > gospels > believers, and eventually rituals) which underlay so much of the Reformation's down-playing of the role of the Eucharist in the church's life and as the locus for encountering the Christ.

Looking at the Emmaus story we can see how communities, still without any Christian-produced text with the status of 'scripture', carried out the activity equivalent to our Liturgy of the Word. One of the formative elements of the early church was their re-reading of Jewish literature in terms of their belief in Jesus as the Christ: those writings foretold him or could now be read clearly through having, at the end of time, a knowledge of the whole divine plan. Many of those writings are still familiar to most Christians as the Old Testament of printed Bibles, more of them are familiar to Catholics and Orthodox through their adherence to more primitive Christian scriptural canons, but many of them have disappeared completely. Reading that literature gave them a series of ways to understand the place of Jesus within a larger pattern of revelation and a set of existential problems for which the work of Jesus was the solution (e.g. grace had been lost in Adam, so Christ as 'last Adam' restores it: 1 Cor 15:22 and 45). We see this re-reading in every early Christian text, but can observe its method very clearly in the first reading and gospel of Sunday 3A. The first reading presents the inspired apostle, Peter, seeing that which was unclear to the prophet David made clear to those who know the Christ, and that which was foreseen being fulfilled in Jesus. The gospel presents two disciples receiving what was, from Luke's perspective (and that of most Christian exegetes until a couple of centuries ago), the ultimate tutorial in exegesis: the Summit of revelation himself revealing everything about himself in the whole scheme of revelation up to that moment in history (vv. 25-27 – and note that v. 27 is the key verse): hence their 'burning hearts' while listening to an exegetical lecture (v. 32)! The early Christians saw themselves as 'the ideal readers' to whom and for whom God had initiated, and now completed, the whole plan of revelation. In making sense of Jesus through 'the scriptures' (i.e. pre-Christian Jewish writings), they could make sense both of themselves and the creation, or at least this was Luke's conviction.

Moreover, it is worth reflecting that (1) while we tend not to understand the Christ-event through re-reading their earlier writings, and (2) contemporary biblical scholarship eschews reading pre-Christian Jewish texts in terms of any supposed 'latent' Christian significance; this notion of preparation-and-fulfilment is still the reason why the church sets Old Testament texts for reading in the liturgy: it is with this logic that the Old Testament text is paired with a gospel reading for each Sunday outside Eastertide (cf. *Instruction on the Lectionary*, n 106 echoing

Dei Verbum, n 16). But are we prepared to interpret in this way in our homilies? Even if we are not, then it is still a central feature of the Liturgy of the Word that we seek to make sense of our lives and world in terms of our collective recalling of the Christ-event: this is why there are homilies after gospel readings!

The particular Eucharistic theology conveyed by Luke through his use of the term 'the breaking of the loaf' is glimpsed by relating his text with that in *Didache* 9, 4 on 'the broken loaf scattered on the mountains' (even if the final form of the *Didache* is early second century and so may post-date Luke, then its individual parts are pre-70 and certainly pre-date Luke) and Paul's imagery of 'one loaf, one body' in 1 Cor 10:16-17. The imagery in all these texts seems to rely on the Jewish image of the people (a single entity: a body) being scattered abroad as a punishment for sin (e.g. 1 Kgs 22:17, Ezek 34:6, Nah 3:18, Hab 3:6) which was linked with the messianic image that when the final acceptable time would come, that process would be reversed (e.g. Jer 31:10, Ezek 28:25). For the Christians this gathering back into a unity, his own body, was what was occurring in Jesus and was symbolised in the Eucharist. The loaf, a single entity ('loaf' is the name of a particular thing: one buys a loaf; whereas 'bread' is the generic name of a foodstuff – and within this symbolic range 'loaf' is a far more sensitive translation than 'bread') is a gathering together of that which has been scattered abroad: the harvest takes place at the right time of completion when the products of the scattered seed grain is gathered (Jesus is the harvester: Jer 31:10 and Lk 3:17) and made into a unity: a loaf. This then becomes the Lord's body which is broken so that disciples can have a share in that unity – taking a part of the loaf, and uniting with it by eating it, is participating in the communion: 'since there is one loaf, we who are many are one body, for we all take a share of the one loaf.'

This approach is not dominant in western theology, and has not been prominent for almost a millennium, but it does peep out in the liturgy (e.g. repeating the 'Lamb of God' chant for the time taken to break up a loaf, or the rite of holding-up loaf fragments at 'This is the Lamb of God') and it is that symbolic code underlying many eucharistic references in Eastertide.

Further Reading:
J.Z. Smith, *Drudgery Divine: On the Comparison of Early Christianities and the Religions of Antiquity* (London 1990).
É. Nodet and J. Taylor, *The Origins of Christianity: An Exploration* (Collegeville 1998).

Second Sunday of Easter Year A

Note

Several themes come together in the liturgy today. (1) It is the Octave Day of Easter: the mystery of resurrection is too great for just one day and so the 'day of resurrection' must be extended until today. It is a day that takes a week to celebrate. (2) It is the Eighth Day and so is symbolically the passing from resurrection to the fullness of new life. It is a passage from rising with Christ in this world through faith, to the final rising in the next Age. That is, just as we celebrate Christ's resurrection now in Easter, so on this day we liturgically anticipate the final end of resurrection in a new and future life. As such, today points forward to the fullness of the kingdom. (3) Historically this day was connected with baptism: this is the day when those baptised at the Easter Vigil stopped wearing special white baptismal garments and took their places as ordinary members of the assembly. Hence its old liturgical name: *Dominica in albis [depositis]*, Sunday when the white garments are put aside. This link with baptism is prominent in the prayers of this liturgy.

Practically this has importance for planning today's liturgy. After the splendour or the Easter Vigil and Easter Day liturgies, and the extra attention focused on the liturgy in Lent, getting back too quickly to the humdrum ordinary Sunday liturgy misses a valuable opportunity to vary the celebration and highlight the centrality of the resurrection in Christian belief. So today it is a very good idea to draw attention to the links between baptism and resurrection (for most people, and indeed most preaching, baptism is seen primarily in terms of identification: 'joining up with the church'). This can be done by way of the Asperges (Missal, p. 388) or more usefully by celebrating a baptism within Mass. In this case avoid wordy explanations and homilies – just say 'Since resurrection time is the time of baptism we will welcome a new brother/sister among us in this celebration', then have the baptism after the gospel and let the event be the preaching.

Introduction to the Celebration
Characteristic of the people who rejoice in the Lord's victory over death is that they gather regularly for 'the breaking of the bread'. In this action we recognise the presence of the risen Christ and are invited to see that as we share a single loaf and cup, so we share in his new life. This new life has the promise of overcoming division, sin, and death: but are we really prepared to share with those around us? And if we are willing to accept forgiveness from the risen Lord, are we also ready to offer forgiveness?

Rite of Penance
The Easter Asperges (Missal, p. 388) is preferable.

Headings for Readings
First Reading
Luke presents us with the key features of life of the Christian group: (1) they are faithful to the teaching, (2) they are committed to the community, (3) they take part in the eucharistic meal, and (4) they have a regular scheme of prayers.

Second Reading
This reading points out the importance of hope for Christians. Hope is not a cosy optimism that 'eventually it will all turn out OK', but the willingness to wait through the trials of this life for the glory that is promised by God. We say at Easter that 'Christ is risen' and 'we have new life', but we still face the sufferings of this life each day. This reading tells us that these should be viewed as trials and tests which can show up for us areas of our lives where the new lifestyle of discipleship, begun in baptism and renewed at Easter, has not yet reached.

Gospel

Christ came among his people gathered on Easter Sunday; then eight days later, today, he came again among them: each time he offered them peace, forgiveness, and the promise of new life.

Or, insert this scene-setter after the greeting and announcement: 'A reading from the holy gospel ... '

In St John's gospel the appearance in the room to the fearful disciples takes place late on the day of Easter. Some of the disciples, Peter and 'the beloved disciple', have been to the tomb, seen it empty, and returned home. Now they have heard from Mary Magdalene that she has seen the Lord. So they wait in fear mixed with confusion and expectation, and debate, and a sense of 'I just wonder if' and of 'it just can't be'. Against such a scene, the gospel continues:

Prayer of the Faithful
President:

On this day of resurrection, we have gathered for the breaking of the loaf. Through Christ present in our assembly let us ask the Father for our needs.

Reader(s):

1. For all Christians, that we may be faithful to the teaching of the apostles.

2. For the sisters and brothers baptised at Easter, that they may be faithful to the community.

3. For all gathering today for the breaking of the bread, that in the shared loaf and cup we may recognise the risen Christ.

4. For ourselves who have received Christ's forgiveness, that we may be forgiving.

5. That those who have died may come through Christ's resurrection to 'praise and glory and honour'.

President:

Father, we believe without sight or touch that your Son has conquered death and stands among us, so hear, we ask you, these prayers for we make them through Christ our Lord. Amen.

Eucharistic Prayer
Preface 1 of Easter (P 21, Missal, p. 424); and since Eucharistic
Prayer I has special variations (i.e. a 'Communicantes' and 'Hanc
igitur' – items 85 and 89 in the Eucharistic liturgy in the Missal)
today, it is an obvious choice. The special quality of the time can
be highlighted by drawing attention to this just before the preface.

Invitation to the Our Father
The disciples were faithful to 'the prayers'. Let us now pray in
union with Christians of all times and places:

Sign of Peace
The Lord's resurrection greeting is 'Peace be with you'; so as his
disciples, let us exchange that greeting.

Invitation to Communion
In the broken loaf, the disciples recognised the Lord, the Lamb
of God who takes away the sins of the world, happy are those ...

Communion Reflection
Some of the chants given in the *Note on Breaking and Sharing*.

Dismissal
Solemn Blessing 7 (Easter Season), Missal, p. 370.

COMMENTARY

First Reading: Acts 2:42-47
Luke's aim was to present an ideal past which could serve as a
model for what actual communities, his audience, should be
striving after. As an ideal for the common life of disciples it functions as a check-list against which every community can measure itself. Firstly there is the stress on the common elements of
being church: they have a common teaching to which they must
be loyal, they have a common set of concerns for those around
them, and they must have a real common experience in gather-

LITURGICAL RESOURCES

ing for a common meal. Secondly, as a community they have a recurring structural feature which gives them identity: they gather in their homes for 'the breaking of the loaf' (mentioned twice) – 'loaf' is a better translation as it brings out that it is a single tangible reality that is shared, not just many individuals having the same kind of food. It is around this feature that other aspects of their discipleship are organised. This text, along with today's gospel, shows us that the regular Eucharist was the central focus of Christian community life in the late first century. If we want to explore its details, we should view today's readings as a theological reflection on the directions for those gatherings that are set out in the *Didache*.

This passage has been labelled in modern scholarship as the 'First Major Summary'; the Second Major Summary is read on this Sunday in Year B, and the Third Major Summary on this Sunday in Year C.

Psalm: 117
Note that verse 22 of this Psalm ('The stone which the builders rejected ...') was prominent in the primitive Christian kerygma in attempts to understand the rejection of Jesus by his people and his vindication by the Father in the resurrection: cf Mt 21:42; Acts 4:11; 1 Cor 3:11; Eph 2:20; and 1 Pet 2:7-8. And it is in this sense, referring to the crucified and risen Lord, whose day we are celebrating, that the Psalm is used here.

Second Reading: 1 Pet 1:3-9
Written in a community under external stress, this is encouragement to Christian courage and fortitude; and it seeks to answer the 'why us' question of those who are suffering by seeing those sufferings as 'the things sent to try us'.

Gospel: Jn 20:19-31
On no other day in the three-year cycle does a text's meaning within its book-setting (i.e. a piece of text within the whole gospel) and its meaning within the liturgy come into so perfect

an alignment – hence its use in Years A, B, and C on this day. The reason for this is not accidental, and most simple: here the structure the evangelist gives to the text is itself the product of the church's liturgical structure, with its weekly celebration of the Eucharist being perceived as its weekly collective encounter with the risen Lord. John's community (like every other Christian community at the time as we witness through the earlier document, the *Didache*) gathered weekly in a private house for the Eucharist and it is against this familiar setting that John imagined the earliest encounters with the risen Christ which he wants to present as prototypical of his own community's experience. The text begins with the Christian assembly on Easter Sunday (v. 19-23). Being together in one room there is a sense of positive identity as 'the disciples,' and of being a distinct group in that the doors are locked. There they experience the Lord becoming present, offering peace and a mission of reconciliation. Thomas's doubt (vv. 24-25) is a sequel which allows a link to the following Sunday, and which is given without a formal time marker: it is presented as a weekday event between two Sunday assemblies. A week later – today in the liturgy – they are again assembled in a house, and again experience the risen Christ. And it is in the context of the church's liturgy (be it the community for whom John wrote or your community to whom you read John) that we have to understand the words addressed to Thomas: it is those disciples who must encounter Jesus sacramentally in the assembly – without the visual encounter of the two prototypical Sunday Eucharists – who are the blessed ones. This passage shows us more forcefully than the synoptics' 'institution texts' (e.g. Mt 26:26-29) the centrality of the Eucharist, a regular weekly assembly, in the life and religious identity of the earliest Christians.

Even a cursory reading of this extract gives one a sense that the text is disjointed: first there is the meeting with the disciples in the house, then the Thomas incident, and finally a remark that sounds like the conclusion of the whole gospel. This initial response to the extract is quite justified as there are three distinct

textual items here; but in the mind of John they are consequences of Christ's resurrection and each item, in some way,
points to the Johannine picture of the identity of Jesus.

The first item is vv. 19-23 on the sending of the Spirit and the
ministry of forgiveness. It picks up two themes that are part of
the tradition as found in Matthew and Luke: first, a demonstration that the crucified Jesus is to be identified with the glorious
risen Son; and second, that the community is given the Spirit to
enable it to witness to the forgiveness of sins. This sending out of
the church as witnesses is part of the glorification of Jesus by the
Father. (Note that there is an echo of John's anti-Jewish polemic
in this text.)

The second item is the story, only found in John, of 'doubting
Thomas' (24-9) – although the theme of disbelief is also found in
Luke. The focus of this story is the acclamation of 'My Lord and
my God' which is the culmination of a series of acclamations
throughout the gospel regarding the identity of Jesus (cf 1:49;
4:42; 6:69; 9:37; 11:27; and 16:30). Crucified and risen, the incar-
nate Word is now fully revealed, hence everyone who comes
after this event and believes is blessed.

The third item is the two verses on the purpose of the gospel
(30-1) which sees the gospel as a series of 'signs' (*sémeia*) revealing the identity of Jesus: the greatest of his 'signs' is the resurrection which shows him to be messiah and Son. The actual phrase
is probably a survival from the conclusion to one of John's
sources, the 'Book of Signs'.

The words of Jesus on the mission to forgive sins come to us
with a long tradition of Christian use and controversy in the
sacramental theology relating to the sacrament of penance.
However, it should be noted that this use cannot be sustained on
the basis of the text apart from a distinct set of assumptions regarding the nature of inspiration and ecclesial authority. One
cannot, for instance, assume that a statement such as 'here
Christ institutes the sacrament of penance' (cf Denzinger-
Schönmetzer n 1710) is the 'simple' interpretation. This view
presupposes that (1) the later canonical forms and propositional

theological elaborations of the Latin church were present latently in the text (i.e. unknown to the author of the text, or more precisely in this style of exegesis: 'unknown to the human author'), (2) that the text is an absolute inerrant record written with the whole history of the church present in the divine mind, and (3) that the actual form of the later use of this text is a deductive unfolding of what was always there. Anyone adopting this approach to the text has a duty to alert the congregation to these basic theological premises as many congregations are no longer familiar with such a starting-point in preaching. Thus the preacher must point out that the first premise is the divine omniscience, and that this is the basis that allows one to view the text as an inerrant revelatory source known infallibly, if as yet imperfectly, in the magisterium of the church. The theological validity of this approach, given our general understanding of the nature of these sacred texts, or its pastoral effectiveness, are separate issues.

HOMILY NOTES

1. There is a theme running through all the readings today – which captures a key sense of the whole liturgy – that we as Christians live in 'in-between' times. On the one hand, we cry out that 'Christ is truly risen, Alleluia' (the great Easter slogan) and death has been put to flight; but on the other hand, we know we must walk by faith for around us there is no shortage of greed, death and destruction. Here is the great tension of discipleship: we must believe that Christ has conquered (or else Christian faith is meaningless) and we must work to bring it about. In short, we live and act in hope. Down the centuries many have tried to resolve this tension in favour of either believing or working (this is the 'Pelagius v Augustine' debate that has polarised so much western theology) rather than seeing in this tension the very structure of human life: we must grow to become what we most truly are. In Easter terms, we know that Christ has conquered and so

life does not end in death, but this new life must be established both in our hearts (through having a new imagination whereby we view the world in terms of what it can become through love, generosity and forgiveness), and in the world through our Christian action.

2. We see this tension of what-God-has-established and what is yet-to-come brought out clearly in 1 Pet. The Christians rejoice in their new birth as sons and daughters of God, but they cannot escape the difficulties and demands of life. The author sought to explain this tension by carrying forward the metaphor of being children of the Father. Whoever is a child of the Father is an heir to the kingdom, but as a human inheritance (i.e. that which belongs to the children) requires waiting, so this divine inheritance is not being given to us yet, but being held for us in heaven. But why does God require us to wait? This time of waiting through difficulties is then explained as God wishing us to undergo a time of testing and purification. While we may not find this explanation convincing, nor like the implications of imagining God using our lives as a trialing-ground – for that invites the impious concretisation of the metaphor in presenting God testing some of his children to destruction – we must confront the same basic question to our believing that that author faced: we believe Christ has conquered, yet we experience death and pain as all too real around us. If we do nothing else in the homily today than acknowledge this basic dilemma of faith, we will have done much.

3. It is all too easy to pretend that the dilemma does not exist or, at least, would not bother us if we were 'proper' believers. One of the common surrogates for Christian faith is presenting Christianity as giving some immediate reward: a happier or more contented life, material benefits, or some notion of having a 'God on your side' – this is the sales-pitch of the tel-evangelists. Equally, many wonder why 'bad things happen to good people' – the nagging doubt about the 'value' of faith when it 'seems to make no difference' whether one is a be-

liever or not. Both positions ignore the basic Christian dynamic: Christ promises us the kingdom, but does so while
challenging his followers to build it in their lives and world.
The kingdom is not a child's wonderland were we are simply
lodged by an indulgent parent, but the completion of our
human work that must engage our wills, our skills, and our
hearts. Thus our faith involves (1) waiting (hope) and (2) the
confrontation of the selfishness that creates suffering in our
world other-focused love (*agape/caritas*). While we may not
want to see these sufferings in terms of a divine testing as
does 1 Pet, we must recognise when we shout 'Christ is
risen', we do so with the sober realisation that suffering is
part of the human condition and that belief requires challenging every attitude and action that contributes to that suffering. Fortitude and courage are Christian virtues.

4. There is another matter we should note today. This liturgy
takes place on 'the octave day' of Easter and, historically, this
day was seen as completing the 'great day of resurrection'
that has lasted since the Easter Vigil. Such a notion of a 'great
day' is beyond the imagination of most people in our society.
For almost everyone this is just another weekend and the
'long weekend' of Easter already seems long past. So there is
a dissonance between the liturgy, and perhaps its president
declaring how special today is, and the average person's
emotions. There is no simple answer to this phenomenon: the
twentieth century saw the secularisation of time into just two
categories of 'work [time]' and 'time-off' where material pro-
duction was the measure of human life. In the process, the religious notion of stressed (high days) and unstressed time
(ordinary time) disappeared, and with it the notion that
human activity fits into a greater harmonious pattern seen in
such regularities as the tides and the seasons. However, this
crisis of sacred time is not helped when the actual liturgy in a
parish has a single tone from Sunday to Sunday and that essential of sacred time, differences between day and day, is
not felt by those celebrating. Today the liturgy expects us to

continue the tone of Easter Sunday in such a way that the feel of this day is notably more special than that of the Sundays that will follow. This presents each community with the need to think about how they celebrate, and how they can mark this time as special.

5. One way of marking the central quality of Easter Day and this Sunday is to pick up the theme from Acts 2 where Luke sees the weekly gathering for the Eucharist as what is characteristically Christian. The symbolism that underlies Luke's eucharistic theology is not that of bread and wine as specific food-materials, but that the baptised participants are united in Christ through each having as their food what is a portion in a single loaf and a single cup: hence his term 'the breaking of the loaf'. However, this aspect of eucharistic symbolism is lost in our practice where we have individual mini-loaves (a round particle indicates a whole unit and is the very opposite of something broken for sharing), and either many cups (symbolic impoverishment) or, even worse, where the cup is not shared by the president with the other participants (symbolic famine). Making this breaking and eating shares of a single loaf, and drinking from a common cup, the central practical part of the celebration, with all its difficulties, delays, and need for explanation, will mark out this day as no amount of words or banners or peripheral decorations can.

Second Sunday of Easter Year B

Note

See Year A.

Introduction to the Celebration

Last Sunday we cried out with joy that 'Today Christ is risen! Christ has conquered evil and death.' This theme is so central for us that we need an extended time to ponder the day of resurrection: so here we are again today thinking about the day he rose. Easter day is the day he told us that our sins were forgiven, it is the day he charged us to be forgiving. On Easter day he gave us new life, and charged us to be life-giving. So as we stand here celebrating resurrection, how do we stand in our lives as people claiming this belief?

Rite of Penance

The *Asperges* or:

For the times when we have failed to forgive, Lord have mercy.

For the times when we have not borne witness to your victory over sin and death, Christ have mercy.

For the times when we have not been life-giving, Lord have mercy.

Headings for Readings

First Reading

This is how Luke, writing several generations after the first days of the Christians, imagined that the early believers lived. He wanted to put an ideal picture before his audience to help them recognise that we can only really grasp the significance of the resurrection when we attempt to build a new style of community in the world.

Second Reading
Jesus Christ comes by water and blood, overcomes death, reveals the Father, and sends the Spirit. This is a summary of the faith of the baptised person: who enters by water into the life of Christ, passes on his victory over death by a style of life that forgives and makes peace, and comes to rest in the life of God.

Gospel
See Year A.

Prayer of the Faithful
See Year A or Year C; or use those given for the Easter Season, Missal, p. 1001.

Eucharistic Prayer
Preface I of Easter (P 21, Missal, p. 424); and since Eucharistic Prayer I has special variations (i.e. a 'Communicantes' and 'Hanc igitur' – items 85 and 89 in the Eucharistic liturgy in the Missal) today, it is an obvious choice. The special quality of the time can be highlighted by drawing attention to this just before the preface.

Invitation to the Our Father
The risen Christ came among his followers and called on them as forgiven people to forgive others. Let us ask the Father that we be true to this vocation:

Sign of Peace
The Lord's resurrection greeting is 'Peace be with you'; standing together as his disciples, let us exchange that greeting now.

Invitation to Communion
Christ stands among us bidding us to be forgiving and to build peace. Happy are those who are called to his supper.

Communion Reflection
Doubt is not the same as indifference.
Doubt is not the same as having no faith.
Doubt is not a disease.
Doubt is not something to deny.
Doubt is not something to be ashamed of.
Doubt is asking how can this be.
Doubt is the probing for what faith means.
Doubt is a wrestling with questions.
Doubt is the growing edge of faith.
Doubt is the starting point of new understanding.
Doubt is the disquiet that can draw us to action.
Doubt is a thirst for a fuller vision.

Dismissal
Solemn Blessing 7 (Easter Season), Missal, p. 370.

COMMENTARY

First Reading: Acts 4:32-35
This is the 'second major summary' that occurs in Acts (the 'first major summary' is read on this Sunday in Year A, and the 'third major summary' on this Sunday in Year C). It is an ideal-image of what the Christian community should be, and what Luke wants it to become. The form is based on the idea of a primal 'golden age' to which we can look back for inspiration. It must be emphasised that this is not actual history but a myth of original purity. The early church had as much difficulty in living up to the demands of discipleship as we have. This is not a guide to what happened, but what Luke – fully conscious of the factions and squabbles of the early church (e.g. as we see in 1 Cor and Gal) – imagined it would be like if we could live with an immediate consciousness of the gospel.

Psalm: 117
See Year A.

Second Reading: 1 Jn 5:1-7
This can be seen as a profession of faith. It answers the credal
question: who are we? The text replies that we are the disciples
who rejoice in, and proclaim, Jesus' victory over sin and death
(the key Easter message and basic meaning of the resurrection).
He shares this with us through the gifts of water (baptism) and
the Spirit (enabling us to profess and witness). So we are the victorious, baptised, Spirit-filled people who follow the command
to love.

Gospel: Jn 20: 19-31
See Year A.

HOMILY NOTES

1. Only one of the three elements in this gospel passage can be
   explored in the homily: to try to do more is to risk confusion
   and overload. I have chosen the image of the risen Christ
   who appears among his followers with the greeting: 'Peace
   be with you', and who follows this up with a sending out of
   the disciples to be bearers of peace and reconciliation.
2. Forgiveness, peacemaking, and reconciliation are not con-
   cepts that we run together in our minds nor automatically
   link to our identity as Christian, yet they are at the heart of
   the meaning of resurrection. Let us note how we tend to react
   to these themes.
3. Forgiveness brings to mind a very individualist notion of
   getting rid of that which hinders me from getting to where I
   want to go: heaven. Forgiveness can be seen as a kind of
   sacred selfishness or a personal escape hatch from doom.
   Seeking forgiveness can then become an introverted process
   of reducing the mystery of God's love into my desire 'to get
   off the hook'.
4. Reconciliation and peacemaking seem to be sideline issues
   for most Christians: one more good work that you might engage in if that is your 'thing'. Having a conscious attitude of
   seeking to overcome division or taking a positive stance to-

wards the question of peace can be seen to be areas where some Christians might feel they have a role, but that these could not be said to be defining issues for Christians. Many First World Christians might even go so far as to say that even if one were uninterested in the building-up of a society of peace one could still call oneself a Christian and a believer in resurrection.

5. When we hear of 'forgiving and retaining sins' we think first of the priest in the confessional in the highly structured environment of the sacrament. The notion of 'retained sins' brings to mind many negative images of being frightened in the confessional and 'the church' wielding spiritual 'power'. This command is therefore primarily a commissioning ceremony of giving out power and authorisation to the apostles and their successors. This range of ideas, limiting forgiveness to a specific sacramental moment often with negative echoes, can seriously impair our seeing the larger significance of this part of Christ's resurrection message.

6. To be a Christian is to be one who is forgiven, and so one who forgives. 'Forgive us our trespasses as we forgive those who trespass against us.' This forgiveness is declared to us in the Father raising Christ from death: death and destruction are not to have the final say in human life. This forgiveness and victory are shared with us in Christ's gift of the Spirit. We are a people who, far from being cut-off from God, have God dwelling within us.

7. This people of the resurrection is then commanded to share this forgiveness and peace in their actions: it is the acceptance of this divine programme that constitutes real belief in resurrection. So the followers are constituted as a group who have a task to fulfill for the whole world: they must be the bearers of forgiveness. It they carry out this task then peace and forgiveness grow, if they do not then guilt and death still haunt us. Forgiveness is not a personal lifebuoy, but a universal task: build the kingdom of truth and life, of holiness and grace, of justice, love, and peace (cf Preface of Christ the

King). This is a ministry that Christ sends us out into the world to perform as his agents. It is a ministry not in some restricted sense of a job or function in the church's administration or liturgy, nor in a special sense of a sacral encounter with a sacred minister (priest), but in the fundamental sense of a service performed to a suffering humanity. The risen Christ looks with love on all who suffer and are in bondage in one way or another, and sends us to bring peace and freedom. This is a central task of us Christians as a group and of each of us. It should be that to know there are Christians is to know that there are people who go around working for peace and proclaiming that God is forgiving.

8. Even in the case of the specific instance of forgiveness we call the Sacrament of Reconciliation we express the belief that the basic mission to forgive and reconcile belongs to the whole group: '... the Father of mercies, through the death and resurrection of the Son ... sent the Spirit ... for the forgiveness of sins ... through the ministry of the church ... ' (the sacramental formula of absolution).

9. However, knowing that peacemaking and reconciliation is central to our role as Christians and our witness as a group is one thing, moving beyond this is something else again. The temptation is to harangue and preach: we must be reconciling! we must be peacemaking! we must condemn violence! and the cries go on and on. But such harangues make little difference in practice. Perhaps it is more useful to become aware of the complexity of our situation. First, we all are in favour of peace and goodness and reconciliation – it is almost axiomatic, like saying 'humans want to be happy.' But, second, while this is what we claim to want, most of us have vested interests in strife in some shape or form: be it in relationships, in the way we earn a living, in our national pride, or in more obviously exploitational activities. We want peace but only in so far as it is equivalent to our victory or at the very least only in so far as our own apple cart is not upset. Third, we must be aware of how precious our own positions

are to us and how we dread having to change our minds or lifestyles. This change is painful and cuts deep. Peace making is only easy for those with no stake in the present situation. Finally, we must note that we as Christians have an abysmal track-record regarding peace. Hence it is all too easy to root around in Christian tradition and find justification for any type of intolerance and this makes the whole notion of peace-making seem less urgent. Memories can be the great authorisation of strife and hatred, and to challenge some long-championed position in theology, politics, business, relationship, or social customs can seem both treacherous and foolhardy.

10. It is in this personal analysis of the contrast between, on the one hand, how big a stake so many of us have in violence, strife, struggle, and a culture of death, with, on the other hand, the command to forgive and make peace, that we individually discover the cost of believing in Christ as the conqueror of death. To even start the examination of this cost of discipleship in our lives is the first victory of peace. Do not ask 'Do I believe in the resurrection' – that can be a cosy religious word-game; but ask: Am I prepared to take the discomfiture, loss of pride, or perhaps loss of income that comes with working for peace, development, and reconciliation (cf 'development [of the Third World] is another name for peace,' Paul VI in *Populorum progressio*)? Peacemaking is never soppy, usually costly, and rarely easy.

Second Sunday of Easter Year C

Note

See Year A.

Introduction to the Celebration

In today's gospel, St John tells us to about an appearance of the risen Christ to the disciples gathered together on a Sunday exactly a week after Easter. John sets the appearance of Jesus on a Sunday because he knows that that is the day when Christians gather for the Eucharist – a practice that marks us out to this day. So like those disciples we have gathered here for the Eucharist, and Christ is now among us. We do not see him here today as on that first Sunday after Easter, but we recall the words Christ spoke on that occasion: 'Happy are those who have not seen and yet believe.'

Rite of Penance

Use the Asperges to make the link between Eastertime, baptism, and the forgiveness that make us into the Holy People gathered for the Eucharist.

Headings for Readings

First Reading

The early community gathered regularly, and their message of forgiveness and healing began to reach out from them to their surrounding. So, despite many being afraid to be seen with them, their numbers increased.

Second Reading

The risen Jesus is the First and the Last, the living one with us today – this is the meaning of the lighting Paschal candle standing among us with its markings: alpha for Jesus is the First, omega for Jesus is the Last, and he is here now, the date, and a living presence lighting up our lives.

Gospel
See Year A.

Prayer of the Faithful
President:
On this day of resurrection, Christ stands among us and offers us access to the Father. So let us place our needs before him with joy and confidence.
Reader (s):
1. For all our sisters and brothers who were baptised at Easter, that the risen Christ may become manifest in them, and for all of us who are baptised that we may bear witness to our hope in the way we work in the world.
2. For those who work for peace in the world and for those everywhere who work for reconciliation of memories or the removal of bitterness, whether they call on God or not, or by whatever name they call on the divine, that they may have a sense of courage to continue in this slow work.
3. That people of goodwill working for peace may feel that Christians everywhere are in solidarity with them or, at least, may not feel that Christianity is part of their problem.
4. For those among us who are in situations of strife or difficulty in their relationships at home or at work, that they may have hope; and for those who are working for reconciliation in our community, that they may see their work's fruit.
5. *Local needs; and silent prayer.*
6. That those who have died may reach the final age of the resurrection in the peace of God.
President:
Father, you have commissioned us through your Son, Jesus Christ, to be your ministers of peace and forgiveness, help us to carry our this ministry and grant us our petitions through that same Christ, our Lord. Amen.

Eucharistic Prayer
Preface I of Easter (P 21, Missal, p. 424); and since Eucharistic
Prayer I has special variations (i.e. a 'Communicantes' and 'Hanc
igitur' – items 85 and 89 in the Eucharistic liturgy in the Missal)
today, it is an obvious choice. The special quality of the time can
be highlighted by drawing attention to this just before the preface.

Invitation to the Our Father
Standing in union with the risen Christ, let us pray to the Father:

Sign of Peace
When Jesus appeared in the assembly on that first Sunday after
Easter he greeted the gathering with 'Peace be with you'; today
each of us has to be his voice in this assembly, so acting as his
voice please greet the disciples here about you with those
words.

Invitation to Communion
Jesus is with us today not in a visible form, but we behold him
with the eyes of faith in this wondrous food. Happy are we who
have not seen, yet believe, and are called to his supper.

Communion Reflection
Read paragraphs 4-7 of the Second Reading of the Office of
Readings for the Wednesday of Easter Week (Breviary, vol 2, pp.
392-3). Introduce it like this: 'A passage from a very ancient
homily for Easter.' Begin at the paragraph, 'This is the feast of
the year ...'; and conclude four paragraphs later, at: 'this is the
day the Lord has made, let us be glad and rejoice in it.'

Dismissal
Solemn Blessing 7 (Easter Season), Missal, p. 370.

First Reading: Acts 5:12-16

Modern scholarship calls this passage the 'third major summary' (the first major summary is read on this Sunday in Year A; the second major summary is read on this Sunday in Year B). Like the other summaries, here Luke wants to present an ideal picture of the earliest church still gathered in Jerusalem. The faithful are meeting regularly and setting up their meeting through the agreement of the whole community. They are witnessing to the Lord in words and mighty deeds, and their witness is beginning to spread out from Jerusalem to the surrounding areas of Judea and Samaria (see Acts 1:8). In Luke's ideal church (1) there are regular meetings which, from an earlier summary, we know are eucharistic; (2) decisions are arrived at by consensus for bickering is one of the problems he wants to oppose; and (3) the witness to the resurrection is always spreading outwards.

Psalm: 117

See Year A.

Second Reading: Apoc 1:9-3, 17-19

This is part of the opening vision of the book. The text has been so edited in the reading that it becomes a vision of the risen Jesus as celebrated in today's liturgy – an exegetical comment of its meaning in its context therefore adds nothing to our understanding of this (liturgical) reading.

Gospel: Jn 20: 19-31

See Year A.

1. Belief in the risen Christ is about sacramental living: 'happy are they who have not seen and yet believe.' It is about dying and rising with Christ and becoming part of him, the church (Col 2:12) – the mystery of baptism; it is about gathering for his meal that transforms us from being individuals into being

'one body for we all share in the one loaf' (1 Cor 10:17) – the mystery of the Eucharist. Baptism is the sacrament of entering, defining the bounds of the body; the Eucharist is the sacrament of sustaining, keeping the body in communion with Christ and between its parts. Both these aspects of the Paschal Mystery keep recurring in the liturgy; both sacraments are inextricably linked with one another, and have been since the earliest days.

2. However, while we may preach these links as abstract items of doctrine, in the minds of most people in the gathering today the two mysteries are as chalk and cheese. A 'christening' is something that belongs to infants and lots of people have the children christened because that's what you do – in all likelihood everyone in the congregation has been to one such ceremony. And, while it 'makes you a Christian' or 'a Catholic,' this is recalled primarily as a social bonding. The Mass, by contrast, is something you go to each week 'if you are religious,' and it is about praying, getting communion (optional), and about 'getting thoughts of the week'. The ministry of preaching has to try to permeate these perceptions and reveal the deeper dimensions of religious practice, and so highlight the core content of Christian faith. Actions tend to break through the crusts of tacitly held perceptions with a far greater effect than formal verbal teaching or preaching (recalling that part of the perception of preaching for many is that it is irrelevant or 'goes over their heads').

3. This could be done by having an infant baptism on this day – the people who are practising and away from the parish on Easter Night may now be back and so can have their baptism today – at the Eucharist. Or, at the very least, by using today (as on Easter Sunday) the Renewal of Baptismal Promises (Missal, pp. 220-221) instead of a declaratory confession of faith. This activity, the baptism or the renewal of promises, brings the mysteries together visibly – and not just on that most special night (the Easter Vigil) but at a regular Sunday gathering.

4. Then taking the cue from the gospel, that the Sunday gathering around the Lord's Table for the Lord's Supper has been a fundamental activity of Christians from the start (long before we had any of the writings now called the New Testament), then make the gathering a real, physical gathering around the table, with a real fraction, and communion under both species from one cup.

5. The fact that the assembly have to engage in the ritual in these unusual ways, not just listening to a homily, may help them engage with the mysteries they are celebrating.

Third Sunday of Easter Year A

Introduction

The Eucharistic assembly has a very definite identity: those who have become one in the risen Christ through baptism, now celebrate that holy union with him in sharing a single loaf and cup – yet this is not how most people think of what they are doing on Sunday morning.

Headings for Readings

First Reading

Our Easter joy is that the grave is not the goal of human life: no tomb could hold Jesus prisoner for 'God raised this man Jesus to life' and through him we have received the Holy Spirit.

Second Reading

We receive both justice and mercy from God.

Gospel

From the earliest times Christians have seen their gathering on Sunday for the breaking and sharing of the bread as their central moment in encountering the risen Jesus. Here Luke presents a story of the apostles on the first Easter Sunday as a prototype for weekly sacramental encounter of his readers: those alive when he first wrote and heard it read at such a gathering; and us today who hear his story at another Eucharistic gathering.

Prayer of the Faithful

President:

Friends, as witnesses to the Father's love, let us place our prayers before him.

Reader(s):

1. That we may bear witness to the resurrection.
2. That we may forgive our enemies.

3. That we may work for peace.

4. That we may know Christ's presence.

5. That we and all who have died may rise in the Lord.

President:

Father, you raised your Son from the dead and so showed us our destiny. Look on us your adopted children, and hear us through Christ Jesus, our Lord.

Invitation to the Our Father

As children of the Father gathered around Christ's table, we pray:

Sign of Peace

Christ stands among us offering us his peace; let us share it.

Invitation to Communion

Here is the broken loaf in which we recognise the risen Lord, happy are we 'who partake of this loaf'.

Dismissal

Blessing n 7, Missal, p. 370.

COMMENTARY

First Reading: Acts 2:14, 22-33

This passage provides a window into some key themes in Christian theology around the beginning of the second century. The most notable is that the person and work of Jesus is to be understood in terms of Jewish texts read as prophetic oracles. Thus David, taken as the author of the Psalms, is viewed as a prophet who makes statements which can only be truly understood by those who know of Jesus. Here the preaching is presented as being directed to Jews who then have their sacred texts made clear to them and in that new found clarity see Jesus as the one raised by God's right hand. In fact, the author's intended audience is a Christian community who understand Jesus within an

entire plan of history. Moreover, in accepting Jesus as the
Chosen One, they see themselves as the divinely intended ideal
readers of those texts originally valued among the Jews; as such
they have inherited the blessings of being the true Israel, and the
final People of God. This passage should be seen, therefore, as a
piece of catechetical explanation within the group, rather than as
a model for apologetics or missionary preaching to those outside the Christian community.

Secondly, we see a way of viewing the resurrection which is
based on the significance of the empty tomb of Christ. Everyone
has a tomb in which they await liberation from the bounds of
death (Hades), even a great king-prophet like David. Jesus too,
as a man, needed a tomb; but, in contrast to everyone else, his is
no longer occupied and this points to what will happen in the
tombs of all his people. This approach, which can be seen elsewhere in early Christian writings (e.g. Jn 5:28), was invoked by
the early church as their rationale for the rejection of cremation
and remained a key element in most writing on 'the resurrection
of the body' (e.g. Augustine, *De ciuitate Dei* 12) during the first
millennium.

Psalm 15/16

Today's readings bring us a concrete instance of a problem of
the liturgy in English which has yet to be addressed by those
producing the liturgical books. A central element of the first
reading (vv. 25-28) is a quotation from the psalms, and appro-
priately the chosen psalm-reflection on that reading is for the
church today to use that same psalm. However, what we read in
Acts (in any version) and in the psalm text (in any version) is not
only different (so destroying the continuity of repeating in our
prayer what we have just heard used by Peter in Luke's text),
but has a different emphasis, and as we read the psalm it is very
difficult to see how Luke derived his interpretation. This dissonance lies in the fact that the only known Old Testament text of
the early Christians was the Old Greek version (the Septuagint)
and Acts 2:25-28 is in perfect agreement with Ps 15:8-11 of that

version (note that the Latin text of Acts differs verbally in minor ways from its Ps 15:8-10). However, that Old Greek version is very different from the extant Hebrew text (where this is Ps 16:8-11) which since the Reformation has been privileged in many church circles as the 'genuine' text which gives the 'true' meaning of the original author. This same privileging of the Hebrew text as 'that with which one should work' has, until very recently, been a characteristic of biblical scholarship, and it is this attitude that is reflected in the selection of a translation for the psalms which is based on the Hebrew text even here where it is plainly at variance with the text (Acts) which it is meant to agree and echo! It would be foolish to attempt to emend this problem in a particular pastoral situation, but it should remind us that we are still far from a lectionary that adequately addresses the liturgical significance of biblical texts.

Second Reading: 1 Pet 1:17-21

Here is a snippet of re-reading by a Christian community of the experience of Israel to explain to themselves the significance of Jesus. It is theology in that it looks back in faith at its history (*fides quaerens*) to have understanding of what is crucial to their present (*intellectum*). Its starting point is that God treats all equally according to their deeds (a notion expressed in 2 Chron 19:7, but made the basis of theological argument in no less than six early Christian documents: here, Acts 10:34, Rom 2:4, Eph 6, Col 3:25, and Jas 1:17). Because of this divine attitude, and their own deeds, they needed reconciliation – this is expressed using a metaphor of being held in captivity, in need of being 'bought back' (redeemed) – and this is achieved by the blood of the perfect sacrifice which reconciles the people. The passage is somewhat difficult to follow for it begins in a formal forensic manner ('no acceptance of persons' is the technical lawyers' phrase), continues the argument using the imagery of slavery / liberation with its rich Old Testament background, and then moves to a third frame of reference: the cultic priesthood language of the temple (most familiar to us from Hebrews) and the annual liturgy of reconciliation carried out by the high priest.

Gospel: Lk 24:13-35

Luke sees the weekly encounter with the risen Christ in the broken loaf of the Eucharist as the central moment of his ideal community's life, and hence he wants to emphasise the importance of the Sunday gathering and add to it further dimensions of meaning. He does this by portraying his archetypal resurrection encounter as a eucharistic encounter. Consequently, he is then able to make that Emmaus meeting, on a Sunday on which the loaf was broken and Jesus recognised, into the basis for each Sunday's eucharistic gathering.

HOMILY NOTES

There is a very strong element of self-reference in today's gospel which carries on into the homily. Here we are now gathered for the Eucharist (which we understand as the weekly encounter of our community with the Risen Lord which takes place in the breaking and sharing of a loaf) reading an early Christian text (the Emmaus story) intended by its author to help his audience understand their gathering for the Eucharist by telling a story of another Sunday gathering around a loaf, except that that gathering at Emmaus is presented as the archetype and explanation of all later gatherings. Luke supposes that all his readers already have this Sunday gathering as part of their practical experience – in our terms, they take 'going to Sunday Mass' as a normal part Christian life – and then he wants to interpret that ritual using the medium of an 'historical' example, his logic being 'look what happened on the first Sunday, therefore that is what is happening now today.'

So the gospel poses us who are actually gathered for the Eucharist with a number of questions to see have we appropriated Luke's vision of what our eucharistic assembly should be:

Do we see our weekly meeting as a moment when we hear the Word?

Do we see our gathering as gathered around the Lord's table?

Do we see our eating together as having a share in the Lord's body?

Do we see our group as one Christian body (a unity formed from individual people) symbolised in the one loaf (a unity from individual grains)?

Do we see this as meeting with the Risen Jesus?

Do we see this as empowering us to go from this meal to proclaim the good news?

These are the question the Emmaus story poses to us at our gathering – they are probably different questions from those it posed to those who were its initial audience – but in answering them we come not only to a deeper appreciation of today's gospel, but to a realisation of its object: a deeper appreciation of the Sunday Eucharist.

It would be an interesting exercise to pose the above questions as one set of poles on a questionnaire scale. The opposite poles would be something like 'I get communion each week at Mass because it makes me holy.' If we compared the Emmaus vision of the Eucharist with the actual perceptions of those who are celebrating with us, we might be rather shocked at the task of evangelisation facing us! One loaf and one cup shared has become the distribution of pre-cut ready-made individualistic roundels – and the cup which we say all should drink from is reserved to the just one person – that hardly speak at all as sacramental signs, much less challenge us to recognise our unity in Christ. Lastly, we might ask ourselves as priests whether we see ourselves as those who preside over the community's breaking of the loaf or those who 'say Mass "with a congregation"'? And whether from the way we act, anyone might see a difference.

Third Sunday of Easter Year B

Note

The notion of the presence of the risen Christ in the church as his forgiving presence appears in several ways in today's readings and prayers. This notion of being forgiven can be highlighted by using the Easter form of the Asperges (Missal, p. 388).

Introduction to the Celebration

We have gathered to celebrate the presence of the risen Lord among us. We are called to be the people who bear witness to his victory over death. We are the people who proclaim the Father's forgiveness to the ends of the earth by being people who are forgiving.

Rite of Penance

For when our actions have belonged to a culture of destruction and exploitation, Lord have mercy.

For when we have failed to witness to the resurrection of Jesus, Christ have mercy.

For when we have failed to forgive or sought vengeance, Lord have mercy.

Headings for Readings

First Reading

In the gospel Luke will tell us that the message of the risen Christ is the message of forgiveness and that this must be preached in Jerusalem, then in surrounding areas, and then to the ends of the earth. Here Luke presents Peter starting off the church's witness to the resurrection by preaching this very message in Jerusalem.

Second Reading

We are called to live close to God by lives of justice and holiness, and we are a people who have our sins forgiven as Jesus Christ is our priest: he intercedes for us with the Father.

Gospel
We have received the gift of peace from the Lord; we in turn must bear witness to this peace and forgiveness.

Prayer of the Faithful
President:
My friends, we gather hear as the witnesses to the Father's love in raising Christ from death; trusting in his love let us place our fears and wants before him.
Reader(s):
1. That may we bear witness to the resurrection.
2. That we may forgive our enemies.
3. That we may seek peace and support all work of it.
4. That we may experience the presence of God in our lives.
5. *Local needs and silent prayer.*
6. That the dead may rise in the Lord.
President:
Father, you raised your Son from the dead and so showed us our destiny. Look on us your adopted children, hear us, and be with us in Christ Jesus, our Lord. Amen.

Invitation to the Our Father
Let us ask the Father to forgive us our sins and bring us to forgive those who sin against us.

Sign of Peace
We believe that Christ stands among us offering us his peace; let us offer our peace to one another.

Invitation to Communion
Behold the risen Lord, the Conqueror of death, the Prince of
Peace; happy are we who are called to his table.

Communion Reflection
If one keeps the homily short one can explore another aspect of
the liturgical mystery of Easter by reading from the account of
the early Eucharist that is found in the Office of Readings today
(Breviary, vol 2, pp. 530-2). It is a long reading but is readily accessible to people, is historically of great interest – and many
people are genuinely interested in hearing an authentic text on
the early church. It highlights not only the early, and still recog-
nisable, structure of the liturgy, but links this with the significance of Sunday, and highlights the connection between the
Eucharist and serving the poor and needy in the community.

It can be introduced with these comments:
Our earliest detailed description of what a Sunday Eucharist
was like comes from a man named St Justin and was written c.
155 AD. He was born of pagan parents in Nablus in Samaria and
became a Christian in his thirties. Later he wrote an explanation
of Christian beliefs and practices which we call the *First Apology*,
which he dedicated to the Roman Emperor Antoninus Pius.
Around 165 he was martyred – we have the account of the court
proceedings – and is usually referred to as St Justin Martyr. Here
is his account of the importance of the Sunday Eucharist for the
Christians and his description of what happened at it for curious
and suspicious pagans.

If the text is read by another, the celebrant could arrange to
interrupt once or twice to point out:
(1) that 'prayer of thanksgiving' is our 'Eucharistic Prayer'; (2)
'memoirs of the apostles', 'writing of the prophets' and 'the address' is the Liturgy of the Word; and (3) to note how he highlights the Day of the Lord (Sunday).

Avoid referring to the collection as an anticipation of contemporary practice. The collection Justin refers to is an expression of Christian care for the poor. It was several centuries be-

fore the need to find the means of financing a professional clergy
caused the purpose of this collection to be changed.

Dismissal
Blessing n 7 for the Easter Season (Missal, p. 370).

COMMENTARY

First Reading: Acts 3:13-5; 17-9
Here we see Luke's understanding of the fundamental Christian
keryma: tell people who Jesus is, and then call on them to
change their lives (usually rendered as 'repent'). To express this
he has this scene of Peter giving one very early sermon of the
church to the primary audience of the Christian message: the
people of Israel in Jerusalem. Peter is among his own people,
they share ancestry, and so he can present Jesus as the one
awaited and build a mosaic picture of him from scriptural (Old
Testament) images. He is the one glorified by the God of
Abraham, Isaac and our ancestors. He is the Lord's servant, the
Holy One, the Just One, and the author of life. Having identified
Jesus with these images, Luke identifies him as the one you (not-
yet-believers) know as you crucified him. Then he further identifies him as the one we (disciples) know as the one God has
raised from the death. So faith in Jesus is in his identity as messiah,
crucified and raised.

   In the second paragraph of the reading he identifies Jesus as
the Suffering Servant in Isaiah, exonerates the people as acting
in ignorance, and invokes one of his characteristic themes of history / divine providence as the effecting of a predetermined plan
of events. The result of this sequence now brings about a specific
moment for the people: they are offered the challenge to change
their lives and turn to God.

Psalm: 4
The use of this Psalm can be understood liturgically as the people taking up the demand of Peter at the end of the first reading:
you must repent and turn to the Lord. This Psalm text can then

be understood as a confident bidding prayer that the Lord will hear and show mercy and favour to his people.

Second Reading: 1 Jn 2:1-5
This section of text is a piece of catechesis on the ethical demands and moral dimensions of the Christian life. To be a Christian is to accept the need to follow the commandments but also to know that Jesus intercedes for us with the Father. In this part of his letter the author adopts a very important theme in the missionary period of Jewish and Christian groups in the first century of the common era. This is to present the faith of Israel – either with or without Jesus – as an ethical option. It is a choice between two ways: one leading to life and light through obedience to a strict code of behaviour as revealed by God but which is primarily ethical; the other is the way of darkness and death which is pursued by ignoring moral restraint and becoming involved in evil or perverse activities. We see these details of the virtues and crimes attached to each way in early Christian documents such as the *Didache* – certainly earlier than 1 Jn – or in many Jewish catechetical texts for converts from the Greco-Roman world.

This reading presents us with an aspect of the early missionary preaching that is not well represented in the canon of the New Testament but which was eminently successful for both Jews and Christians at this time. Its presence in the liturgy today reminds us that the formation of those baptised at Easter continues in the Easter season and that a central part of mystagogy is the introduction to the moral lifestyle of Christians.

Gospel: Lk 24:35-48
This extract, when we take away the linking verse ('Then they told what had happened on the road, and how he was known to them in the breaking of the bread') which is a scene-change code, consists of two units with very different theological purposes which are tacked together by Luke by the simple formula: 'Then he said to them' (v. 44).

The first item (vv. 36-43) is Luke's version of one of the resurrection accounts that must have formed part of the early Christian preaching: the appearance to the frightened and doubting disciples gathered indoors. We find it in Luke in a less explicit and less detailed form than it is found in John (20:19-29) which was read last Sunday (cf and compare the commentary on that reading, above). The key elements in this appearance is that the Lord is suddenly and mysteriously present among his frightened (and disbelieving) followers, offering them the greeting of peace. There is an undercurrent of doubt and disbelief at the heart of this story though it is adapted in different ways by John – where it becomes the Thomas incident – and here where all the disciples see and touch the wounds and all see him eating. Like John who implies a criticism of Thomas for disbelief, Luke is embarrassed by this doubting and puts forward the notion that it is a special kind of doubt which he calls 'disbelieving for joy'. Luke wants to stress that Christ is really, which for him is here equivalent to materially, risen and does this by stressing the continuity between the crucified and risen Jesus. He then reinforces this assertion and shows there is no basis for doubt by twice appealing to this syllogism: ghosts are not material – a principle, Christ now is material – a fact, therefore Christ is not a ghost – hence he is truly risen.

The second item (vv. 44-48) is a theme very close to Luke's heart which appears in many shapes and forms in the gospel and Acts: the wholly revealed Christ, i.e. crucified and risen, stands at the centre of space and time. The whole of human history and the whole history of the people of the covenants has been preparing and leading up to this moment. God has been effecting his plan for the Christ. Now it is revealed and it is to be witnessed to by the disciples. Likewise, Christ stands at the centre of God's space and his message spreads outwards in every direction from Jerusalem through the witness of the disciples.

HOMILY NOTES

1. Luke, both in his gospel and in Acts, has a picture of the world as made up of concentric rings. At the centre is Jerusalem (the holy city where the Lord has chosen to dwell), then the surrounding countryside and region (the land of the chosen people), and finally the lands beyond this again (the lands of the nations). He sees the witness that Christians must bear to the victory of Jesus over death, and so the forgiveness of humanity, as spreading out through these rings starting from the centre. It is like the ripple effects in a pond.

2. Our attempts to build a world of peace and goodness tend to fail as we give up on plans as useless: 'What's the use? It'll be all the same no matter what we do!' This forgets the incarnational dynamic of action: we may think global, but we act local. The Lord came to save humanity as one human in one place at one time. His impact ripples outwards in time and space – from one man in Palestine it has now touched each of us. The place to seek for peace is at the centre of our own lives, then in our immediate personal world, then in the world that touches our lives, and then beyond. We make our impact where we can and then let the ripples spread outwards. Do not despair at the dark clouds and the seeming impossibility of peace and justice, but act with justice in a single case in one's own life and avoid surrendering to the darkness.

Third Sunday of Easter Year C

Introduction to the Celebration

We are Easter people. That means we believe that in the event of the first Easter we see God's plan for the universe and for each of our lives. The Christ has been raised to a new life and he shares that with each of his people. The grave is not life's goal, but joy in the presence of the Father. But if we look forward to the coming kingdom, we must also live our lives in such a way that our world grows more like that world that God wants: we must act in ways that give life, enhance life, and not succumb to the ways of death and destruction. Let us spend a moment recalling that we are called to witness to life and reject the ways of death.

Rite of Penance

In Eastertime, the Asperges is preferable.

Headings for Readings

First Reading

This reading reminds us that we are witnesses that the Father has raised Christ from the dead and made him our leader and saviour.

Second Reading

This reading is a vision of Christ in glory with the Father, receiving the praise and worship of the whole creation.

Gospel

The shorter form is preferable today or one is presented with two distinct themes: since it is preferable to preach on just one of these themes, reading both just adds material that can distract from a unified presentation.

Shorter form:

The risen Lord showed himself to the apostles by providing

them with a meal, so too today we encounter the risen Lord in this holy meal.

Longer form add:

And the Lord called on the apostles to continue his work of caring for his people.

Prayer of the Faithful

President:

Sisters and brothers, in Eastertime we should be more conscious than usual of our being a baptised people. We have died with Christ and risen with Christ, and so with Christ we can now pray to the Father.

Reader(s):

1. That the whole church of God will be obedient to his will, and enabled by the Spirit to bear witness to the resurrection.

2. That this community may encounter the risen Jesus every time it comes together to celebrate his Supper.

3. For all who serve in public office, that they may be strengthened to reject what is false and do what is just and right.

4. For all who labour to bring us the bounty of the creation, that they may respect it and see its wonder.

5. *Local needs.*

6. For all who are in need, for the sick, the lonely, the oppressed, that God will heal, comfort, and liberate them.

7. For everyone here, that we may be given new inspiration through the resurrection of Christ.

President:

Father, you and your Son receive the praise of all creation; hear our petitions and come to your people in their needs through Christ, our Lord, Amen.

Invitation to the Our Father

Gathered in the name of the risen Christ, with him, let us pray to the Father:

Sign of Peace

We pray that the Father forgive us as we forgive others. Let us show our desire to forgive others by exchanging a sign of peace with those around us.

Invitation to Communion

'The Lamb that was sacrificed is worthy to be given power, riches, wisdom, strength, honour, glory and blessing.' This is the Lamb of God who ... .

Communion Reflection

Our God is the God of all humans.
The God of heaven and earth.
The God of the sea and the rivers.
The God of the sun and moon.
The God of all the heavenly bodies.
The God of the lofty mountains.
The God of the lowly valleys.
God is above the heavens;
and he is in the heavens;
and he is beneath the heavens.
Heaven and earth and sea,
and everything that is in them,
such he has as his abode.
He inspires all things,
he gives life to all things,
he stands above all things,
and he stands beneath all things.
He enlightens the light of the sun,
he strengthens the light of the night and the stars,
he makes wells in the arid land and dry islands in the sea,
and he places the stars in the service of the greater lights.
He has a Son who is co-eternal with himself,
and similar in all respects to himself;
and neither is the Son younger than the Father,
nor is the Father older than the Son;

and the Holy Spirit breathes in them.

And the Father and the Son and Holy Spirit are inseparable. Amen.

(Found in the writings of Bishop Tírechán, c. 700, who attributes it to St Patrick).

Dismissal

Blessing n. 7 [Easter Season] (Missal, p. 370).

COMMENTARY

First Reading: Acts 5:27-32, 40-41

By the time Luke wrote, the break between Christianity and Judaism was complete: they were now separate religions with very different fortunes in the Greco-Roman world. However, Christians were aware that their memory was rooted firmly in Judaism of the time of Jesus and this memory could not be ignored. These clashes between the apostles and the Jewish authorities in Jerusalem – whereby those authorities seek to repress the apostles' preaching, but the latter must continue despite the authority of the high priest – serve to form the background to the splitting apart of the Jews-who-believe-in-Jesus from their then co-religionists.

Second Reading: Apoc 5:11-14

This is the second of a series of visions of the Lamb that run through this book (Apoc 5:6-8; 5:12-13; 6:1; 6:16; 7:9-10; 7:14-17; 8:1; 12:11; 13:8; 13:11; 14:1-4; 14:10; 15:3; 17:14; 19:7-9; 21:9-14; 21:22-23; and 22:1-3) and form one of its great unifying themes. The Lamb is the risen Christ now enthroned in glory at the Father's hand, high above even the most sublime of angelic creatures, and in this vision he is to receive his due: the praise of the whole of the creation.

Gospel: Jn 21:1-19 (shorter form: Jn 21:1-14)

This comes from the additional material that is found at the end of John, but which has been present in the text from as far back as our manuscript evidence allows us to see. The story is of an appearance in which the risen Christ is at first not recognised, but then through the course of the encounter their eyes are opened to see who he is, so that they dare not even mention their initial lack of recognition. The risen Christ is both different and the same. He is also still with the community of disciples guiding them and providing for them; and it is most significant within a Johannine community – for presumably it was from such communities that the 'appearances' of this additional chapter come – that he is recognised in the course of eating a meal: this fits with a principal Johannine theme that the risen Christ appears in the course of the weekly gatherings (ch 20) where he presumes on the experience of his communities that these weekly Sunday gatherings are gatherings for the Eucharist. The message here seems to be that as the first disciples found it hard to recognise the risen Lord when he ate with them, so too the community must recognise the risen Lord without his earthly form in their eucharistic meals.

Over the centuries the feature of this passage that has drawn more attention from exegetes than any other is why the gospel records the number of fish: 153 of them. The most likely solution is that given by Augustine that since 153 is a triangular number it indicates that in all the risen Lord does is to be found the trait of perfection (Augustine considered 'triangular numbers to be perfect – and in this he was probably in line with the mind of the original author). A triangular number is made up by adding 1+2+3+4 and so on, and when you add 17 you get 153, so it is the seventeenth triangular number. Such little details serve to remind us just how foreign are many of the thought patterns of those whose texts we read from our own. However, as some exegete once remarked, one could imagine all the exegetes from Origen to the most recently deceased scholar being lined up in heaven before the Johannine author and being upbraided for all their ingenuity, and the author saying that there were 153 because that's the number I got after counting them!

HOMILY NOTES

1. We frequently use the language of being witnesses to the resurrection, but what does that really mean and how does it
   impact on our lives?

2. Bearing in mind the limitations of the homily format as a way
   of communicating (see 'Homily Notes' for the First Sunday of
   Lent, Year B), this is a question that can be offered to people in
   the assembly to think about and share with their neighbour.

3. If the congregation come to recognise the difficulties posed
   by this question for actual living, from a sharing with those
   near them that lasts five minutes, it will be five minutes well
   spent. The conclusion to the period of sharing could be simply the acknowledgement that 'being witnesses to the resurrection' sounds lovely, but actually doing something about it
   is a far from easy. It is only after reflecting on this difficulty
   that we as a community move along the road towards being
   real witnesses.

Breaking and Sharing:
Making More of the Fraction

The Eucharist's central symbolism is that we break, and then share in, a single loaf and drink from one cup filled with wine. We see this brought out in the account in Paul: 'the Lord Jesus on the night when he was betrayed took a loaf of bread, and when he had given thanks, he broke it ... In the same way he took the cup ... For as often as you eat this bread and drink the cup, you proclaim the Lord's death until he comes' (1 Cor 11:23-6). The imagery is that of having a share in what has a unity: scattered grains of wheat become a single loaf (*Didache* 9:4), and then each share is not a case of the individual getting his/her 'bit' but participating in the unity which is Christ. This whole symbolism has been lost to us as we can see in the language we use: we speak of 'getting communion' – an individualist agenda – rather than 'sharing in the common loaf' or 'sharing in the communion' with Christ – such phrases would denote a communal and ecclesial agenda. The situation is then made worse in that we have reduced the symbolic meal to a token: we still have a breaking (the fraction) but it could not be less important than it is: the minimum number one can break anything into is two – so that is all we do, and then we do not even share the second piece for most priests put both parts together and consume them. The fraction cannot be seen, and the assembly get pre-cut round 'breads' so that there is not even a hint in the actual elements of one of the basic sacramental messages. The same degradation of symbolism happens with the cup: we announce the Lord's words: 'Do this, as often as you drink it, in remembrance of me' (1 Cor 11:25), but for many this then does not happen. So we join in a sacramental meal, but a core part of the sensible base of the mystery – the actual drinking – is reduced from the level of the symbolic reality which marks the point of human entry into the mystery of the covenant to that of a token.

A frequent objection is that a fraction into many pieces

would take too much time, but this assumes that this is 'waste time' (the liturgical analogue of hanging around the kitchen while the kettle boils for a cup of coffee), rather than a central part of the whole symbolism of the Eucharist: if we are all to be sharers in the one loaf (see 1 Cor 10:17), then this takes time and should be done deliberately and not as if it were some practicality to be got over. What we do at present is the equivalent of the TV cooks' trick: 'Here is one I prepared earlier.' A similar argument of time and convenience is used by those who do not share the cup with the assembly, but the reply is the same: if the symbolism of the new covenant in Christ's blood is eating and drinking in this holy meal, then we have to accept that this takes time. The present reductions to 'get the communion over' quickly have their secular analogue in the 'drive-through' facilities at fast-food outlets. If the actual eating and drinking is going to be rushed, then that is to make the mystery something you 'get and go' – so we should not confuse people with the language of a 'sacred banquet.'

This present situation arose as a result of the major shift in theology in the middle ages which emphasised the elements, not as symbols, but as vehicles for divine presence where 'getting,' 'having', and 'adoring' the host (where 'host' referred more directly to the consecrated form of bread rather than to the Victim), rather than to the participation in the sacred banquet. However, we can still see reminders of the earlier approach. In the National Museum in Dublin lies the Derrynaflan chalice and paten. That paten is a good-sized dinner plate, c. 36 cm in diameter. This measurement shows they were still using a loaf, and breaking it as part of the actual celebration – and textual evidence informs us that, on occasion, it had to be broken into about 70 pieces. Turning to the chalice we find that its shape is eminently suited to the practical problems of having 'one cup' that can provide communion to a sizeable number of people. Our chalices resemble a stem glass (ideal for one person's use), while it has handles for giving and taking back with ease and without spillage. Rough calculations shows that it held just under 1.5

litres of wine without fear of spillage. Such an amount provides, on average, about 75 mouthfuls which fits well with the figure for the number of fractions.

But this all took time, and indeed had to have its meaning explained: so while these actions were taking place there were special sequences of prayers/chant known as *Confractoria*. This has all but disappeared in the Latin rite except for the triple repetion of 'Lamb of God, who takes away the sins of the world'. Originally, this was repeated as many times as was needed to cover the time taken by the deacons to break up the loaf to provide particles for the Assembly. When this was no longer needed, because of the introduction of unleavened bread (which is better for reservation), less frequent communion for the laity, and pre-cut round mini-loaves, it was retained vestigially in the form we now have it. However, note that in the Missal, n 131, p. 510, there is now this rubric: 'This [the Lamb of God] may be repeated until the breaking of the bread is finished, but the last phrase is always "grant us peace".' This rubric seems to suppose that in an ideal world there would not be a ciborium with pre-cut individualist mini-loaves (much less the idea that a ciborium would be taken out of the tabernacle for use at the Eucharist), but that communion would be from a single loaf that is broken.

Here some early medieval chants – originating in Ireland – in translation. They could be used at any Eucharistic celebration, but are particularly suited to Eastertide or Corpus Christi. Every line is taken from scripture, and as assembled they present us with a sophisticated Eucharistic theology – albeit one that seems unfamiliar.

For the breaking of the loaf

[1] They knew it was the Lord, Alleluia;
    In the breaking up of the loaf, Alleluia.
    The loaf we break is the body of Jesus Christ, our Lord, Alleluia;
    The cup we bless is the blood of Jesus Christ, our Lord, Alleluia;

For the remission of sins, Alleluia.
Lord, let your mercy rest upon us, Alleluia;
Who put all our confidence in you, Alleluia.
They knew it was the Lord, Alleluia;
In the breaking of the loaf, Alleluia.

[2] O Lord, we believe that in this breaking of your body and pouring out of your blood we become your redeemed people;
We confess that in taking the gifts of this pledge here, we lay hold in hope of enjoying its true fruits in the heavenly places.
The structure of the prayer would suggest that the first section (They knew it was the Lord, Alleluia) was repeated.

During the distribution of Communion
[1] My peace I give you, Alleluia
My peace I leave you, Alleluia.
Those who love your law have great peace, Alleluia;
They do not stumble, Alleluia.
Bless the king of heaven who comes with peace, Alleluia;
Full of the odour of life, Alleluia.
O sing him a new song, Alleluia;
Come, all his saints, Alleluia.
Come, eat of my loaf, Alleluia;
And drink of the wine I have mixed for you, Alleluia.

[2] Ps 23 is recited.

[3] He who eats my body, Alleluia;
And drinks my blood, Alleluia;
Abides in me and I in him, Alleluia.

[4] Ps 24 is recited.

[5] This is the living bread which comes down from heaven, Alleluia;
   He who eats of it shall live forever, Alleluia.

[6] Ps 25 is recited.

[7] The Lord fed them with bread from heaven, Alleluia;
   Men ate the bread of angels, Alleluia.

[8] Ps 43 is recited.

[9] Eat, O friends, Alleluia;
   And drink deeply, O beloved ones, Alleluia.
   This is the sacred body of our Lord, Alleluia;
   The blood of our Saviour, Alleluia;
   Feast, all of you, on it for eternal life, Alleluia.
   Let my lips declare your praise, Alleluia;
   Because you teach me your commands, Alleluia.
   I will bless the Lord at all times, Alleluia;
   His praise always on my lips, Alleluia.
   Taste and see, Alleluia;
   How sweet is the Lord, Alleluia.
   Where I am, Alleluia;
   There shall my servant be, Alleluia.
   Let the children come to me, Alleluia;
   And do not stop them, Alleluia;
   For to such belongs the kingdom of heaven, Alleluia.
   Repent, Alleluia;
   For the kingdom of heaven is at hand, Alleluia.
   The kingdom of heaven has suffered violence, Alleluia;
   And violent men have taken it by force, Alleluia.
   Come O blessed of my Father, inherit the kingdom, Alleluia;
   Prepared for you before the foundation of the world, Alleluia;
   Glory be to the Father ... ;
   Come O blessed of my Father, inherit the kingdom;

As it was in the beginning, is now, and ever shall be,
world without end;
Come O blessed of my Father, Amen, Alleluia.

What we have is a psalmody (4 psalms – cited here in Hebrew numeration – and their antiphons: items 1, 3, 5, and 7) which were used in the normal manner of the Roman rite (antiphon, psalm, 'Glory be', antiphon) followed by a prayer (item 9) re-echoing the Lord's call to take, eat and drink. There are enough psalms to cover quite an extended period – this was not a 'get and go' liturgy – and in any renewed use of this during the distribution of communion it could be tailored to the size of the assembly by omitting one or two of the psalms. The next challenge will be to see can these sequences not only be used for a real fraction and sharing of one loaf and one cup, but to put them to music.

If you are introducing a lengthy fraction or distribution communion under both species, then these ancient *confractoria* and communion chants offer materials that can be adapted for use, shortened or repeated, to provide a meditative background to breaking and sharing.

Fourth Sunday of Easter Year A

Note

There is an emphasis in the gospel and the prayers of the liturgy today on Christ who, risen from the dead, continues to care for his people: Christ the Good Shepherd. This emphasis often leads to an emphasis on 'vocations', understood as seeking to attract young people to the priesthood and religious life. Whatever of the actual effectiveness of using the liturgy as a place for recruiting pastors, it actually deprives those present who are not thinking of the priesthood or religious life of an opportunity to reflect on the nature of all Christian ministry as the on-going presence of the Christ among his people and in the world. It is this presence of the risen Christ, which becomes physical in the different tasks and witness that are necessary in each Christian community, that must be highlighted today as part of our celebration of the Easter message.

Hence some practical demonstration of all the ministries that are needed in one actual community could take place after the homily or be expressed in others ways such representatives of various ministries reading the Prayers of the Faithful. For example, there could be a commissioning of readers or ministers of the Eucharist or for some other task in the community. The point to emphasise is that each of these people, in offering to carry out this task of service to their sisters and brothers, is participating in the work of Christ as the shepherd of his people.

Introduction to the Celebration

Who do we follow? This is the question that today's gospel puts before us. Many of us would like to think that we follow no one, that we make our own decisions and choose our own paths. Yet, our experience tells us that we are often led – look at advertising – and often led astray: look at how many brigands have incited human beings so that the worst of crimes and destruction have been justified? But the choice of Christ as our shepherd is the choice to bear witness to the victory of life, and love, and forgiveness over the forces of death, domination, and vengeance. So where do we stand in terms of calling ourselves disciples?

Rite of Penance
Option c vii (Missal, pp. 394-5) is appropriate.

Headings for Readings
First Reading
To become a follower of the Good Shepherd is to acknowledge a need to change our way of living and to begin to live as children of God.

Second Reading
Even after choosing the Christian way, we stray off the path, so we must acknowledge our need to return to Christ and begin afresh.

Gospel
Where do we want to belong? In the fold of Christ or in the camp of the brigands, thieves, and those who bring destruction?

Prayer of the Faithful
President:
As a community who have chosen to acknowledge Jesus as our shepherd, let us pray for one another, the whole community of faith, and all humanity.
Reader(s):
1. That we may become aware of our task to bring mercy into the world.
2. That we may see the use of our talents to build up the Christian community
3. That those with special ministries in our community may have the strength to carry out their service.

4. That no Christian community may be deprived of the Eucharist through lack of someone suitable to preside at it.
President:
Father, we acclaim your Son as our shepherd. Through him, hear and answer our prayers, Amen.

Invitation to the Our Father
Christ our shepherd leads us to the Father, so let us pray:

Sign of Peace
Let us now express the commitment to peace and forgiveness that we have taken on in choosing to follow Christ.

Invitation to Communion
Behold the loaf: as the shepherd gathered his scattered sheep into a flock, this loaf has gathered many grains into a unity. So may it gather us into the unity of Christ, who takes away the sins of the world. Happy are we who are called to share it.

Communion Reflection
George Herbert's poem 'the Call' (Breviary, vol 2, p. 613*).

Dismissal
Blessing n 7 (Easter Season), Missal, p. 370.

COMMENTARY

First Reading: Acts 2:14. 36-41
This is Luke's vivid picture of the first day of the church's preaching, and he identifies the message as 'repent and be baptised.' This is a variant on that found in Mk 1:15 where it is presented as the basic preaching of Jesus. The apostolic preaching is to turn around and take on the mantle of Christ (be baptised, believe in the gospel). Luke wanted to set out what he considered to be the kernel of the apostolic preaching: knowing what God had done, 'be baptised in the name of Jesus Christ for the forgiveness of your sins, and you will receive the gift of the Holy

Spirit.' In order to do this he invented a sermon which he put
into the mouth of Peter, as the leader of the apostles, as the very
earliest – and so the core – preaching of the church.

Second Reading: 1 Pet 2:20-25
Christ is the one who has suffered for his flock, and deliberately
identified with the Suffering Servant of Is 53 which is quoted
four times here. This part of 1 Peter is concerned with giving
maxims for Christian living, in this case that the Christians
should suffer patiently following the example of Christ. It is this
patience by the Suffering Servant, by Christ, and by his disciples
which is seen as bringing salvation and healing. The identification with Christ the suffering servant and shepherd is brought
about by conversion (JB: 'come back') which places us under
Christ the bishop (*episkopos*; JB: 'guardian') who keeps watch
over us.

   This notion that Christians should suffer injustice in civil
society, rather than take an active role in opposing it, is probably
to be explained in that this text originated in a community that
was under severe stress from the surrounding society, if not out-
right persecution. However, 1 Peter has often been appealed to
in history in a fundamentalist sense by many down the centuries
to argue that Christians should suffer injustice in civil society –
as here – rather than take an active role in opposing it: being passive in the face of social injustice is 'the Christ-like way' – it
therefore reminds us that false exegesis is not only defective in
terms of human understanding, but traduces the gospel into
that which enslaves people. And, any social implication drawn
from this reading should, therefore, not be treated in isolation
but set against the whole of the church's teaching on building
the society of justice and peace.

Gospel: Jn 10:1-10
This is the beginning of a section of the gospel that draws directly
on Old Testament sheep imagery (Gen 49:24; Ps 23; Ezek) to describe the ideal leader/priest. The text's proposed audience is

the Pharisees, and the topic of who are the ideal priests to serve in the temple seems to be just beneath the surface, the text's message to its readers is that Christ alone is such an ideal leader. Others have come to re-dedicate the temple and claim the mantle of shepherd, but these were not righteous priests; now the righteous leader of the people has come who brings them home to the Father. The two parables (1-5 and 7-10) are really parallel rather than the latter explaining the former; they have these images in common: (1) Christ likens himself to a gate and this leads to safety; (2) there is a threat to the sheep from outside (a false shepherd, thief) and this leads to destruction. Because of the nature of this section where the relation of Christ and his followers is developed using similes (*paroimia* = a dark saying: JB: 'parable') it has always attracted allegory from interpreters.

The parables are complex, presenting interpreters with more problems than consistent solutions, and consequently have always attracted allegory. Unfortunately since we do not have the original key to these figures, such attempts at decoding the text are, at best, pious guesswork adapted to the need to preach something about the text. However, one line of allegory which does seem inappropriate is that which sees this text as providing a model for pastoral ('shepherd-like') ministries in the church (for example this Sunday is often presented as 'good shepherd Sunday' and becomes 'Vocations Sunday'), for the stress within this piece of text is that Christ is *uniquely* a shepherd as the perfect High Priest, not simply a Shepherd which others could imitate in some '*alter Pastor bonus*' manner.

HOMILY NOTES

1. In many places this is 'Recruitment Sunday': 'we need priests because without priests there will be no Mass – so if there are some generous, unmarried men in the congregation, why not join up now!' However, whether or not such appeals have any effect, it is best to avoid the whole topic as it abuses the liturgy by turning the moment in the assembly's week when its president is charged with helping his brothers and sisters

reflect on the mystery of Christ into an advertising slot. Preaching is a sacred task and no other end, however noble, can justify replacing the Sunday homily with a piece of promotional work.

2. Since the gospel text is opaque, and the use of allegory as its key usually results in something that is little more than a free association of ideas, it is worth inviting people to explore the dynamic underlying Luke's 'sermon' in Acts, for this brings us face-to-face with what the evangelist saw as the kernel of the Christian vocation. So instead of a formal discourse, invite the assembly to work through the text meditativly, noting its main features.

3. The text can be conceived as trinitarian in structure. It supposes that the kerygma's audience, both the audience described in the text and the text's audience, begin from a position of belief in God who has brought them into existence, sent them his revelation, and exercises a providential care for them. This is the starting point of faith in God, who once the Son has been recognised will be acknowledged as Father; and with it goes a recognition of human need and incompleteness. This notion of providential care and the human predicament of sin is clearer when the whole text of Acts 2:14-41 is read – which could be summarised in a few words.

The Father has sent us, his children, his Son. Then we are given a list, of sorts, which set out what we receive through Jesus and his victory over death – we should note that Luke locates his sermon in the context of Easter, the Paschal mystery, and its proclamation:
– Jesus's life, death and resurrection reveal the life of God;
– through Jesus we are re-made as a community: the People of God;
– Jesus calls us to share in his Paschal Mystery and to enter his communion in baptism; and
– Jesus draws us to repentance, a new vision, a new lifestyle. We as baptised people have received the gift of the Spirit.

We are those 'whom the Lord our God will call to himself'.

4. Such a recollection of the structure of the Paschal Mystery is appropriate to Eastertime. Moreover, the text of Acts lends itself to this narration of 'the wonderful act of God' which every Sunday Eucharist celebrates. A fitting conclusion to a homily whose style is a meditative pondering of a text is to simply read the final sentence of this section of Acts 2:42, which Luke imagines as the on-going effect in the hearers' lives of their conversion on the day of Pentecost (the verse that opened the reading on Second Sunday of Easter), and this makes a good transition, after some moments of silence, to the recitation of the Creed.

Fourth Sunday of Easter Year B

Note
See Year A.

Introduction to the Celebration
One of the gentle images that we find applied to God in the Old Testament is that the Lord is the shepherd of his people: The Lord is my shepherd, there is nothing I shall want. We Christians apply this title to Christ the Lord. He is the good Shepherd who knows his sheep and lays down his life for them. We may find this language of sheep and flocks and shepherds strange, but beneath the imagery the belief it points to is at the heart of our faith: God is gentle, concerned, caring and just.

Rite of Penance
Option c vii (Missal, p. 394-5) is appropriate.

Headings for Readings
First Reading
Luke wanted to capture the immediacy of the first Christian preaching. One of the ways that they sought to understand the identity of Jesus was to apply an image from the Psalms: the stone rejected has become the corner stone. Jesus was rejected and put to death by humanity, but he has been raised and glorified by the Father.

Second Reading
We are loved by God, we are the children of God, we can dare to address God in familiar terms.

Gospel
In trials the shepherd must not abandon the flock, and if needs be he lays down his life for them. This is a key image in our understanding of Jesus and Christian love.

Prayer of the Faithful
President:
We gather here as community with many different needs, talents and responsibilities. Let us pray that we will grow in awareness of the tasks we are called to perform for one another, the whole community of faith, and all humanity.
Reader(s):
1. That every Christian may become aware of the specific ministries they are called to perform for their sisters and brothers.
2. That every Christian may see the use of their talents as a way of sharing in Christ, the good shepherd.
3. For those with special ministries in our community here, that they may not be discouraged and may inspire us.
4. That we may be thankful for the ministry we receive, and be gentle in our giving and receiving from our brothers and sisters.
5. That no community may be deprived of the Eucharist because of the lack of someone suitable to preside at it.
6. *Local needs.*
7. For all who are suffering, ill, or cannot be with us at this Eucharist, that the Lord may be with them and that they may know our concern for them.
President:
Father, you gave us your Son as our shepherd, hear our prayers and grant our needs though that same Christ our Lord, Amen.

Invitation to the Our Father
Think of the Love that the Father has lavished on us, by letting us be called God's children; and that is what we are, and so we can pray:

Sign of Peace
Let us express our desire that the Peace – the token of the presence of the risen Lord – be among us here.

Invitation to Communion
Christ is the shepherd who has gathered us as a flock around his table; happy are we who now partake of his supper.

Communion Reflection
In the different areas of my life
– as an individual with needs
– as part of a family
– as a member of society
– as a Christian
– as a worker
how many different skills and services do I need from others?
Thank you Lord for those who help us and minister to us.
In the different areas of my life, how can I use my skills and talents
– to help those in need
– to show mercy
– to bring hope and light
– to witness to the God of love
– to establish peace and justice
– to witness to resurrection?
Lord, that we may recognise our gifts and talents and use them for building your kingdom.

Dismissal
Blessing n 7 [Easter Season] (Missal, p. 370).

COMMENTARY

First Reading: Acts 4:8-12
This is part of a section of Acts where Luke sees the church undergoing trials which provide it with the opportunity to show its belief in inspired words and demonstrations of power. The context of this speech is an examination of the fisherman-turned-leader, Peter, before the mighty council of the Sanhedrin. The drama is that the uncultured fisherman is able to respond to the questions put to him with such ease: he is a despicable one

made powerful by the power of God, and so like Jesus himself: rejected yet raised to be the cornerstone.

We should note three points about this speech. First, Luke draws the dramatic scene so beautifully that he can lull us into thinking of this as a historical incident. This forum is designed by Luke to provide a platform for a demonstration of the power of the keryma (cf Lk 12:11). Second, that the 'rejected stone becoming the cornerstone' theme was a major element in the early preaching to explain the mystery of the resurrection following the rejection of the cross (cf the note on the Psalm for the Second Sunday of Easter for references). Third, this text with its clear stress on the Jewish leaders as those who crucified Jesus ('the one you crucified') has a sordid history in Christian anti-semitism. It is one of those texts which we have to approach with the utmost caution as it comes with blood on it.

Psalm 118 [LXX 117]
See the commentary for the Second Sunday of Easter Year B.

Second Reading: 1 Jn 3:1-2
Recognising that Christians are God's children has three consequences, each of which parallel an idea found in John's gospel: (1) Christian do not belong to the world – as a Jesus was not received by it (cf Jn 15:18-9; 17:14-6); (2) they must lead Christ-like lives (cf Jn 17:17-9); (3) they know there is an even greater future (cf Jn 17:24).

The notion found in v. 2 that to see/know is to become like what is seen/known is a basic idea in Greek thought and religion. Here it is taken over, building on the notion that the end of life is to come face to face with God: when we see/know God, we shall be divinised through this vision.

Gospel: Jn 10:11-18
That the identity of the Christ as recognised by the disciples is an important element in this passage. It draws directly on the image of the Lord as the shepherd of his people (Gen 49:24 and

Ps 23), and indirectly on the notion of the condemnation of the wicked shepherds who abandon their flocks (Ezek 34). At the end of that passage, in the Septuagint, we have this declaration: 'they will know that I am the Lord their God and they [are] my people, says the Lord. You are ... the sheep of my pasture and I am the Lord your God' (vv. 30-1). For John the people are able to identify Jesus as the noble, ideal, and good shepherd as he is the one who does not abandon the flock but faces the wolves despite the cost. In seeing this, they recognise Jesus as the Lord spoken of in the covenant oracle in Ezekiel. So as the good shepherd, Jesus is intimate with the Father. There is an analogy here: as we are one with the shepherd, so he is one with the Father. This shepherd is the one recognised as Lord by both the flock and the Father ('I am the good shepherd; I know my own and my own know me, as the Father knows me and I know the Father') and so Christ is the intermediary (priest) and communication of the Father.

The reference to laying down his life freely and taking it up again is difficult and there is no fully satisfactory explanation. It is clearly connected with the theme of Christ as the obedient one who redresses Adam's crime. It is also clear that John rejects a docetic understanding – Jesus could not be really killed as he is an immortal essence – of Christ's victory over death. This is perhaps its most important message in the liturgical context of Easter: Jesus really died and was raised, and that we must beware of seeing the 'resurrection' as the result of the divine impassability or of psychic immortality – both positions which effectively destroy the significance of the resurrection in our human lives. We should note that appeals either to the divine omnipotence ('Jesus was God so they could not kill him') or immortality ('Jesus showed that in the end it will be OK as our souls are immortal') are far more common among Christians, and among general perceptions of Christian belief, than most preachers or teachers imagine. It is perhaps worthwhile in the Easter homiletic context to point out how alien these docetic or gnostic notions are to Christian faith. It is possible that the formulation here is apologetic: how could Jesus be one who was intimate with God, if he could be killed with criminals – surely if God loved him he would have intervened and stopped such a crime (this type of objection and apologetic can be found in Mt 12:53). If this is its purpose, then John's answer to the objection is that Jesus is the human being who acts with perfect freedom – a freedom not even limited by death.

It should be noted that in the image of the shepherd dying for the flock there is a vivid inversion of values. The sheep are there for the shepherd, not vice versa. While a shepherd might be unlucky in loosing more than it was worth in trying to defend his livelihood, to deliberately put one's means of life above one's life is foolish. This is therefore a piece of parable wisdom which uses the enigma of the situation to demonstrate the generosity of the divine love and care.

HOMILY NOTES

1. The language of shepherding, of sheep, and of flocks is, historically, very much part of the church's self-understanding. We refer frequently to 'pastors,' 'pastoral work,' 'the flock,' the pastoral staff (crosier), 'the defence of the church from wolves,' and so forth. This language is often objected to by Christians today as patronising power-language. 'While before God we acknowledge our need to be disciples, when men set out to pastor us it is often all too clear that they treat us like sheep' (remark of someone to me after hearing the Good Shepherd gospel in 1995). Moreover, most of the images of this shepherding are power-oriented: crosiers are things people get 'raps of' in common language and in the formal language of the law bishops are appointed to, or resign from, 'the actual pastoral government'. For someone in a formal position of authority, e.g. a priest 'in full uniform' at an ambo, to say that 'Jesus left us a pastoral ministry in the church' can seem like a piece of 'user-friendly' 'official-speak' meaning 'the command structure has divine sanction' so do not challenge it. From the point of view of communicat-

ing it is irrelevant whether this is true or not, this is how much of the shepherd / sheep language is received. It must be used with an awareness that it is a debased currency and that ecclesial structures built with this language may also be in need of revision.

2. The identification of the presbyteral ministry with the work of the Good Shepherd on this Sunday presents that ministry as an elite group which stands in distinction to those for whom they are pastors: they lead, guide, defend, and stand to that group as Christ stands to the whole church. These are very direct and powerful symbols, but symbols we use comfortably as they seem hallowed by use. However, it is important to note how problematical this whole symbol system is and how it can create a very false view of the nature of the church. How often do we use two-tier language of leaders / led, clergy / lay, or military language or 'army of priests' or 'the troops'. Such metaphors presuppose a univocal view of authority where the work of Christ is virtually that of the ordained, and this can be seen in terms of a hierarchy. Any genuine discussion of ministry, from the most private ministry of one Christian to another to that of Petrine ministry seen around the globe, must begin with the fact of each baptised person having a skill / gift / talent in a unique way, in a specific situation, so that another can experience the presence of the caring Christ, and thus the kingdom can in some particular way be realised.

3. Focusing on the ordained priesthood as a direct continuity with Christ runs to risk of failing to note that his priesthood is unique: he has an unique relationship to the Father, and he establishes an unique relationship with us which is like it. Likewise, an emphasis on 'vocations to the priesthood and the religious life', if not seen as an exceptional expression of the basic reality of each person needing to be aware of their call to minister, creates an imbalance in the our preaching and involves the possibility, not unknown in practice, that the basic nature of vocation might be ignored and people

might reduce 'vocation' and 'ministry' to these high-visibility tasks.

4. So the basic question we must address in homilies today is how are we to view ministry. Each of us lives in a connected series of worlds: family, close friends, the people we work with, the local community, the Christian community assembled, the town, county, country, Europe. We interact at all these levels: we need them and contribute to them; we are needed by these as well. This is most obviously the case in the worlds that are close to us: we need others and they need us. This human interaction is the concrete base of ministry. We are brought towards the perfection we all desire and pray for, the kingdom, by the drawing love of the Father in Christ, but this becomes a visible fact through human hands and minds and voices. In each situation we find ourselves – and our spheres of ministry are all unique to us and of different extents – others are helping us towards the goal (i.e. those who minister to us: spouses supporting and encouraging, children making us love less selfishly, people who help us make life run smoothly from petrol pump attendants to politicians (note we use the language of ministry here: 'ministers' and 'civil servants'), to those who witness to the truth and help us towards understanding such as teachers, to those who help us in sickness, to those who provide food, and those who have special skills in the Christian community.) And we help others towards the goal (our ministry). To be a Christian is to be aware of the relationships that bind us and to have an attitude of care and contribution because we believe that in Christ the kingdom is not a dream but a divine promise.

5. To believe in the risen Christ involves seeing life with hope. We join in the task of life as more than just sets of contracts ('I scratch your back, you scratch mine'). Contracts may be necessary to protect us from exploitation, but we believe that there is something more and we are called to witness to it. To act as a Christian is to be aware of how we affect others, and

are affected by others, for good or ill, and to act knowing that Christ acts as a good shepherd: he stands by us and brings us into a life of love such as that he shares with the Father. From the Father to the Son, from the Good Shepherd to us, and from us to others: a pattern of love and care where the basis of interaction cannot be a system of contracts alone, but must draw on a generosity that flows from being members of a family.

6. To talk about specific vocations, e.g. ordained ministry, before we make clear our Christian vision and give it visible expression in our external Christian structure, is to assume that the ordained minister is just one more 'service provider' – like the electrician or the solicitor – in a world of contracts: we need certain religious things for our survival, then let us 'buy them in' from the experts (priests in their special place of work: church buildings) and all can look on the priesthood as a job and the church as merely the functional organisation that organises the services required. This picture of priesthood and ministry – historically not unlike the tasks assigned to the various priesthoods of early imperial Rome – can be all too real and draws both non-Christians and Christians, indeed many priests, into its web. To reflect on the risen Shepherd is to challenge this view.

Fourth Sunday of Easter Year C

Note

See Year A.

Introduction to the Celebration

One of the images applied to God in the Old Testament is that he is the shepherd of his people: The Lord is my shepherd there is nothing I shall want. And, he will send a new shepherd to Israel who will gather all those who have been scattered – which is seen as a result of sin – into one flock. We Christians believe that Christ is our shepherd, leading us to the fullness of life. We may find this language of 'sheep' and 'shepherds' strange, but beneath the imagery is our belief that God is gentle, caring and just.

Rite of Penance

Option c vii (Missal, p. 394-5) is appropriate.

Headings for Readings

First Reading

We are a light for the nations, so that Christ's salvation may reach all humanity.

Second Reading

All humanity has a place in the Lord's kingdom.

Gospel

We are the flock of Christ and have received eternal life from him.

Prayer of the Faithful

Use the Sample Prayer of the Faithful n 8 (Easter Season), (Missal, p. 1001).

Invitation to the Our Father
Through baptism we can call on the Father, so let us pray:

Sign of Peace
Christians are to relate to others in peace and forgiveness; let us express this now.

Invitation to Communion
Christ is our shepherd, and he is the Lamb of God who takes away our sins. Happy are we who are called to share in this banquet.

Communion Reflection
Use some of the chants translated in the *Note on Breaking and Sharing*.

Dismissal
Blessing n 7 [Easter Season] (Missal, p. 370).

COMMENTARY

First Reading: Acts 13:14, 43-52
By this point in Acts, the gospel is presented as reaching place after place, group after group. In each place the gospel is the fulfillment of long held hopes, but it also encounters opposition: both movements are seen in this reading. However, Luke wants to point out that despite setbacks, the movement out to the ends of the earth is continuing: 'but the disciples were filled with joy and the Holy Spirit.'

Psalm: 99: 1-3, 5; R/ v.2
This psalm invokes the theme that Israel is the Lord's flock and is always in his care; in Christian reading this becomes an image of the church. While usually the psalm is a response to the first reading, today it is an anticipation of the theme of the gospel.

Second Reading: Apoc 7:9, 14-17

This is one of the visions of the Lamb, and it is the vision which describes the universality of the redemption of the Lamb. It does not fit very well into the liturgy today, as it appeals to the range of imagery which sees Christ as the Lamb of God, but today the focus of the liturgy is the imagery of Christ as the shepherd. Trying to move between these sets of images (Christ as Lamb and Christ as shepherd) can cause a dissonance of metaphors. A possible solution is to omit the second reading today, or replace it with that from Year B.

Gospel: Jn 10:27-30

As it stands, this reading lacks context and it is difficult to make sense of it – the only rationale for its selection here seems to be that it invokes the image of the shepherd again (first found in John at 10:2) and the earlier parts of ch. 10 which use the image had already been selected for Years A and B. So, having opted for the theme of Good Shepherd Sunday, this was the only gospel text that was available! The reading makes sense if set in its full Johannine scene which begins at 10:22 and ends at 10:39. The scene is a festival in Jerusalem and Jesus is being challenged by the Jews to keep them in suspense no longer: is he the Messiah or not? (v. 24). Jesus will only tell them that his works in the Father's name testify to him. His own know him and follow him, and so these are brought into the domain of the Father. He and the Father are one, but as Jn 17:1 makes clear, this union includes the community of the disciples. This answer by Jesus causes consternation, and they attempt to stone him, a further statement on his works and about his relationship to the Father, and the gospel moves ever closer to the showdown of his arrest and crucifixion.

HOMILY NOTES

1. Preaching today is difficult. For a start this is often referred to as 'Good Shepherd Sunday' and attempts to attract people to the priesthood and religious life – yet, while there is sheep

imagery in the gospel, it is not the familiar image of 'the good shepherd'. Second, using the homily as a place for advertising the ordained priesthood may be counter-productive! Clergy today may be more of an object lesson in what to avoid, than an attractive example. If you do pick up this theme, bear the following in mind. (1) Be careful not to ignore the fact that every Christian is called to some specific ministry in the church – high visibility ministries are but one variant on the general call to serve the Body of Christ. (2) The ministry of Eucharistic presidency must be presented as something that exists within the whole body of the church and not as a 'class apart', which is the device used in recruitment of 'specialists' in the employment market. (3) Harping on about falling numbers is a waste of time: people can both count and observe the age profile of clergy. Time should be devoted to giving a deeper understanding of what ministry is all about. (4) We do not preach in a vacuum: people have seen – are seeing – the scandals in the church, the failures of administration to take action, the general sluggishness in facing issues. So honesty about the problems within the priesthood today is a pre-requisite, or what is said is dismissed as obscurantist. Refuge in the distinction between the shining ideal and the sordid affairs of individual situations likewise does not appease people, and in any case one cannot speak of some ideal church – it is the real historical church that is the vehicle of the gospel. If you cannot face speaking in such blunt terms about the state of the presbyterate, then it is perhaps best to leave the topic alone.

2. If one opts to preach on the gospel text, the situation is not helped by the fact that the reading lacks context. However, the shepherd / flock imagery is part of the basic stratum of the kerygma (see the Eucharistic Prayer in the *Didache* which predates all our other textual references to the theme). From the *Didache* we can get some idea of the world of images that lies behind today's gospel. In Ezekiel the scattering of the people of Israel is seen as a result of their sins, and there is the

promise that YHWH will one day send a good shepherd –
unlike the wicked shepherds who led the people astray –
who will gather the isolated people and make them into one
flock of the Lord. This is the theme that the *Didache* takes up:
Christ has gathered all the scattered individuals and formed
them into a new, transformed body – his own. This is the
cause of their joy as followers, which they see celebrated in
the Eucharist, and for which they see themselves as offering
thanks with the Son of David to the Father. This is the theme
that can be derived from today's gospel: Christ has called
each of us, he knows each of us by name, he has gathered us
to form the church and this assembly.

3. This theme of Christ the gatherer, the true leader, and the one
    who has made us into this people now at the Eucharist is a
    valuable one to explore. It also points out that all Christians –
    whether they are called 'shepherds' / pastors or not – have to
    see themselves as followers of Christ.

Fifth Sunday of Easter Year A

Introduction to the Celebration

We gather for the Eucharist not as a group of individuals each here for her or his own needs: rather we gather as a community called by God to work together. This is the meal that bonds us to one another and to Christ; with Christ we become God's people offering worship to the Father; from Christ we draw strength to build a society focused on God's loving plan for the creation; and in Christ we are called to turn from selfishness and strife to a life of peacemaking and gentleness.

Rite of Penance

The Easter form of Asperges (Missal, p. 388) is preferable.

Headings for Readings

First Reading

In this reading we hear of the plans being made to fulfill two central concerns of the church: to look after the material needs of the poor in the community, and to preach the word of God.

Second Reading

Here is one of the richest images of what we are called to become in the church: just as a great building must have many stones each set correctly, and must have a good foundation, so each of us must play our distinctive part in building the kingdom, and all of us must be founded on Christ.

Gospel

Jesus goes ahead of us to prepare a place for us with the Father: he is our Way, our Truth, and our Life.

Prayer of the Faithful
President:
On this day of resurrection, Christ stands among us offering us access to the Father. So let us place our needs before him with joy and confidence.
Reader(s):
1. For all our sisters and brothers baptised at Easter, that the risen Christ may be manifest in them.
2. For those seeking their way, for those seeking the truth, that their quests may lead them to peace.
3. That people of goodwill working for peace may feel that Christians everywhere are in solidarity with them.
4. For those who work and care for the community with the hungry, the poor, the marginalised, the sick, that the Lord may support them.
5. That those who have died may come through Christ into the Father's house.
President:
Father, you are known to us through your Son, Jesus Christ. Hear now our prayers for we bring them to you through Christ, our Lord. Amen.

Eucharistic Prayer
Preface of Sundays in Ordinary Time I (P 29, Missal, p. 432) is preferable to any Easter preface: it picks up the central theme from the second reading.

Invitation to the Our Father
'I am the Way, the Truth and the Life. No one can come to the Father except through me', so with Christ we pray:

Sign of Peace
The Lord's resurrection greeting is 'Peace be with you', so as his disciples, let us exchange that greeting.

Invitation to Communion
Christ says that we should not let our hearts be troubled, but
trust in him; happy are those who are called to his supper.

Dismissal
Blessing 7 (Easter Season), Missal, p. 370.

COMMENTARY

First Reading: Acts 6:1-7
Coming just before one of his irenic summaries (v. 7) which
stress the harmony and unity of the apostolic church, Luke con-
structs this incident as a validation of the role of deacons by giving their origin as an apostolic initiative. In the early second century the various administrative patterns found in the churches
were being harmonised in a uniform structure of bishop, presbyters, and deacons. By means of this incident Luke presents the
group known as 'deacons' as having emerged organically within
the original church and as having a specific role in it. Here the
deacons are those who are to organise the domestic arrange-
ments while the apostles preach, yet a few chapters later (e.g. the
case of Stephen), when he records traditions about their actual
work, we find that the deacons are among the early preachers of
the gospel. This passage is of little historical value for the early
church, but Luke's vision of what the church should be – and
which he articulates by way of an imaginary golden history – is
still a vision that deserves our allegiance: a group conscious of
its common purpose and identity, caring for those in need and
proclaiming the good news.

Second Reading: 1 Pet 2:4-9
This passage is badly cropped in the lectionary: the natural unit
is 2:1-12 which is a second century post-baptismal instruction
with the satisfying unity of a little nugget of primitive preaching, probably one used after Easter with those who had just become Christians. In this vv. 1-3 set the context: the audience are
new-born babes (v. 2) who have tasted the Lord (v. 3 quoting Ps

34:8) – which is probably a reference to the Eucharist – and so they must have a new morality and act as new people (v. 1). The last verses continue the theme: v. 10 gives another image of the church, this time drawn from Hosea, while vv. 11-12 are a concluding exhortation to live up to the new life just begun.

In the passage we read, the key theme is that Christ is the 'Living Stone' – here used as a formal title for Christ – which is then developed using a rich tapestry of 'stone' images from the Old Testament. It is not clear in the sources that are used (Is 28:16 which is quoted; Is 8:14; Ps 118:22 and cf Mt 21:42) whether the stone is a cornerstone or the keystone over a door / in an arch; hence the JB covers itself by using 'cornerstone' and 'keystone'. This ambiguity allows the passage to be read in several ways: Christ is both the foundation, and the key structural member, and the stone which keeps the whole edifice from falling. It appears as if 1 Peter wants the whole range of this imagery to be exploited in terms of the role of Christ within the new community based on baptism. The baptised are a 'spiritual house' and Christ founds it, supports it, and draws it together. The notion of a 'spiritual house' was obviously one familiar to the audience as it is also found in use among the Qumran community. Also reminiscent of Qumran is the notion of the church as a holy priesthood – a perfect group who live in accordance with God's law, and who can, through Christ, make an acceptable sacrifice. On this point many commentators have seen a Eucharistic theme underlying the passage, but this probably should not be pressed too far. It seems that the offering is the life and prayer of the church. 'The church is not to be made up of individuals who are cold and dead, but who enrich their environment with life-giving love' (Bo Reicke). This community can then be described using images from Isaiah (43:20 – chosen race; 43:21 – people set apart to offer praise) and Exodus (9:6 – royal priesthood, holy nation). The final image in the passage to be read draws on the notion of baptism as enlightenment and God dwelling in inaccessible light.

Gospel: Jn 14:1-12

This is the opening of the final discourse in John and the context is the Last Supper: the questions raised all concern his impending departure from the disciples. Within John's situation the discourse concerns the abiding presence yet visual absence of Jesus from the church. Jesus is not visually present to the church for he is before the Father acting as our intercessor; he alone is our access to the Father.

HOMILY NOTES

1. One of the mysteries that finds least resonance in modern western society is that of the church. We view life as isolated individuals, rather than as members of a group where the group is considered more real than the individual. This individualism grows apace: a few centuries ago the kin group was the source of identity, then it was reduced to a smaller family unit, then to the 'nuclear family,' and now even that notion seems 'to threaten individuality'. The view of the church has likewise changed: from being a wider and more profound bond than any other, it became in the sixteenth century the vehicle for getting one's religious needs served; then to being simply a cultic administration, and now for many who wish to call themselves Christian it is no more than a hindrance, a set of arbitrary external forms challenging their individual liberty.

2. This sets up a tension for the preacher. On the one hand, the church's structures have a record of abusing power – the more objectionable as it was done in the divine name. And, there is an on-going danger in all administrative minds, such as those who rise in religious hierarchies, towards closet totalitarianism: the notion that is it is the group that must survive and the individual is just a replaceable bit that can be jettisoned. In the community of Christ where the highest is to feed the little lambs (Jn 21:15-7), avoiding such totalitarian action must be a primary moral imperative. On the other hand, the mystery of the church is central to the good news.

Christ gathers us into a unity, we act as a group in union with him, we are a people, a community, a body of different members with Christ as our head. Baptism is not an individual ticket to salvation, nor simply a declaration of a religious stance, rather it makes us into a member of community which is the body of Christ on earth. Since we are made by God for membership of this community, and known through and through by him, in this group we do not surrender our individuality to the collectivity but each is called to be a unique part of the whole: no one can make Christ present in a particular place, situation, and time, or in just the same way that you or I can. Each unique person and situation can become a place of the incarnation. As such we can praise uniqueness without endorsing a lonely individualism, praise collective endeavour to build the kingdom without invoking a totalitarian vision. But having this vision, and seeing our talents as gifts to be used in conjunction with others, while recognising the other's different vocation, is difficult; and indeed is one of the tasks we must face in growing in holiness.

3. Preaching this primary Christian mystery of the church took many forms in the early kergyma: we are most familiar with the body metaphors in Paul, but it can also be found in the pastoral language of flocks and shepherding in the gospels, or in a series of Old Testament religious images such as 'Israel' in Galatians, or as in today's second reading. However, of them all the building metaphors of stones, corner-stones, and so on, are perhaps the easiest to take on board.

4. All the parts of a building are different (doors, windows, wires, pipes) and individually of not much use. But when fitted together the whole is greater than the sum of the parts. We can ask which we would like to get rid of: the wood, the plaster, the glass? It is the rich variety of parts that are different and specific to tasks and location within the building that makes the whole so worthwhile. Alternatively, the church building may contain an arch of stone or bricks which can be

used as a visual aid. All the bricks look the same when viewed one by one. But in an arch each has to be set slightly differently to the bricks each side of it. Without any one brick, or if two are set in same way, then the whole is weakened and cannot achieve its purpose and the bricks are just a heap doing nothing. The arch is a unity, but for its unity it depends on each having its distinctive role. Both building and arch need a mind that co-ordinates the parts, an architect who links the parts to the larger purpose: as members of the church we believe Christ is that guiding source of unity.

5. In 1 Peter there is a crucial distinction made when using the building metaphor: we are *living* stones. We are not like bricks which can only be moved by someone else. We must use our initiative, and see what is needed to advance the kingdom for which we pray 'thy kingdom come.' Being living stones we are not tools / materials in the hands of another, but all are fellow workers with one another and Christ. Being a Christian challenges the modern myth of lonely self-advancement; our vision is one of using our individual creativity in conjunction with others to build a kingdom worthy of being presented by Christ to the Father.

Fifth Sunday of Easter Year B

Introduction to the Celebration

We gather as people who have been grafted into Christ by baptism, as the people who have heard his voice and who seek to follow him in our lives, and to join with him in prayer in thanking the Father. In today's gospel we are reminded that this discipleship is not a passive affair: we are made part of Christ so that through us the Father's kingdom can come closer to all humanity and so that, through us, his will can be done on earth as it is in heaven.

Rite of Penance

The Easter form of Asperges (Missal, p. 388) is preferable.

Headings for Readings

First Reading

Saul, having had a revelation from Christ on the road to Damascus, had changed from being a persecutor of our sisters and brothers, to seeking to be a disciple. However, it is not enough that he just wants to join the church, he has to convince the rest of the church that he is serious, and learn what it demands and means to be a member of Christ.

Second Reading

Discipleship is not just words, it means taking on a lifestyle and its demands.

Gospel

Discipleship is not just being part of the life of God in Christ, it is about bearing fruit though doing the Father's will.

Prayer of the Faithful
Use the Sample Prayer of the Faithful n 8 (Easter Season), (Missal, p. 1001).

Invitation to the Our Father
'We need not be afraid in God's presence, and whatever we ask him we shall receive,' and so we pray:

Sign of Peace
The Father commands 'that we believe in the name of his Son, Jesus Christ, and that we love one another', so let us offer each other a token of that love.

Invitation to Communion
To remain in Christ is to partake of his supper; happy are we who are called the Banquet of the Lamb.

Communion Reflection
Edmund Spenser's poem 'Easter' (Breviary, vol 2, p. 608*)

Dismissal
Blessing n 7 [Easter Season] (Missal, p. 370).

COMMENTARY

First Reading: Acts 9:26-31
This is a transition moment in Acts. Luke sees history evolving in definite steps: there are now churches in Jerusalem, Judea, Galilee, and Samaria (the evangelical homeland), now Saul/Paul is upon the scene and has joined with the disciples. Now the next step can begin: the moving out from the homeland to the nations. First through the preaching of Peter, being then followed on a much larger scale by Paul. So in this reading we have the transition linked with the introduction of a key character for later in the grand plan.

Second Reading: 1 Jn 3:18-24
This passage is a statement of the confidence that Christians should have before God, but this is linked to the test of acceptance by God which is willingness to 'do what pleases him' (see Jn 8:29). This leads the author on directly to a summary of the commandments and a summary of Christian identity that is trinitarian in its structure: the author addresses the follower of Christ about living in God [the Father] who lives in them by the Spirit.

Gospel: Jn 15:1-8
That Jesus is the true vine is one of the important images in John for the relationship of the community to God. In this he takes over the Old Testament images of Israel as the vine, and the pruning image from the prophets (e.g. Jer 5:10 or Ezek 17:7). The relationship of 'remaining in' Jesus is the foundation for the confidence that the community has in its prayer to the Father.

HOMILY NOTES

1. During this whole period of the year, the focus is on discipleship. In Lent the emphasis is on recognising the blockages that exist in our lives in following Christ and repairing damaged relationships with God and our neighbours. In Easter it is about growing in discipleship.

2. Discipleship is not a rush of enthusiasm, but a long term commitment to following Christ, collaborating with Christ, to having a relationship with the Father through Christ. And, in every long-term relationship there is need for re-focusing, replenishing, restoring, and reconciliation.

3. Discipleship is also about 'discipline' in the sense of training and the building of habits of behaviour. To be a disciple of Jesus requires training in a particular way of living, it requires the acquisition of specific skills, and it requires the practice to know how to put those skills into practice in our lives. For example, to follow Christ requires that we have developed some skills in prayer – not perhaps the elaborate

schemes for prayer that some teachers of prayer have developed over the centuries, but it does require knowing the basic prayers of the Christians. But the skill of praying requires the practice of regular prayer and the prudence to know that sometimes one has time to pray and sometimes one does not. A Christian lifestyle demands sympathy for the poor and those suffering injustice, but this sympathy is a skill which entails recongising injustice and knowing that it is not part of God's plan, and the prudence to know how to do something about it.

4. In the early church there were little manuals for leaders and mentors in the community to use with those who were about to become Christians, to impart the basic Christian skills to them. We often translate these as 'manuals of teaching' (e.g. the *Didache* is one of them), but a more careful look at their titles and content shows that they should be seen as disciple-making guides and that they were not concerned with 'doctrine' or 'teaching' such as is found in a catechism, but with imparting the habits and skills so that the newcomer would know how to behave within the new community she or he was entering. Hence, they impart a series of 'do' and 'do not' rules, they guide on how and how often to pray, when and why to fast, when and how to assemble for the Eucharist. To become a Christian, that is to rise with Christ in baptism at Easter, was to have started the life-long process of acquiring the skills to be grafted onto Christ.

5. This notion of skilling is not one often used today within the context of preaching, yet everyone knows it from his or her workplace. Every job has a prescribed skill-base – you must have the skills and the experience to use them or the job is not yours. Adverts read: 'you will have high standard IT skills, competence in HR, ...' – and if not, you are not 'our kind of person'. Equally, people do not just have skills, they need re-training, in-service training, continual professional development. As current management speak has it: 'without continual staff-development, you are de-skilling your workforce.'

This is exactly similar to the situation with the skills of discipleship and being the sort of person that can be described as 'Christ-ian'.

6. While we readily link Lent with this sort of returning, reforming, restoring, it is equally true of the time after Easter: during this time the newly baptised are supposed to be getting the mentoring they need to be full disciples; but also all the baptised are supposed to be refining their skills, and retraining, and up-dating their understanding of discipleship, here lies the focus of today's gospel. We are all grafted into Christ and have entered the service of the Father, but our belonging requires that we bear fruit. Have we the skills and the practice in the skills to recognise that we are not just passively 'grafted on'; we are grafted on in order that we can bear fruit. Note that in each image the point at issue is not belonging, but activity which fulfills the purpose of that to which we are grafted. We are not 'in Christ' as a cup of water diffused in a barrel – a passive image, but made part of vine and the vine only makes sense when it yields the grapes for which it was planted and tended.

7. It is from this perspective of discipleship being costly, demanding commitment, and serious long-term training that we can read this gospel in Eastertime. This is how we are to unbderstand its references to pruning, and dead wood being thrown-away and burnt. Discipleship is being someone with the vision to see the kingdom in outline and the skills to help build it. It requires a dynamism that the word 'following' does not convey in English, and it requires a commitment to the coming of the kingdom and to doing the Father's will on earth – this is the fruit we must show for being part of Christ.

8. 'It is to the glory of my Father that you should bear much fruit, and then you will be my disciples.'

Fifth Sunday of Easter Year C

Introduction to the Celebration
The Paschal Candle burning before us alerts us to the fact that on these Sundays after Easter we are trying to grasp the mystery of what it means to follow Jesus who has risen from death and who is sharing his new life with us. Jesus has called us out of darkness, he has renewed us in baptism, he calls us to give new life to the world, and he beckons us to the glorious city beyond history where we shall be one with him in praising the Father.

Rite of Penance
The Easter form of the *Asperges* (Missal, p. 388) is preferable.

Headings for Readings
First Reading
We are called by the risen Jesus to belong to the Kingdom of God, but on our way to that Kingdom we have to be ready to endure many hardships.

Second Reading
The destiny to which the risen Christ calls us is to belong to the Holy City, the New Jerusalem, where God lives among men and women.

Gospel
If we are to live the new life of baptism, then we must live by the New Commandment: we must love one another.

Prayer of the Faithful
President:
At baptism each of us became a child of God and so a brother or sister to every other Christian, and so as a family we pray for

each other; at baptism we also became a priestly people and so we can now stand in God's presence and make intercession for our needs, those of our fellow Christians, our fellow humans, and the whole creation.

Reader(s):

1. For all Christians, that we will become aware of being a baptised people, and act accordingly.

2. For all human beings, that we will become aware of the mystery of love that sustains us, and become more attuned to the presence of God in the creation.

3. For all who are suffering, that they may not loose hope, and that their sisters and brothers will help them.

4. For us in this community, that our gathering now at the Lord's supper will help us to love one another more.

5. *Local needs.*

6. For all who have died, that they may rise in the New Jerusalem.

President:

Father, your risen Son has shared his new life with us; grant our needs now, and welcome us into his presence at the coming of the New Heaven and the New Earth for we ask this through Christ our Lord, Amen.

Eucharistic Prayer

The renewal of the creation, which is a theme in the second reading, is also found in Preface of Easter IV (P 24, Missal, p. 427).

Invitation to the Our Father

Looking forward to the kingdom when God will dwell among us, let us pray:

Sign of Peace

Christ, risen and standing among us, offers us his peace, let us exchange that same peace with one another.

Invitation to Communion
This is the Lamb of God, who calls us to love one another and
who shares his life with each of us. Happy are we to be gathered
here around his table.

Communion Reflection
Edmund Spenser's poem 'Easter' (Breviary, vol 2, p. 608*).

Dismissal
Blessing n 7 (Easter Season), Missal, p. 370.

COMMENTARY

First Reading: Acts 14:21-27
This is the conclusion of Luke's 'first missionary journey' and its
larger purpose is that it is on this journey that Paul recognises
that the Good News is not only for the Jews, but all the nations –
see the last verse of the reading – and so the gospel has now entered the third phase of its dissemination (the first phase was in
Jerusalem, the second in the surrounding lands of the existing
Chosen People, the third phase is in the lands of the nations out
to the ends of the earth).

Now having inaugurated this phase, the scene is set in Acts
for the formal ratification by the Jerusalem church for this activity
and the way that Paul is preaching 'The Way' without circumcision or dietary laws. There has been a continual tendency to
read these passages as simply 'an account of facts' (e.g. they then
got to Lystra, and then did something else) and this exegetical
tendency would no doubt have pleased Luke as a comment of
his skill as a stylish ancient historian, but that is to miss the fact
that this is theology being presented as history. The actual ex-
pansion of belief in Jesus and membership of churches was a
very haphazard and messy business, and caused a great deal of
turmoil among many different parties of Jews who had become
Christians – indeed some of these Jewish-Christian parties were
so unable to cope with the widening people base of Christianity

that they eventually became detached sects. However, Luke wants to present this messiness as simply 'little local difficulties' which can be ignored and forgotten within the grand design of God: if, he seems to argue, Christians can see the 'big picture' and see it as God's will (hence 'all that God had done with them'), then they should accept the breadth of Christianity that is found in his time even if it is different in its ethnicity and practices from that of the earliest followers of Jesus.

Psalm

The most appropriate response to all the Psalms in Eastertide is simply 'alleluia'. However, it seems just too short! Against this should be weighed three points: (1) The Liturgy of the Word can be very wordy without a reflective pause to let things sink in. The Psalm is supposed to be a reflection on the first reading, but a long response just makes it another thing to be remembered – 'alleluia' is very simple. (2) This is a key word of rejoicing for Eastertide. (3) Sung responses require a choir or special musical skill, a simple triple 'alluluia' is within the musical competence of most people.

Second Reading: Apoc 21:1-5

This is the author's vision of the eschatological church: the perfect assembly offering the perfect liturgy with God dwelling in the midst of his people. It is worth noting that in contrast to the popular modern meaning of 'apocalyptic' and also in contrast to many ancient apocalypses, this account ends on a high point of glory and happiness: it is a new creation, not a great crunch! The new creation in this reading is not a simple extension of this universe 'made perfect' nor an utopian vision – as many fundamentalists today try to interpret it, but rather it exists in a wholly different order of existence: it is the new creation after all we know ('the first earth') and all we can imagine ('the first heaven') have passed away, and it is God's gift to humanity ('coming down ... from heaven') so that he can dwell with us.

Gospel: Jn 13:31-35

The setting is the Last Supper where the new commandment follows on from the washing of the feet of the disciples, and the opening verses of the passage introduce John's interpretation of the event of the cross: the Son of Man being glorified and so God being glorified in him. This interweaving of two themes here (the first introducing a theme that appears later in John (ch. 17), and the second to that which has gone before (13:4-17) and will be picked up again in ch. 15) makes this passage appear disjointed when read as a reading at the Eucharist. One way around this is to recall that the Eucharist itself is a participation in the death and resurrection of Christ and so a participation in the glorification of the Son of Man; but the Eucharist is, like the Last Supper, the gathering of the disciples with the Lord and so the place to hear the new commandment.

HOMILY NOTES

1. Some words keep coming up in Eastertime: 'new life,' 'new creation,' 'renewal,' 'new birth,' 'baptism,' 'being a baptised people,' and you could add many more to the list. However, these words all suffer a burn-out in meaning for people. Baptism is just a fancy name for a christening which is just a party after a new baby – and even those who are regular church-goers will have been to many such family events where they know that christening is an event and that's the end of it. As for 'new' and 'renewal', these words belong to the stock and trade of advertising. The effect of this exhaustion of meaning within words is that some of our most basic beliefs about the life that the Christ shares with us become, when expressed in phrases like 'he gives us new life', sounds that are indistinguishable from trite clichés.

2. So can meaning be restored? The two great means of restoring religious symbols – and words are just one kind of symbol – are (1) re-inventing rituals which capture the imagination anew, and (2) reflection which brings those symbols into new alignments within our minds (so baptism is not

linked to a private family occasion nor new life with someone offering a 'lifestyle makeover').

3. If the theme of new creation, new life through baptism is to
be explored and given back its 'saltiness' then the homily and
the rest of the ritual need to gel together. So make more of the
sprinkling with water at the beginning that involves movement and action and touch by all concerned: effective ritual
always needs at least these components if it is to be affective.

4. At the homily time ask people to reflect with those near them
what saying 'we are a new creation' means to them? Does it
have implications for how we treat one another? Does it
mean replacing the instinct for vengeance with that of forgiveness? Does it have any implications for how responsible
we must be with the earth's resources and care of the environment?

Such questions touch some of our most deeply held beliefs in contemporary western societies – areas of belief
where often we do not want the light of Christ to penetrate
lest it cause us discomfort. But it is only in discomfort that the
basic symbols of our faith can be renovated from flippant
phrases into life-giving words.

Alternative credal formulae

One of the signs of the times seems to be – for there is nothing more difficult to see than one's own time and culture – a desire to recover a Christianity that speaks to us from 'our roots' and which somehow has a freshness in comparison to the tired formulae with which we are familiar either in Christian discourse or in the liturgy. Moreover, even for those people who are not consciously seeking alternatives to current ways of praying and thinking, there is still the fundamental problem of liturgy that 'what we do everyday, bores us' (St Augustine). Hence, we must be always on the look out for alternatives that can add variety to our celebrations, and cause us to look afresh at texts which have become stale through over repetition.

Creed formulae

An example of this tiredness is the communal recitation of the creed in the Sunday liturgy. Most people, if asked, would adopt the now widely current explanation of its nature that it is a statement of 'core beliefs' and as such valuable – but the actual recitation seems to suggest that it is only a long technical tract imperfectly remembered. We do re-set it within its baptismal context on occasion (e.g. on Easter Sunday) but this rejigging of the creed into its more basic question-and-reply format is not seen as illuminating the meaning of the recitation on other occasions, but as a discreet act of 'renewing baptismal promises'. Moreover, the creed most often used – commonly called 'Nicene' – contains technical terms which were crucially important to fourth-century theologians when a baptismal liturgical text was pressed into service as a canon of orthodoxy, but which do not speak directly to ordinary people as expressing their belief.

The Missal does offer the alternative of the so-called 'Apostles' Creed' which has the advantage that it is more easily seen as originally a set of questions at a baptism. However, when it is used, the fact that it does not echo in the memory means that unless people read it, then one slips back into the 'Nicene Creed' and the result is a cacophony rather than an expression of unity in Christ in faith. Clearly, while we need to retain familiarity with both these texts, we need to add other expressions of faith to our liturgical repertoire. The obvious first choice is to use the Renewal of Baptismal Promises from the Easter Sunday liturgy (Missal, pp. 220-1) more frequently. This indeed happens in many places on the Sunday of the Baptism of The Lord, and it is a practice that could be extended further, especially when then theme of baptism appears elsewhere in the liturgy on a particular Sunday. However, do we need even more alternatives?

Alternatives?

It is easy to prepare alternative liturgies using 'the blank page and ink' method. However, this approach has two major disadvantages. First, any liturgy or text produced usually so reflects the concerns of the moment and the group that produces it that it is too limited as an expression of the whole faith of the community that has to use it. So while those who wish to invent afresh praise the 'spontaneity' and 'relevance' of their creations, they forget that the alternative names for those qualities are 'idiosyncratic' and 'ephemeral'. Second, the most basic fact about Christianity as a religion is that it is historical in its beliefs. The Christ came at a particular time in a specific place and culture, and so it lives as a religion within a tradition, and so its liturgy must represent this chronic continuity and link people not only to their beliefs and one another in the present, but to the communion of believers throughout the Christian age. These are ideas that are neither easy to present today, nor felt to be of great importance, but if we forget them within our liturgy we loose that union in Christ which is the very purpose of our gathering. Seeking alternative credal formulae must be a quest for the new and for our own past.

Here are two formulae with deep roots in the past: one in the liturgy of early Christian Britain, the other in early Christian Ireland.

1. Here is a translation of St Patrick's confession of faith which, for the most part, represents the sort of creed he would have learned in Britain in the fifth century and no doubt used continually in his ministry. We should note, however, that the creed was not recited as a part of the eucharistic liturgy until the eighth century.

> There is not, nor ever was, any other God – there was none before him and there shall not be any after him – besides him who is God the Father unbegotten: without a source, from him everything else takes its beginning. He is, as we say, the one who keeps hold of all things.
>
> And his Son, Jesus Christ, whom we declare to have always existed with the Father.
>
> He was with the Father spiritually before the world came into being; begotten of the Father before the beginning of anything in a way that is beyond our speech.
>
> And 'through him all things were made,' all things visible and invisible. He was made man, and having conquered death was taken back into the heavens to the Father.
>
> 'And he has bestowed on him all power above every name in heaven and on earth and under the earth, so that every tongue may confess that our Lord and God is Jesus Christ.'
>
> In him we believe, looking forward to his coming in the very near future when he will judge the living and the dead, and 'will repay each according to his works.'
>
> And '[the Father] has plentifully poured upon us the Holy Spirit', the gift and pledge of immortality, who makes those who believe and listen into 'sons of God' the Father 'and fellow heirs with Christ.'
>
> [This is] who we profess and worship, One God in Trinity of sacred name.

This text has both the theological sophistication we expect from credal formulae, but it also has a certain rugged grandeur.

There has been much discussion as to whether this is related to the 'creed of Nicaea and Constantinople' or not, but all that discussion misses the essential point: creeds were in use in the baptism liturgy and as part of the catechetical process from the first decades of Christianity. By the time of the great councils (325 and 381) their basic trinitarian shape was already fixed in the liturgy and everyday use – it was this practice that gave the councils their model, not the councils which gave a model for ordinary use. Patrick takes over a creed that he knew by heart, that he had used in baptising and teaching, and since it was his own deepest profession of what he believed, makes it the basis of his entire recital of God's gifts.

This text could be used as part of a renewal of baptismal promises or elaborated for use in other ways. It could be recited by a single individual as a piece of prose, or broken up into questions inviting 'Amen' as a response.

2. The second text is from Tírechán's collection of traditions about Patrick (*Collectanea de Sancto Patricio*). Christians in Ireland are fortunate in having several credal expressions within the tradition which have not only proven their value by long, if not recent, use, but which reflect perfectly the Latin tradition of creed-formation within baptismal liturgies, and which pick up some of the themes about the value and beauty of the creation that are appealing at the present. Nowhere are these qualities more obviously found than in this creed:

Our God is the God of all humans.
The God of heaven and earth.
The God of the sea and the rivers.
The God of the sun and moon.
The God of all the heavenly bodies.
The God of the lofty mountains.
The God of the lowly valleys.
God is above the heavens;
and he is in the heavens;
and he is beneath the heavens.
Heaven and earth and sea,

and everything that is in them,
such he has as his abode.
He inspires all things,
he gives life to all things,
he stands above all things,
and he stands beneath all things.
He enlightens the light of the sun,
he strengthens the light of the night and the stars,
he makes wells in the arid land and dry islands in the sea,
and he places the stars in the service of the greater lights.
He has a Son who is co-eternal with himself,
and similar in all respects to himself;
and neither is the Son younger than the Father,
nor is the Father older than the Son;
and the Holy Spirit breathes in them.
And the Father and the Son and Holy Spirit are inseparable.
[Amen].

So where did this come from? Sometime in the late seventh century, Bishop Tírechán set about 'collecting' traditions about St Patrick. In his book, the *Collectanea* (section 26), he invents a dialogue and scene around a passing mention by Patrick in his *Confessio* that many of the sons and daughters of Irish leaders have been baptised and become monks and nuns (*Confessio* 41 and 42). Tírechán develops his scene by 'naming the nameless' and making it a meeting of the two daughters of the king of Tara by a well (a deliberate echo of Christ meeting the Samaritan woman in Jn 4). One woman asks Patrick about the Christian God, and as his reply Tírechán puts the statement of faith into Patrick's mouth – for Tírechán assumes that the confession of a creed is a central part of the process leading to baptism. As to the ultimate origins of the text we can do little more than guess that it was a piece of liturgy known to Tírechán.

Writing in the later seventh century, it is virtually certain that Tírechán never encountered a creed as part of the Eucharistic liturgy, and so we must assume that he imagined this text solely in terms of catechesis and leading people towards baptism. So how is this text related to the liturgy? It may be, as some have suggested, a baptismal hymn – it has a metrical quality in Latin – based on the questions-and-answers. It may be an elaboration of a declaratory creed – indeed it could be that it is an elaboration of either the 'Apostles' or 'Nicene' creeds and doctrinal formulae as they were used in the teaching of theology and as declarations of orthodoxy by clergy on those occasions when the law demanded that such declarations be made. But whatever its origins, we have here an ancient text whose beauty is such that it deserves to find a place in the liturgy once more.

Its use of nature imagery and its emphasis on the manifestations of God in creation might make us – had we not the manuscripts to prove otherwise – think that it was written to order by a committee of modern ecotheologians. Its sense of Christian faith in the Three Persons as that which can find echoes in every aspect of life makes it seem like something that was written only yesterday, yet it has been tried in the sieve of time and not been found wanting. How it can be used in the liturgy is a matter of the style of different congregations, but if the collective rumble of the 'Nicene Creed' is replaced from time to time with a single voice reciting this text, and the invitation made to the assembly as to whether we can say 'Amen' to that statement, then it can be a refreshing encounter with the basics of our belief.

Using alternatives like these may appear to some to be unnecessary innovation in the liturgy – a sop to those with itchy ears, while to others the fact that it has been dug out of an ancient Irish source might seem just part of a doctrinal atavism – a sop to those who want the romanticism of the past, but the wise steward of the liturgy is the one 'who brings out of his treasure' both 'what is new and what is old' (Mt 13:52).

Sixth Sunday of Easter Year A

Introduction to the Celebration
We gather to celebrate in the presence of the risen Lord. We are called to be the people who bear witness to his victory over death. We are the people who proclaim the Father's forgiveness to the ends of the earth by being people who are forgiving.

Rite of Penance
For when our actions have belonged to a culture of destruction and exploitation, Lord have mercy.
For when we have failed to witness to the resurrection of Jesus, Christ have mercy.
For when we have failed to forgive or sought vengeance, Lord have mercy.

Headings for Readings
First Reading
The good news spreads out from Jerusalem as persecution scatters the followers of Christ.

Second Reading
Here is one of the hard lessons we have to hear: how should we behave when threatened as Christians?

Gospel
Christ shares his life with us, and so we are caught up in the life of God, Father, Son, and Holy Spirit.

Prayer of the Faithful
President:
My friends, as witnesses to the Father's love, let us place our prayers before him.

Reader(s):
1. That may we bear witness to the resurrection.
2. That we may forgive our enemies.
3. That we may seek peace and support all who work for it.
4. That we may experience the presence of God in our lives.
5. That the dead may rise in the Lord.
President:
Father, you raised your Son from the dead and so showed us our destiny. Look on us, your adopted children, hear us, and be with us in Christ Jesus, our Lord. Amen.

Invitation to the Our Father
Let us ask the Father to forgive us our sins and bring us to forgive those who sin against us.

Sign of Peace
Christ stands among us offering us his peace; let us offer our peace to one another.

Invitation to Communion
Behold the risen Lord, the Conqueror of death, the Prince of Peace, happy are we who are called to his table.

Communion Reflection
One of the pieces translated in the *Note on Breaking and Sharing* is appropriate in Eastertide.

Dismissal
Blessing n 7 (Easter Season), Missal, p. 370.

COMMENTARY

First Reading: Acts 8:5-8, 14-17
Luke sees the gospel spreading outwards in concentric circles (Acts 1:8): first, Jerusalem, next Judea and Samaria, and then to the world. This passage marks the beginning of the second phase: the believers having been driven from Jerusalem by per-

secution, now inaugurate the mission to the larger area of the land of Israel, prior to going out to the gentiles. So God's reign is advanced by these opponents of the believers: for Luke there is a divine plan at work in history and it will not be thwarted. In the reading in the lectionary we are told of the initial contact with Samaria, and then the 'follow up' of the apostles going there so that they could receive the Spirit. Behind this passage is the desire of Luke to present all the churches as having an apostolic link in their origins, so there is a single faith and one church.

The passage raises a serious difficulty from the point of view of the modern reader. Despite the fact that the first appearance of Simon Magus is not read (vv. 9-13) with its emphasis on the miraculous powers of the apostles, the miraculous plays a large part in this reading: miracles, the expulsion of demons, and physical healings are the proofs that the new group have the correct credentials for calling on the power of God. This is a position which we have withdrawn from both theologically and in preaching, and usually pass over in silence. Unfortunately, this silence is often interpreted by those listening as a deliberate attempt to ignore the difficulties or even to continue preaching what we know is false. Given that many in the congregation may have a false notion of verbal inerrancy about scripture (i.e. they think that the church holds that it is literally true in every detail, they know it is not so, therefore the whole thing is a fraud) which is fostered by the use of phrases such as 'gospel truth' meaning every detail is true or 'the bible of car maintenance' meaning everything you need to know is there and it can be trusted, it is worth pointing out in explicit terms that this is not our understanding, and that these texts – no more than our own understanding – are not immune to the limitations of their time and culture.

This text, with its distinction between baptism and the sending of the Spirit, has sometimes been appealed to as the distinction between the sacraments of baptism and confirmation. Apart from being the product of a false hermeneutic, this is theologically unacceptable as it would imply that the Spirit is not received in baptism and that baptism is not a full sacrament unless confirmation is received.

Second Reading: 1 Pet 3:15-18
This passage, part of a moral instruction to new Christians on appropriate behaviour, is one of the most demanding texts we read in the liturgy. Written in the context of actual persecution it is guidance on how Christians are to react to threats, insolence, and violence – and was probably written to distinguish the way Christians should act from those Jewish insurgents who took military action against the Roman authorities. Christians are to give an account, an apology, for their beliefs, but to defend their position with courtesy. They are 'not to fight fire with fire' by responding to insults and intolerance in like manner. Their example is to be Christ; if they follow him in their suffering they will share in his victory for he is risen.

Gospel: Jn 14:15-21
This text is John's most succinct presentation of how he understands the inner life of God revealed to Christians. The Son, sharing in our humanity, asks the Father to send the Spirit to dwell within us. Through our relationship with Christ, we possess the Spirit, and are brought into the presence of the Father. The Christian life for John is not simply a discipleship, nor a service or following of God, but much more: it is an abiding in the trinitarian life of God.

HOMILY NOTES

1. The demanding stance on how Christians are to react to persecution in 1 Peter makes this a fine occasion to reflect on the ever present question of Christians and violence.

2. It is interesting to note the number of times that public figures quote scripture without knowing it (e.g. 'going the extra mile for peace' (President Clinton) is an allusion to Mt 5:41) and it is cited both with approval and non-approval. Invariably when one hears quotations on non-violence cited,

they are implied to be feeble and silly, if not downright wrong: thus 'turn the other cheek' (Mt 5:39) is not presented as the statement of wisdom, but of a stupidity that acquiesces to evil. While few who declare themselves Christians take the hawkish position of 'take 'em on, take 'em out!', there is an awareness that one must stand up to bullies, those who abuse power, those who trample on other's rights, especially those who abuse the weak, poor, defenceless. This dilemma has lead to the traditional unwillingness of the church to adopt a pacifist position. Pacifism has a simple attractiveness, but the pacifist must ask this question: is it right for me not to oppose someone who if not stopped will destroy not only me, but others who may not be able to stand up for themselves? While using force can appear immoral, pacifism too can be immoral in that I am passively collaborating in suffering being caused to others. Thus I may, in the exercise of my freedom, be destroying the freedom of others. Pacifism poses moral problems, and can be a selfish opting out of our moral responsibilities to others weaker than ourselves. This is a dilemma; but we are certain that those who set out to dominate others act evilly, and a wilful hawkishness cannot be reconciled with Christianity for which force is always a last resort.

3. However, the situation envisaged in 1 Peter is slightly different: how should Christians react when they are being persecuted as Christians – it is their behaviour precisely as Christians that is the issue. They are to give an account of their beliefs but to do so with courtesy. Put another way, they do make their stand known, but do not 'fight fire with fire'. They cannot have recourse to methods of bullying, force, or intolerance, for that would betray the Christ in whom they seek to live. As Christ chose the way of gentleness, so when challenged Christians must act with gentleness: otherwise their words preach one thing, their actions another. This is a hard lesson: the recurrence of the notions of crusade and *pro Deo et patria* (God gets first billing, but usually takes second

place) testify to this. And sadly these notions are far from dead, as various right-wing Christian groups demonstrate in their readiness 'to fight for gospel values'. Their very militancy compromises the Christ they wish to serve.

4. 1 Peter makes deep moral demands on us. As a Christian how fitted am I to give an account of my faith? Is my understanding of the Christian message a few 'do's and don'ts' and some scraps of information remembered from school? Do I appreciate there is a Christian manner of action? Am I conscious of how others are persecuted for their beliefs, or feel a sense of solidarity with Christians who suffer elsewhere? As a member of a body which was born in persecution and whose head suffered on the cross, am I sensitive to the pain of all who are oppressed, and seek to alleviate their persecution? Is a document such as the Universal Declaration of Human Rights something that I consider should interest me as a Christian? Do I support those who support human rights? Painful questions, but can we be true to our origin if we shy away from them?

Sixth Sunday of Easter Year B

Introduction to the Celebration

We are the people who live in Christ's love: by dying he has destroyed our death, by rising he has restored our life, and we look for him to come in glory. So now let us celebrate his presence among us.

Rite of Penance

The theme of Easter is already receding from consciousness by today, so the Easter form of the *Asperges* may serve as a reminder that we gather on Sunday as a baptised people to celebrate the resurrection.

Headings for Readings
First Reading

God has no favourites: everyone who does what is right is acceptable to him.

Second Reading

God is love, and everyone who loves is his child and knows him.

Gospel

We see how much God loves us: he sent us his Son and his Son was prepared to lay down his life out of love for us whom he calls his friends.

Prayer of the Faithful
President:

Friends, God loves us and has shown us this love in the life, death, and resurrection of Jesus. With Jesus who is among us we have access to the Father to express our needs.

Reader(s):

1. That we may bear witness to the resurrection.

2. That we may forgive our enemies.
3. That we may work for peace.
4. That we may know Christ's presence.
5. That we and all who have died may rise in the Lord.
6. *Local needs.*
President:
Father, we seek to love you and each other and so be the friends of your Son. Hear us in all our needs, and come to aid us through Christ, our Lord, Amen.

Invitation to the Our Father
Through Christ who calls us friends we have come to know the Father, so let us pray:

Sign of Peace
We are all made friends in Jesus Christ and have been called to love one another. Let us indicate this new life to one another with the sign of peace.

Invitation to Communion
This is the Lamb who calls us friends and invites us to be guests at his table, happy are we to be here.

Communion Reflection
One of the pieces translated in the *Note on Breaking and Sharing* is appropriate in Eastertide.

Dismissal
Blessing n 7 (Easter Season) Missal, p. 370.

COMMENTARY
First Reading: Acts 10:25-26; 34-35; 44-48
This is one of Luke's stories to show that the faith was to spread to all nations but without the demands of the Jewish law. The dietary laws – principal means of defining the people as Jews – have no more force: God has no favourites.

Second Reading: 1 Jn 4:7-10
This is a summary restatement of a theme of love found in all the Johannine writings: God is love, this is revealed in Jesus, and the new commandment follows from this: love one another as God in Christ loves you.

Gospel: Jn 15:9-17
Set at the heart of the Last Supper discourse, this passage re-states, yet again, the new commandment of love, and establishes the nature of the bond between those celebrating the Eucharist in Johannine communities: they can be seen as friends of the Word. The intimacy implied in friendship in the ancient world is something that is lost on us today, but it was used to describe the highest level of human intimacy.

HOMILY NOTES

1. Finding suitable ways to give a broad overview catechesis of what we believe in by saying Jesus rose from the dead and has shared his new life with us is something that has con-cerned preachers from the very beginning as we can witness, for example, in 1 Peter. What is needed is a rounded state-ment, that is accessible, memorable, and pictorial. The most frequently chosen image has been that of baptism – but while this is the foundational Christian symbol, its power for many today is limited as it is too often seen just as a family occasion or as rite for infancy. So even when we preach about it, we have to face the dissonance that an actual baptism may for those concerned involve more worry over the name to give the child than the ritual or its reality.

2. However, we must still use our great symbols and continue to expound them. One way of doing this is to take the prayer for the blessing of the water at baptism at the Easter Vigil (Missal, pp. 213-214) and go through it by way of a medit-ation with comments. This serves to recall that we are in Eastertide and calls up all the great images of Christian memory.

Sixth Sunday of Easter Year C

Introduction to the Celebration

At Easter we recalled that we have died and risen in Christ in baptism. Today let us recall that, as his people sharing his life, we must be people of the Light.

Rite of Penance

The theme of Easter is already receding from consciousness by today, so the Easter form of the *Asperges* may serve as a reminder that we gather on Sunday as a baptised people to celebrate the resurrection.

Headings for Readings

First Reading

Christians are to avoid all that might give credence to false gods in the minds of other people, and to abstain from evil: then they will be following God's law.

Second Reading

We look forward to the coming of Christ again in glory when he will gather the whole church from every time and place, and he will be our unending Light.

Gospel

Christ has shown us the Father's love and he sends the Holy Spirit among us who keeps the life of God present in our hearts.

Prayer of the Faithful

Use the Sample Prayer of the Faithful n 8 (Easter Season), Missal, p. 1001.

Eucharistic Prayer
Preface III of Easter (P 23, Missal, p. 426) is a good choice as it invokes the image of Christ the priest and harmonises with the gospel when we read a portion of the High Priestly Prayer.

Invitation to the Our Father
Christ our high priest has given us access to the Father, and so we can dare to pray:

Sign of Peace
The risen Jesus offered his followers the greeting of peace. Let each of us now be Christ's voice and offer that greeting of peace to each other.

Invitation to Communion
Behold the Lamb of God, our temple, our place of encounter with the glory of God, whose radiance lights up our lives. Blessed are we who share in his banquet.

Communion Reflection
George Herbert's poem 'Easter' (Breviary, vol 2, p. 614*-615*)

Dismissal
Blessing n 7 (Easter Season), Missal, p. 370.

COMMENTARY

First Reading: Acts 15:1-2, 22-29
This is an abbreviated account of Luke's conference at Jerusalem that is intended to show his audience just how amicably, in the Holy Spirit, all the difficulties that confronted the earliest generation of Christians were resolved in harmony and a spirit of love. Luke sets it out with two purposes: first, to show that the gentiles are equally part of Christ as those Christians who were converts from Judaism; and second, as a model to Christians in his own time about how they should resolve their quarrels over how Christians should live, how they should resolve their ritual

squabbles, and how they should welcome all other Christians from the whole church.

As it is found in today's reading, the text lacks coherence and is hard to follow (e.g. circumcision is mentioned in the opening verses and then we hear nothing more about it in what follows), so it is probably best to draw little attention to the details but to point out that it is part of Luke's message that all disputes between Christians should be sorted out in patient conference and in mutual love.

Second Reading: Apoc 21:10-14, 22-23
This is the vision of the final church: the perfect gathering of all the followers of the Lamb in the New Jerusalem. In reinterpreting the vision of the new city from Ezekiel, the author places Jesus as not only the End of the history of Israel, but extends that to being the End of all humanity. This is the theme of 'I am the Alpha and Omega' which has a place in the liturgy at Easter by being inscribed on the Paschal Candle.

Gospel: Jn 14:23-29
This is part of the conclusion to one Last Supper discourse in John where Jesus speaks about his departure, and in that context how he will remain present to his community. He has two gifts to the church: the Holy Spirit and peace. The Spirit is the one who continues the teaching of Jesus by keeping it in the memory of his disciples, and does not introduce a new or additional teaching. Peace is the gift that enables them to remain in love with each other and with the Father.

HOMILY NOTES

See Year B.

The Ascension of the Lord Year A

Introduction to the Celebration

The mystery we have been celebrating since Easter is that of Christ's victory over death: death is not the end. Today, we reflect on another aspect of that mystery: when on earth he was present only in one place at a time to a small group of disciples; now seated at the right hand of the Father he is present to all his disciples at all times. Ascension is not about Christ's absence, but about his presence in a different way to that which he had before his death. He now is present in our hearts and minds, and requires us to make that presence a visible one in the way we live our lives, work for justice, and seek the kingdom.

Rite of Penance

Option c vii (Missal, p. 394-5) is appropriate.

Headings for Readings

First Reading

This very dramatic story by Luke seeks to express the visible absence of Jesus from his people in terms of his floating away through the clouds. Because we can picture this colourful scene so easily, we often forget that this just a story intended to point out some basic Christian beliefs: Jesus is not physically with us, then it is our task to be his witnesses and we must proclaim his good news. In this task there is no room for slacking – hence the detail of the two men in white – and we must remember that Jesus will come again to judge the living and the dead.

Second Reading

Here we have an image of the victorious Christ in heaven: he has been raised by the Father and has the whole creation beneath him. He is the head of the church, and so we make him visible in the creation. The image is a complex one: on the one hand Christ is the Lord of creation exalted above all things; on the other, he is connected to each of us as giving us life, inspiring us, beckoning us, and calling on us to make him present in life.

Gospel

The story of Jesus going up into the heavens which gives us the idea for today's feast – and which has so often been the subject of paintings – is only found in one gospel writer: Luke. In the others, the transfer of the duty of making the Father known from Jesus to us is portrayed in different ways. Today we read Matthew's account of this change where the image is one not of departing, but of a transfer of authority, and a command to the church to carry on his work until the end of time.

Prayer of the Faithful

President:

On this day when we recall that we are the visible presence of Christ and that he has given us a mission to perform, let us ask the Father for the strength we need for our tasks.

Reader(s):

1. That we will grasp the implications of the mystery of the ascension in our lives.

2. That we will be the witnesses of Christ to the ends of the earth.

3. For those who are scandalised by the church, or by those who are seen to represent it, that they may not be prevented from finding Christ.

4. *Local needs.*

5. For those who have died, that they may see the risen Christ face to face.

President:

Father, we gather as disciples of your Son. We believe that he is now present at your right hand, and also here in our gathering. Grant us what we ask that we may be your Son's visible presence until he comes again. We ask this though Christ our Lord.

Eucharistic Prayer
Ascension I (P 26) is preferable as it focuses on Christ as our priest. Note the special addition if you opt for Eucharistic Prayer I.

Invitation to the Our Father
Gathered with the risen Christ, conscious that we must carry on his work of advancing the Father's kingdom, let us pray.

Sign of Peace
Peace was the Lord's parting gift to the disciples. Let us express now our desire to live in peace with others and with God.

Invitation to Communion
Christ has been taken from our sight, but let us recognise his presence now among us in this broken loaf. This is the Lamb of God ...

Communion Reflection
There is a lack of symbolic action in today's feast to make it stand out from other celebrations. A possible solution is to re-use the old ceremony of formally extinguishing the Paschal candle after communion (in the pre-1970 rite it was done after the first gospel). This can be done with a minimum of words, e.g.:
'Lord, as this candle reminded us that you had risen and conquered darkness, so may we know that while this flame burns in each of us beyond this place, then it is not extinguished. Amen.'

Dismissal
Blessing n 8 (Ascension), Missal, p. 371.

COMMENTARY

First Reading: Acts 1:1-11
1. This text presents us with both exegetical and pastoral difficulties. Exegetically, it brings us into the world of the religious mythology in which the New Testament was written: an image of heaven above the spheres above the earth, of won-

drous entries and departures from the world, and where nu-
minous beings appear and communicate with men.
Likewise, the author presents the ascension as an historical
event that took place in our time and space, i.e. you could
locate it with a map and a watch. Understanding this worldview is the difficulty of all exegesis of ancient religious texts.
To the Christian exegete it poses an additional problem: what
is beneath this myth that actually tells us something about
the revelation of God in Christ? What is the message beneath
this time conditioned covering?

2. Pastorally, it poses a related problem: since this is the classic
   text for the 'event' of the ascension, many who are there may
   not have paused to consider that this is not history. Taking
   advantage of this lack of reflection by some of their congregation, many preachers have then taken a position of 'not disturbing simple faith' because of the doubts of the 'few'.
   However, thus leaving people with their (presumably passively held) fundamentalist views unchallenged is not leaving people in any kind of faith – simple or otherwise – but in
   ignorance. And, for Catholics at least, ignorance cannot be a
   virtue.

3. Furthermore, hearing of 'the marvellous' in the readings
   without any attempt to translate it into our mental framework is something that is seriously disturbing to many people who find themselves unable to take these tales seriously
   and interpret the silence from preachers as implying that to
   those with 'faith' such problems do not arise and that these
   mythic presentations are to be accepted as facts. These
   doubters rarely surface in the parish setting as those with difficulties frequently assume that they know what answer they
   would receive if they asked their local priest. Instead, they
   'vote with their feet' using this syllogism: they believe all that
   stuff; I cannot; therefore, I have no faith and should not be
   there.

4. Each preacher has to pick the level for his congregation, yet
   must communicate that this scene is not to be understood as

an historical account of the last moments of Jesus on earth. Rather it is a story-vehicle-for-a-truth-that-cannot-be-fully-expressed (a myth) that Jesus is no longer with us, yet is with each Christian, and both individually and collectively we must make him visible. If people can go away with the notion that this is 'what happened back then,' and without any challenge to this un-Catholic reading of the text, then this preaching and celebration have failed.

5. In the passage it is Luke's intention to set up a theme for his understanding of the mission of the church: the gospel must take root everywhere for it is greater than all boundaries (even those held to be sacred for generations); and this must happen through us. Luke sees the message spreading out in concentric circles: Jerusalem (the focus of revelation until the time of Christ); the Jewish homeland (those who were alerted to his coming); and then out to everyone on earth. The rest of Acts is then the account of this task being successfully carried out. We might see it as making Christ's message present in ourselves, in our immediate circles of family and friends, and then in our work and environment. This spreading is as difficult and requires as much suffering as did the early spread of the message through the cities of Judea, Asia, Greece, and Italy: a spread characterised by reversals, misunderstandings, and martyrdom.

6. There seems to be something rude involved in shattering fundamentalism – hence many avoid it and relinquish the ministry of teaching to those who shatter icons for effect or in opposition to Christianity – but it brings this reward. Freed from looking backwards and treating this feast as a commemoration service for an historical event long past, this feast can be seen as calling on us to grasp our mission: we are to be the visible presence of Christ in our world. In the past this text was read as the 'scriptural warrant' for the miraculous event of the ascent of Jesus and so the 'justification' for this festival. However, in all likelihood the Lukan story is an attempt to give a vivid background to a mystery already

being celebrated liturgically within his community – an endeavour which engages Luke on several occasions in Acts.

7. The church believed that every aspect of the life of Jesus was significant to them and that, far from being a now-dead founder who dwelt beyond this realm with God (a perversely simple view of resurrection that is not found in any early Christian document), he was present everywhere with them now. This was not expressed as a theological formula, but within the myth of the Ascension whereby he was with them through they being in him, and consequently they were charged with being his presence. As this was preached it took to itself an 'historical' location within the narrative sequence of life, death and resurrection, and was then given this brilliant narrative form by Luke. But the basic story must already have been part of the celebration of Christians by Luke's time as he takes it as the key moment in his own overall narrative: the junction between the times of the earthly Jesus (his gospel) and the times of Jesus acting in the church (Acts).

The Psalm: 46

Psalm 46 is used today because of its imagery of 'the Lord goes up' which seems to point to Ascension, where Lord is read by Christians as referring to Christ. In order to bring out this point it requires that 'goes up' be replaced by 'ascends' in both the response and the psalm.

Second Reading: Eph 1:17-23

Using a different set of mythological images to Acts, the author of Ephesians here seeks to describe the mystery of the risen Christ: at once he is victorious over all limitation and evil, beyond the creation, and with the Father; yet also he is active in the salvation of his people and present through those whose lives are joined to him in baptism. This text on Christ at once near and far away, at once immanent and transcendent, the end and the means, stands behind many of the key developments in the Latin theology of the sacraments.

Gospel: Mt 28:16-20

Often referred to as the 'Great Commission,' this imposing image which concludes Matthew is functionally akin to the ascension stories in Lk 24:45-53 and Acts 1:1-11. The work of Jesus in making the Father known must be carried on by the church which is uniquely constituted with his authority (a point made more explicitly here than in Luke-Acts). The mission is presented as focused on baptism and an early liturgical formula is incorporated into the text. It is significant for our understanding of Christian origins that while for centuries, after the New Testament canon became fixed, people looked back to this text as the basis of the baptismal formula and trinitarian structure of the creeds, in fact Matthew is derived from the actual liturgical life of the author's community.

HOMILY NOTES

1. Luke's images are so powerful, full of colour, and the sense of ending and going away are so strong that they dazzle us and we fail to see through them to the mystery they present. Our response to this image must not be that of asking 'how did it happen?' but 'what does it tell us today about the Christian life?' The key question is this: 'if Jesus is not present as he was before the crucifixion, then how is he leading us, teaching us, and being present to us?'

2. We live in the 'Age of the Church': the Lord is not present as once in Palestine, nor as he will be after this world; rather he is to be seen through the works and words of those who are united to him through baptism: the church. The church is not an organisation to promote his cause or ideology, but the people who see themselves as acting as a group, in union with the Christ they cannot see, to bring about the kingdom. Many people each doing their bit, seeking to be honest and loving in their actions with others, and doing so as they know that these are not just random actions but made into a united endeavour by Christ towards making the Father's kingdom come about.

3. To celebrate the ascension is to be aware that here and now one must act as a part of the church: this is how Christ is present in the world. Likewise, it is to acknowledge a moral responsibility: if one bears the name 'Christian' and people are scandalised by our failures – and the more someone publicly identifies him/herself with Christ as in the case of clergy and religious, the greater the offence – then this is people taking us at our word that we are Christ's body on earth. To say one will represent Christ (i.e. make him present here and now) is an awesome mission. Older textbooks used to point to a distinction of individual failures versus collective holiness (still found in the liturgy: 'look not on our sins, but on the faith of your church'), but this, while answering a theological problem, must not distract us from the existential predicament of the Christian: to be a disciple is to be aware of the dignity one is given in making Christ present. Moreover, examining our actions in the light of that fact is part of the cross of discipleship.

4. We are not just people who rejoice that God loves us, while keeping our eyes fixed on Christ as the glory of the Father; we have to build a world of justice, truth, and peace. If we believe that Christ has ascended, then challenging corruption, untruth, intolerance, and all that enslaves should be characteristic symptoms of the presence of Christians in a society. The ascension is not a cosy feast: it should make us feel uncomfortable. Have we just been standing idle looking into heaven?

The Ascension of the Lord Year B

Introduction to the Celebration

There is an air of finality about today's festival. Our focus is on the retelling of a story declaring that Christ has returned to the Father, and so we think of it as the 'end' of the Christ event or the 'end of Easter' – in times past there was a custom of extinguishing the Paschal Candle after the gospel to signify: 'he is gone'. But the air of finality must be presented in a different way – it is not the final song to mark the sorry close of a party, but the joyous finality of a building job completed: Christ's presence is no longer limited to a small group in one place at a particular time, now his presence is diffused throughout creation through his body the church. It is this mystery of Christ's presence we celebrate today: we are not here to recall some 'event' that 'happened' on some fixed day in human historical time. Ascension is not about Christ's absence, but about his presence in a different way to that which he had before his death. He now is present in our community, and as a group we must make him present by testifying to him before the world as the community of justice, peace and love.

Rite of Penance

Option c vii (Missal, p. 394-5) is appropriate.

Headings for Readings
First Reading
See Year A.

Second Reading
The Year B option (Eph 4:1-13) is to be preferred since vv. 8-10 contain a theological reading of the notion of 'ascension' that is contemporary (early second century) with the liturgical reality that was inspiring Luke's formulation of the story as 'historical' narrative. The lectionary's shorter form is useless as it omits the key verses.

The presence of Christ is now not limited to one place or a few people: he had gone to the very heights and depths of reality and proclaimed his reconciliation. We, his people, must not be frightened by either dark powers or human evil; rather we must be ready to oppose evil, confident that Christ, who has conquered death, is with us. In contrast to Luke's picture of Jesus floating gently way, this letter has him actively taking on the high and mighty powers that threaten us and making them captive.

If you opt for Eph 1:17-23, then See Year A.

Gospel

Christ challenges us to proclaim him and make him present in every corner of the creation. Each of us is called to this task if we want to call ourselves Christians, and when we carry this out, he is with us.

Prayer of the Faithful

President:

Today, recalling that Christ is present throughout the creation and that his challenge to us is to make this known, let us ask the Father for the strength for our mission.

Reader(s):

1. That we become sensitive to Christ's presence in the creation.

2. That we will be the witnesses of Christ to the ends of the earth.

3. That those who have had Christ obscured for them by the false-witness of Christians may discover God's love.

4. *Local needs.*

5. That all who have died, whose faith is known to God alone, may rise in the presence Christ.

President:

Father, gathered as disciples in your Son's presence, we believe that he is present too at your right hand. Through his intercession hear the prayers of your children now and always.

Eucharistic Prayer

Ascension I (P 26) is preferable as it focuses on Christ as our priest. Note the special addition if you opt for Eucharistic Prayer I.

Invitation to the Our Father
Gathered in Christ, conscious that we must advance the Father's kingdom, let us pray.

Sign of Peace
Ascending to the heights, he gave gifts to women and men, and the greatest of his gifts is peace. Let us express our sharing in this gift with one another.

Invitation to Communion
The disciples recognised the Lord was still present with them in the breaking of the loaf. Let us now recognise him present in our midst. Behold the Lamb of God ...

Communion Reflection
There is a lack of symbolic action in today's feast to make it stand out. A possible solution is to make a special event of sending out Eucharistic Ministers to extend Christ's presence from the Eucharistic Assembly to all those who are house bound in the community. That which extends presence of Christ in the world, such as this sacramental extension, makes real the mystery we name today as 'ascension'

Dismissal
Blessing n 8 (Ascension), Missal, p. 371.

COMMENTARY

First Reading: Acts 1:1-11
See Year A.

The Psalm 46
See Year A.

Second Reading: Eph 4:1-13

Ephesians was written probably towards the end of the first century by someone thoroughly familiar with Paul's thought, but who also was a theologian with a very distinct vision of his own; but which he did not put forward under his own name but Paul's, using the common ancient convention of pseudonymity. One of this author's great themes is the church – a mystical and universal unity – as the on-going reality of Christ. The actual churches seem to have little interest for him. In this text we have his great plea for the unity of this mystery while at the same time recognising its variety in ministries (this is a list of ideal ministries, not a list of charisms). In order to develop this theme he quotes Ps 68:19 – in a form which is not otherwise found in Hebrew or Greek – of an ascension on high (hence the use of Eph 4:1-13 in today's feast in several ancient lectionaries as well as our own) and a giving of gifts. This is then interpreted as being a 'descent' – why? Because an ascent to give gifts to men makes no sense! So we see this author has a three tier universe: the heavens where dwell the heavenly beings and the righteous, earth where mortals dwell and where both angels from above and demons from below can mingle, and under the earth where the demons and the damned dwell. In order to establish this 'great mystery' of the church, the Lord had to descend to earth and establish it (the incarnation) and then leave his gift: the various ministries. From what he says at 2:20 it appears that he sees 'apostles' and 'prophets' as belonging to the initial moment of the church, which leaves preachers, pastors, and teachers as the key ministries of his own community.

As *the* statement in the New Testament about the unity of the church, this text is well suited to today where the presence of Christ-in-the-church-rather-than-physically is the centre of the celebration.

See also Augustine's homily for this feast, based on this passage, in the Second Reading of the Office of Readings for today (Breviary, vol 2, pp. 627-8).

If you opt for Eph 1:17-23, then See Year A.

Gospel: Mk 16:15-20

Here we have the conclusion of Mark's gospel as that gospel is commonly found in printed editions, and so it adds to the tone of finality that can pervade the liturgy today. Moreover, it seems to accord well with the theme, with its challenge from Jesus to them to proclaim the Good News to all creation, and that having said that he was taken up into heaven. However, we are dealing here with the famous 'last eleven verses' (16:9-20) which did not originally belong to this gospel and are a later conflation from Matthew and Luke added to Mark, as 16:8 seemed too stark an ending for a gospel. Indeed, apart for the traditional ending, which we read today, there are several other endings extant. But the fact that sometime in the second century (possibly before Justin's time, (died c. 165) and certainly prior to Irenaeus, (died c. 202) this ending was added, is crucial for our understanding of this feast: it is the mystery of ascension that that community felt had to be included in any account it would receive of the Christ-event. They saw and celebrated that event as one where they were the continuation of the work of the Christ: they were being upheld by his presence so that not only was he 'at the right hand of the Father' but with them in their trials protecting them. And if Christ was with them, they were going everywhere preaching and making him present.

So, in the three readings we have three different ways of viewing this early Christian belief in their on-going life in Christ. All three assume that this is something that animates the community, and are incomprehensible in their imagery of Christ in the heavens unless that mystery was already part of their liturgical life prior to these writings.

HOMILY NOTES

1. Today's feast celebrates our belief in the presence of Christ in the universe and sets it in a tension with the demand that we then be the vehicles by which that presence is made manifest. It is his presence in us that makes the demands of discipleship upon us that we must proclaim him. The mystery of as-

cension is that his presence with us and our witness to him cannot be separated.

2. But do we take his presence in the universe seriously? Do we believe he is present in every poor person, every sick person, every prisoner? Mt 25:34-46 can be read as the 'other side' of this mystery: in today's texts we think of the beginning of the ascended presence of Christ in the church; in Mt 25 we have a reflection on the eschaton and when that presence in the disciples ceases.

3. Do we take seriously the notion that there is no area of the universe from which Christ's presence is excluded? So Christ is present in every creature (see Jn 1:3) and in every aspect of human life. But there are powerful forces that would want to silence those who preach concern for the environment or, at least, argue that ecology is not something with which the church should concern itself. Or in the human universe, there are many who see Christian concerns in politics, economics or medicine as meddling and would like to limit church concerns to 'Jesus and religious matters'. But this feast is our proclamation that Christ is now to be found everywhere as the risen one forming a kingdom for his Father, and so in every area of existence his followers must be witnessing to him. In rising from the dead, the whole creation has been transformed and is a 'religious matter'.

4. 'To be witnesses' (*martures*) and 'proclaim' (*kéruxate*) were key terms for the early church: one was descriptive of what they must *be*, the other a command as to what they must *do*. But, by the second century, both were very expensive words. A misty sweet image of Jesus floating away, alongside an arcane discussion about 'whether you can trust "the bible"' in its creative poetic narratives such as Acts 1, fails to do justice to this mystery on both counts.

The Ascension of the Lord Year C

Introduction to the Celebration

The image we have of the Ascension is that of departing, going away, disappearing; but our belief as Christians is that it represents the silent presence of Christ everywhere in the universe. He is no longer limited by earthly conditions – to be in one place at one time in his presence to his followers – but now dwells in the heavens with the Father: present in every gathering of his people – so he is present among us now, present whenever his people are in need, present in hearts calling us to be disciples and to be his hands, and feet, and voice in our lives. To celebrate this feast today is not to recall a past event – that day long ago 'when he went up to heaven' – but to rejoice that Jesus is our living Lord, with us now, leading and guiding us, because he is not tied down to a moment in earthly history.

Rite of Penance

Option c ii (Missal, p. 392) is appropriate; or if you intend to preach on the Christ the High Priest, then replace the Rite of Penance with the Rite of Blessing and Sprinkling Holy Water using prayer C (Missal, p. 388).

Headings for Readings
First Reading
See Year A.

Second Reading
The Year C option has the advantage that it allows you to present the Ascension in terms of Christ the High Priest – a theme also picked up in Preface I of the Ascension.

In this reading we have an image of the dwelling-place of the Father as a temple, and at the heart of this is a sanctuary where our need for salvation can be presented to the Father. But who can present our needs in this heavenly place: only Jesus who has risen on high, and as our great priest intercedes for us, obtains the forgiveness of our sins, and gains for us as a people an eternal dwelling place.

If you opt for Eph 1:17-23, then See Year A.

Gospel

Today we read the story – only found in Luke in his gospel which we are about to read now, and in his book of Acts which we have just read a few moments ago – of the mystery we are celebrating. Jesus commanded that the forgiveness of sins be preached to all and then was carried from their sight but was still with them in their hearts and in their gathering: that is how Jesus is with us here now, and still commanding us to make known the forgiveness of sins.

Prayer of the Faithful
President:

Friends, as we assemble today we remind ourselves that although Jesus is no longer with us a visible individual, he is present in others, and one special way that he is present is when we as his priestly people gather together and pray in his name to the Father.

Reader(s):

1. That we, and all Christians, will continue to witness to Christ's victory over sin, evil, and death.

2. That those with responsibilities for the world's resources will recognise that these resources belong to all humanity and must be distributed with justice.

3. That people everywhere will be more sensitive to the hidden presence of God in the world.

4. That those who are hungry, those who are oppressed, those deprived of justice, may know God's love through the presence and action of the disciples of Jesus.

5. *Local needs.*

6. That those who have died may ascend to the right hand of the Father.

President:

Father, recalling that Christ the mediator between you and us, has passed beyond our sight, we ask you to hear the prayers of his people, for we make them as a priestly people in Christ Jesus, Our Lord, Amen.

Eucharistic Prayer

Ascension I (P 26) is preferable as it focuses on Christ as our priest. Note the special addition if you opt for Eucharistic Prayer I.

Invitation to the Our Father

Standing here together, united in Christ as his people, let us put our prayers before the heavenly Father:

Sign of Peace

Charged to be witnesses to the Lord's forgiveness, let us show each other our willingness to be forgiving.

Invitation to Communion

Until he comes again, let us rejoice in the Lord's presence in our sacred banquet. Behold the Lamb of God ...

Communion Reflection

If we believe we have encountered the risen Christ in sharing the loaf and cup, then today we recall that we are to witness to forgiveness and reconciliation. This is always a demanding project. Reconciliation in a world of great disparities in access to food, medicine, and education cannot be divorced from development, work for a just distribution of the earth's resources, or from care for the creation as God's gift. So, this day provides a good opportunity to bring this task before a community, and if it is announced before hand, there could now be a collection of money for promoting development. This is a suitable theme for this moment in the Eucharist as if we are reflecting on being fed at the Lord's banquet, having thanked him for his goodness, then this outpouring to others in need is a suitable response. If the Lord is really present, then we must really work to witness to reconciliation not merely use nice words; and in our world real commitment means committing resources, i.e. cash.

Dismissal
Blessing n 8 (Ascension), Missal, p. 371.

COMMENTARY

First Reading:
See Year A.

The Psalm 46
See Year A.

Second Reading: Heb 9:24-8; 10:19-23
Hebrews is often considered one of the more difficult parts of the New Testament to preach, partly because of its language of temples and angels, and partly because its understanding of priesthood has been confused for many Christians since the Reformation by trying to find in it a theology of ordained ministers in the church who are 'sacrificing priests'. Let us dispose of the latter objection first: the author of Hebrews was concerned to find a way to make sense of what the church believed had been happening, and was continuing to happen, in the birth, death, and resurrection of Jesus. The letter is a christology, not a theology of Orders. And, as long as one tries to apply any part of the letter to an understanding of the specific identity of presbyters, one will lose the thread. The letter is concerned with presenting Jesus as the great priest (*hierea megan*) (10:21) – a person and office unique in the creation, but because he has associated us with himself as his people, we (all who are baptised: 10:22) are made a priestly people.

The rationale of Hebrews depends (as well represented in 9:24-8) on the reader having an amount of information on the standard ritual explanations of what happened in the temple in Jerusalem, current in particular strands of Judaism around the time of Jesus. According to this strand of Judaism, the high priest, e.g. Annas, acted as the representative of the whole of Israel and even the whole world (see Wis 18:24). Once a year he entered the sacrament of God's presence, the Holy of Holies, to re-establish the links between God, his people, and the creation. This was accomplished sacramentally by smearing (literally, 'atoning' – think of our word 'toner') the blood of a goat (cf Lev 16:9), and thus effecting reconciliation. The author of Hebrews presents this ritual as an imperfect foreshadowing of what was to come in Jesus. It was imperfect as the old high priest was imperfect, it was passing (needing annual renewal), and it was a substitute's blood and it took place sacramentally (i.e. in a temple which was a sacramental model of the true abode of God on high). Now, argues Hebrews, a perfect priest has come, has used his own blood (the death on the cross), whose action is not transient but done 'once for all time,' and it is done in the real abode of God, his heavenly temple. As a presentation of the death of Christ and his 'redemption' (to use one image)/'atonement' (to use the image of the Letter to the Hebrews) it has been a central plank of how Christians have understood the Christ-event. Christ's coming, his death, and his ascension form together the new and complete rite for human reconciliation; and for the author of the Letter this was all 'sketched out' before hand in the temple rites prescribed under the Old Covenant. Aquinas captured this well for those familiar with our understanding of sacraments: as the sacraments (*signa*) of the church point to the realities (*res*) to come in heaven, so the sacraments of the old Law pointed to the reality of what Christ does for humanity. Because Christ is the real priest compared with the earlier shadows (first part of today's reading), we who are linked with our priest (we are linked with him by being sprinkled with his blood and pure water – our sacramental bonding to him) enter the heavenly court as his people – hence being a priestly people.

If you have used the sprinkling with holy water at the beginning of today's Eucharist, it is worth noting that the sprinkling is seen as this uniting with Christ as the perfect priest, and then being so united, we as a priestly people can then, with him, address the Father and make intercession in the Prayers of the Faithful. So today, the Ascension is our ritual celebration of his entry into the true heavenly sanctuary, just as Good Friday was the celebration of his sacrifice, his shedding his blood for our reconciliation.

If you opt for Eph 1:17-23, then See Year A.

Gospel: Lk 24:46-53
The story of the Ascension – as it belongs in the imagination of Christians – is derived from these verses in Luke and the related verses from the opening of Acts as read in the first reading. For the problems of this text see the notes on Acts 1:1-11 given for Year A, and for background to this text see the *Note on Celebrating Ascension and Pentecost.*

HOMILY NOTES
1. Preaching on the priesthood of Christ, and so of our identity as a priestly people, always seems such a difficult task that most of us try to avoid it! Yet, if Ascension Day is our ritual celebration of his entry into the true heavenly sanctuary, just as Good Friday was the celebration of his sacrifice, his shedding his blood for our reconciliation – and this in one of the classic ways that the tradition has understood this mystery – then it is something we should not try to avoid. The temptation is to treat the Ascension as simply some sort of historical recollection of 'the final act' of the earthly Jesus (see the *Note on Ascension and Pentecost*), and to forget that the theology of Hebrews is one of the basic ways by which we as Christians understand the mystery of the Cross (see the note on today's alternative second reading).

2. However, to open up this vision of today, and of the sacrifice / redemption of Christ, we need a convenient vehicle. The liturgy provides just such an entry-point in today's magnifi-

cent preface (Preface of the Ascension I, P 26; Missal, p. 429).
So the homily could take the form of a meditation on that
preface with a few glosses of explanation. Alas, when this
preface is simply spoken out in the Liturgy of the Eucharist
today, it is all over so quickly that its beauty and theology
can be simply missed – so a meditation on upon it will prepare the assembly to appreciate it more when actually used.

3. 'Today the Lord Jesus, the king of Glory' – we are speaking
    now about our living, risen Lord, we are not recalling an
    event two millennia ago. And, we are celebrating today –
    through the mystery of our baptism we are being brought
    into the actual ascension now, for we are with Christ who is in
    the Father's presence giving us and all people his reconcili-
    ation. The ascension is a means of giving us images that
    speak to us as image-loving-beings of what Christ's love is all
    about.

    'The conqueror of sin and death.' Jesus is the one who suf-
    fered and died on the Cross, and this shedding of blood
    showed his love and obedience to the Father and so has de-
    stroyed our death.

    'Ascended to heaven while the angels sang his praises.'
    Our celebration today is that Jesus is the true high priest,
    higher than the angels (see Heb 1:5-13), who has entered the
    true temple – the Father's presence.

    'Christ, the mediator ... and Lord of all'. Jesus is priest and
    Lord.

    'Has passed beyond our sight, not to abandon us but to be
    our hope.' We are not abandoned nor do we look backwards,
    but look forwards with confidence because Jesus has pre-
    pared the way for us.

    'Christ is the beginning, the head of the church.' We are
    united with him in baptism; we have been sprinkled with his
    pure water and are able to stand before the Father because
    we belong to him. We are a priestly people because he is our
    Way, our high priest.

    And, the preface concludes with the pithiest statement of

what is meant by Christian hope/confidence that is no mere optimism: 'where he has gone, we hope to follow.'

This is why we can say in the line leading to the Sanctus (when we claim that our praises at this eucharistic assembly become joined with that of the heavenly assembly) that the joy of his resurrection and ascension renews the whole world: Christ the priest has reconciled the world to the Father, and soon we will celebrate the presence of the Spirit whom the Father has sent among us for the forgiveness of sins (see the formula of absolution).

4. When a text has been used with glosses as a meditation, it is then useful to conclude the meditation by reading the text through again from beginning to end without comment to let the hearers 'own' the words that have been commented upon.

Celebrating Ascension and Pentecost

Sequels?

In our perception of the liturgical cycle of festivals, Ascension and Pentecost seem to be the great 'sequels'. They are less feasts we look on directly, than celebrations that mark the ending of Easter, the close of a season, or recollections of the 'final moments' of the Christ-event. This view is easily explained by the fact that both are seen as 'based upon' the 'events' narrated by Luke in the last sections of his gospel and opening sections of Acts. In this view, Luke (alone among early Christian writers) records a final blessing (Lk 24:50) and a final instruction (Acts 1:6-9) near Bethany (Lk 24:50) after which Jesus was taken up (Acts 1:2) in heaven (Lk 24:51 – but the text is problematic) from 'the mount called Olivet' (Acts 1:12) and 'a cloud took him from their sight' (Acts 1:9). Meanwhile, the eleven (Lk 24:33 and Acts 1:13) worshipped him (Lk 24:52). After which two strange figures – traditionally interpreted as angels – tell them they will see Jesus come again as they have seen him go (Acts 1:10-11). This is the story of 'the ascension' as the final event of Jesus with 'the twelve' (actually at this point in the narrative there are only eleven: Acts 1:15-26). The story is a conflation of two distinct strands of tradition – Acts has a more elaborate ascension story than that in the gospel – that existed within Luke's communities. It has become the dominant image of the ascension within the churches, and it is within the frame of this image that the conclusions of the other three gospels are read. And, it is the force of liturgical recollection feeding our memory that drives our readings of our sacred texts. This process is the very life-blood of the tradition that binds Christian communities over generations and gives us a coherent common imagination. However, probing this common memory in terms of some of the alternative imaginary structures used in the earliest communities offers us today a valuable perspective on these celebrations of Ascension and Pentecost and allows us to see some of the interests of those early communities and their preaching about their Lord, prior to the Lukan historicisation.

Luke's time-framing

Luke's structure in Acts for the events after Easter day is based on two fixed moments, Easter day, and Pentecost falling fifty days later. Between these moments he has Jesus present for forty days (Acts 1:3) which produces our Ascension Thursday, and then ten days later comes the day 'the [restored] twelve' (Acts 1:15-26) have been told to expect (Acts 1:4-5) when they were filled with the Spirit (Acts 2:4). This is again the great image of Pentecost in subsequent Christian imagination, with 'the twelve' and Mary in a room with tongues of flame over each head (Acts 2:3). The inclusion of Mary with 'the twelve', although a staple element in western iconography, is a later conflation: Luke has Mary and Jesus's brothers (never part of the iconography as Jesus's four brothers disappear from Christian memory with the rise of the notion of Mary's post partum virginity) praying with 'the twelve' while they await Pentecost (1:14), but none but 'the twelve' are assumed to be present for the tongues of fire (2:1).

The origin of Luke's time-frame lies in the liturgical continuity of many of the earliest communities of the followers of Jesus as one more Judaism – notions about 'Judaism' as a monolithic religious system is an anachronous projection of outsiders – among the rainbow of different religious groups which made up 'Israel' – i.e. the people referred to in 'the scriptures' which all these groups had as a common reference point. The followers of Jesus constituted one such Judaism and so shared many rituals with other Judaisms, and these rituals formed and bonded them together as a people. We, looking back as Christians, tend to note either new rituals (e.g. baptism) or the breaks with ritual (e.g. the discontinuance of killing a paschal lamb) between Christians and Jews – hindsight, mixed with our history of Jewish-Christian antagonism, highlights discontinuity – but communities in their actual life tend towards ritual continuity, and, as modern liturgists since Anton Baumstark have noticed, are most dogged in their continuity in the cycle of major annual events. We observe this ritual doggedness all around us: while authority changed the texts of Roman Rite swiftly after Vatican II, usages, attitudes, and memories are taking generations to adapt; the midwinter cult of the sun continued for centuries until is was christened as Christmas, and it still continues as a festival for people who are post-Christian for many generations. So it was for communities who were following Jesus, but whose sacred year still included the great festivals of the other Jews around them. This was obviously going to be the case with the Passover which because Jesus's death took place at that time was soon to be interpreted within the structure of that feast – note Paul's statement for the Corinthians, celebrating the feast as part of their liturgical year, linking theologically the Christ's death with that of the lambs of the feast: 'Cleanse out the old leaven that you may be a new lump, as you really are unleavened. For Christ, our paschal lamb, has been sacrificed. Let us, therefore, celebrate the festival, not with the old leaven, the leaven of malice and evil, but with the unleavened bread of sincerity and truth' (1 Cor 5:7-8). But equally that other feast, Pentecost, regulated in its date by the Passover remained part of the ritual year of the followers of Jesus. As with Passover, Paul (1 Cor 16:8) provides our earliest evidence that it was a feast which marks a definite fixed point in the year among those who believed Jesus to be Lord.

By the time of Jesus, Pentecost (the Greek term meaning 'the fiftieth day' is second century BC) had been given a variety of meanings having originated, probably, as a thanksgiving feast to mark the end of the barley harvest. It had been linked with the earlier Passover festival within priestly traditions as 'the Feast of Weeks', the conclusion of a week of weeks (7 times 7 days) – see Lev 23:15-16 – and the time to make an offering of new grain. It had also been located within an annual pattern of festivals that were seen as recalling God's acts of deliverance of Israel in history (Deut 16): a theme that would resurface within the meaning given to the festival by Luke. Within some of the Judaisms of the period – such as those which held Tobit and Maccabees as part of their scriptures, and as such are Judaisms that can throw extra light of the early disciples of Jesus, the feast had become a notable special family meal with 'an abundance of food' which was seen as distinctive of Israel marking it apart from Gentiles living around them (Tob 2:1-2), and a time for thinking about Jerusalem and the temple (2 Macc 12:30-32). It was a time for pilgrimage to the temple and for recalling the Covenant. This last point would later be the central explanation of the feast in rabbinic Judaism when it was the annual memorial of the Law being given on Sinai.

Christening Pentecost

What did Pentecost recall for the earliest of Jesus's disciples who kept this feast? The simple answer is that we do not know; but in all likelihood it retained whatever particular strand, or combination of strands, of explanation which that group used before hearing of Jesus. However, we can be fairly certain that prior to Luke, or outside his community, it did not have any specifically Jesus-centred meaning. We know this by contrasting it with the Passover which was very clearly linked to Jesus, given his death during the feast, and so gained a theological Jesus-centred rationale very early in the life of his followers (by Paul's time). Hence by the time the gospels were written, Passover had generated several distinct theologies – i.e. explanations of practices held dear by the communities; Pentecost, however, is mentioned in only one place and the explanation given by Luke is without rival in Christian memory.

So how did Luke 'christen' Pentecost? We could think of the development of the Christian festival as a process in a series of three stages with three underlying dynamics. The followers of Jesus kept to the ritual year with which they were familiar, and if this included a devotion to the temple, then this was no doubt coloured by their faith in Jesus (cf. Acts 2:46). The practice of keeping the festival was, as is the way of rituals, more stable in its physical structures – things done, foods eaten – than in its explanation, and annually the focused effort was devoted to the celebrating rather than concerning themselves with 'what it all meant'. It is, by the way, the conceit of academics and teachers to imagine that meanings are prior to parties and to lament that what they imagine as, in the final analysis, being a classroom play is treated as an end in itself by those playing: there was a party on 25 December, before 'Jesus' was claimed as 'the reason for the season', and whether or not people are interested in reasons for seasons, they know that they shall enjoy the party and know what they must do in it!

At some later stage, that link between the festival and the temple would have become more tenuous, partly since after 70 AD the temple was no more, and partly as the Jesus-followers, while retaining many rituals from the Judaisms around them, no longer could relate their activity to a group with which they were at odds. In this situation the explanations used for their rituals would have been open to new imaginative constructions. The third stage was Luke's own desire to find suitable historical moments to which he could attach the beliefs of the community in such a way that they were 'tied down', easily pictured, and related to one another in a unified sequential narrative of God's saving deeds. The community believed that Jesus had promised them the Spirit (see John 14:26); they believed the Spirit was with them (see Rom 5:5 and Paul shows no interest in a 'Pentecost event' or John 20:22 where the Spirit is imparted by Jesus on Easter Sunday); now they could look to a moment, already special to them, as the point in time when it happened and to a suitable symbolic picture of what the event was like. Just as later 25 December became the moment to celebrate the birth of Jesus and the crib, the theologically laden image, Luke fastened on Pentecost and turned a shimmering belief in the Spirit's presence into a solid image. The success of this christening of Pentecost was, again as with 25 December, due in no small measure to the fact that he grafted his narrative onto a well-embedded practice in the churches.

Ascension

Luke stands apart from the other gospel writers in his interest in seemingly fixed dates (e.g. 3:1) and historical situations for pieces of teaching (e.g. 11:1). So now having linked Easter and Pentecost, there was the need to locate Ascension. Since forty days was already in the tradition as the time Jesus spent in the wilderness (Mk 1:13 followed by Lk 4:2), that was a suitable length to have after Easter and before Pentecost. Unlike Pentecost, there is no evidence that there was any celebration by the communities on this fortieth day after Easter, nor is there any evidence of a celebration of Jesus's taking leave of the church. With Paul, who takes the celebrating (for whatever reason) for granted (1 Cor 16:8), there seems to be no interest in such an 'event': 1 Cor 15:3-8 simply attests to the resurrection appearances among his followers as that which he must hand on, and this is echoed later in Mt 28:20 which is intent on Jesus's continuing presence. It would seem that this day within our liturgical year may be solely based on Luke's historicising narrative skills.

History and Ritual

It can seem strange to us, who tend to approach our celebrations as part of a community of faith through books and explanations, that Luke's creative work could build so easily an image that has become a key part of our imagination as Christians. Our problem arises in that we seek out historical explanation like a dog following a scent; and since we read these texts historically, we tend to slip silently into imagining the texts as history, rather than the work of a preacher using the human love of historical narrative to convey his message. In the process, Luke tapped into, wittingly or unwittingly, three powerful dynamics in human understanding. First, cyclical practices are among the most intransigent elements of our imaginative world: regular celebrations bind us together and mark our passing lives for us. Meanings are secondary for they can come and go and are re-interpreted by each generation – there are new theologians and

theologies in every generation, but it is the ritual of the party itself that forms the continuity of generations. We have celebrated
Pentecost, so have generations after Luke, so have followers of
Jesus before Luke, and those same people were celebrating the
festival before they had heard of Jesus. For each generation and
culture the meaning is something new. What binds us into a
continuity is that we have each taken part in a festival at a fixed
moment in the year – as indeed, in all probability, did Jesus himself. The second dynamic is that when a practice is already embedded in a community's practice, then it is an ideal vehicle for
the diffusion of a new meaning. And, thirdly, a solid picture
forces itself on the memory like no abstraction can. The priestly
theology of creation is remembered from the stirring images of
Genesis, not from the subtle reflections of the Wisdom writings;
the coming of the Spirit is remembered as tongues of flame
rather than as the forgiving divine presence of John 20.

Preaching today
De-historicising these feasts is a more significant task than simply that of searching out the history and structure of the ritual
year of the earliest Christian communities. In locating Christian
faith in the witness and praxis of the church – its true home –
rather than in an individual ascent to a 'wonder' or in a
preached claim that we ought to remember a single moment as
'relevant to us', it can reveal to us other aspects of our believing
often buried under a weight of history.

   In the first place it reinforces the fact that each of these feasts,
especially Pentecost, should be celebrations that are significant
times for the local church to bond and just to party about being
what it is. The fact that we – from our first days as the community
following Jesus – are able regularly to gather, affirm each other,
rejoice, and in so doing witness to who we are, is far more important than any particular aspect of the mystery we might recall on a particular day in the year. It is celebrating as Christians
that is important. Linking that to a special interest in the Spirit's
animating presence in the community at Pentecost is more fit-

tingly seen as a 'good excuse for a party' rather that 'the reason' or 'the cause' for it, whereby the celebration merely becomes an annual obligation. The true festivals of a community do not need the extra sting of 'duty' to bring about their observance!

Second, within the legacy of the tradition there is not just one theology of either Christ's transformed presence in the church (Ascension) nor the Spirit's animating presence (Pentecost), but many. These can be seen in the range of readings given for these feasts in the lectionary, but these readings' message and vision is usually drowned out by the power of the Lukan historicisaton. For the Ascension, each year we have as the Second Reading, Eph 1:17-23 with its very different view of how Christ is now with each church scattered across the earth. In that reading we see an early community's faith that Christ is no longer confined to one place but is everywhere within the creation, and they, as the church, are making him present as witnesses (*martures*). Moreover, by the early second century this was not some pious feeling of being a 'force for good in the world', but making Christ present through witnessing to him was literally the call to martyrdom. This theology of Christ now not-being-confined as he was before his death – the irony that death which was meant to confine his influence actually made it possible for him to be everywhere in the creation is the basic belief that drives all the early theologies of the Ascension and is what Luke tapped into – is even more visible in the Alternative Second Reading for Year B: Eph 4:1-13. Christ has taken our enemies captive and nowhere is immune from his salvation. The creation has been transformed by his gifts. While the alternative to Eph 1:17-23 for year C, Heb 9:24-28 and 10:19-23, brings us into the very different world of temple theology in early Christianity, where Christ is the one who, as our eternal priest, is joining our temporal, earthly liturgy here and now with the perfect liturgy of heaven. This reading recalls a wondrous theology of Christ's presence which was widely found in the western church until the eleventh century, when it was displaced by the new theology of Christ's presence as the Blessed Sacrament, but which still pops up at the end of the preface ('may our voices blend with theirs') and in 'that your holy angel may take this sacrifice to your altar in heaven' in Eucharistic Prayer I. In year A the gospel focuses on Christ's continuing presence, for within Matthew's theology he has never left the church (Mt 28:16-20). While for year B (Mk 16:15-20) the situation is more complex. This is the famous 'long ending' of Mark, which is a later addition built from a reformulation of elements of Matthew's and Luke's texts. Thus we have the continuing presence of Matthew *and* a statement that Christ has been taken up and is at 'God's right hand'.

For Pentecost the range of ways at looking at the Spirit's presence is even more wide-ranging. There is a good selection of Old Testament texts given for the Vigil Mass which show the whole spectrum of how we, as Christians, have appropriated 'the scriptures' of the first communities who followed Jesus as our own. There is the Spirit who can confuse the tongues of the proud and give voice to the people of God (Gen 11) which is the text that had the greatest influence on Luke in Acts. There is the Spirit who reveals the awesome majesty of God in fiery moments of revelations (Ex 19). The Spirit who is 'the Lord and giver of life' animating the dry bones (Ez 37) and who inspires 'sons and daughters to prophesy, old men to dream and young to see visions' and is even prepared to inspire slaves and women – so that even these creatures cannot be ignored (Joel 3). While the range of early Christian writings (Rom 8, 1 Cor 12, Gal 5, Jn 7, Jn 14, Jn 15, and Jn 20) present the Spirit as continually present, inspiring, interceding, and forgiving – which in the case of the Day Mass where the Acts 2 is the only First Reading, broaden our appreciation of what we confess as Christians about the Spirit.

Thirdly, the power of historicisation is that it produces a strong image, for it uses scenes from our everyday existence to convey that which is only grasped in 'a mirror darkly' (1 Cor 13:12): the presence of God. Here lies also the attractive power of preaching Pentecost in terms of 'the birthday of the Holy Spirit' or 'the birthday of the church.' The weakness is that we become distracted from the mystery to the details and wonder about

whether it was a 'miracle' or not, or even worse become so dis-
gruntled with the contradictions and worldview of the miracle
that we loose sight of the mystery altogether. De-historicisation,
far from being a 'threat to faith', is often the ground-clearer to let
us behold the mystery of faith with its proper fascination.

Seventh Sunday of Easter Year A

Introduction to the Celebration

Today falls between two great feasts: Ascension and Pentecost. We Christians have an ancient memory that between celebrating each of these mysteries we should stay together in prayer seeking to know more profoundly who we are as Christians, and we do this in reflection and prayer together. So we must realise that we form a single body, each a sister or brother for we have been baptised into Christ and have accepted his challenge that we will witness to him before all creation.

Rite of Penance

Replace with the sprinkling with Holy Water. The 'alternative' opening prayer ('Eternal Father', Missal, p. 272) is preferable.

Headings for Readings

First Reading

This is Luke's description of how the earliest community of disciples behaved between the time of the Ascension and Pentecost.

Second Reading

Bearing witness to Christ has led many to suffer down the centuries. In this reading, written to sisters and brothers who were suffering for their faith, the author tells them that their sufferings are a means of union with Jesus who has suffered. In the plan of God even our misfortunes can bring us closer to the mystery of God's love.

Gospel

This is the great prayer of Christ to the Father as the High Priest of the new and eternal covenant.

Prayer of the Faithful
President:
Sisters and brothers, by ascending into heaven Christ has con-
ferred on us as a community the dignity of being a 'priestly people', so now let us stand before God our Father and intercede for
ourselves, our brothers and sisters, and all humanity.
Reader(s):
1. That like Mary and the apostles we will remain united in
prayer and witness to the resurrection.
2. Remembering the unity of the earliest church between the
Ascension and Pentecost, that we will be more devoted to working for Christian unity.
3. Recalling the mission to witness to Christ's love, let us pray
for peace and reconciliation between peoples.
4. Conscious of the fears that afflicted the early churches, let us
pray for all who suffer for their beliefs, and all who are victims
of prejudice and discrimination.
5. *Local needs.*
6. Recalling that Christ has ascended to be with the Father in
glory, that he will welcome into his kingdom all our departed
sisters and brothers.
President:
Father, we gather each week as your people to thank you and to
intercede with you for our needs. Hear us gathered now as you
have listened to the gathering of Mary and the apostles in
Jerusalem for we seek to follow Jesus the Christ, your Son, our
Lord, Amen.

Eucharistic Prayer
Preface of the Ascension I (P 26) is preferable as it focuses on
Christ as our priest.

Invitation to the Our Father
Gathered together as the church, let us pray:

Sign of Peace
To exchange the sign of peace is to convey to one another the
greeting of the risen Christ, and to affirm each other as members
of his body.

Invitation to Communion
Christ bids us to be his people by gathering around his table.
Happy are we who gather here for his supper.

Communion Reflection
Introduce the solemn silence with the reminder of the phrase
from Acts: 'All [the apostles] joined in continuous prayer, together with several women including Mary the mother of Jesus,
and with his brothers' – let us now pray together in silence.'

Dismissal
Blessing n 8 for Ascension, Missal, p. 371.

COMMENTARY

First Reading: Acts 1:12-14
This is the continuation of the Lukan narrative in the linking
period between Ascension and Pentecost See the note on
Celebrating Ascension and Pentecost.

We should note that the gathering is made up of 'the twelve',
interpreted as 'the apostles', some women, and the close family
of Jesus. By the time that Luke wrote, the first and last of these
groups were no longer significant in the organisation of the
churches which had then become focused on bishops. However,
there was still a clear memory that Jesus's brothers – the notion
that Jesus was without real siblings would not develop until the
late third/early fourth centuries – and especially James had
taken a key role in leading the Jerusalem church. Moreover, 'the
twelve' – a group of great significance during Jesus's life – did
not continue in a central role. They became part of the basic
memory, but not part of the basic system of the churches: seen
here in that 'the twelve' are indistinguishable from 'the [twelve]
apostles'.

Psalm: 26

The psalm expresses the continuing presence of the Lord, and the desire that he should hear prayer. This psalm text picks up the theme of the People of God praying together and asking that their prayers be heard, which is the picture presented in the First Reading.

Second Reading: 1 Pet 4:13-16

By the time that this letter was written (late first/early second centuries) there was a steady harassment of Christians by the general population: Christianity was a strange, new fangled, alien religion, and for that reason attracted the sort of suspicions, prejudices, and harassments that go with being 'different.' It is this general suffering and the pain of discrimination and insults that should be seen as the background to the letter's references to 'suffering' rather than some highly organised persecution. The letter, which may have been written as part of a training of new converts for it contains much baptismal material, wants the Christians to face this suffering because of the name of Christ realistically, and recognise that it is one way of being united with Christ. It presents the same view of persecution and blessedness that is found in Mt 5:11.

Gospel: Jn 17:1-11

This is part of the 'farewell discourse' and is very well suited to the time being celebrated today in the liturgy. It is part of his taking leave of the disciples, and the farewell takes the form of a prayer for the disciples who have to carry on his mission, and for all those who will then come after him. Although in the scene in the gospel text, Jesus is still with his disciples, yet he speaks the prayer to the Father, and its language is structured as if he had already left. The content of the prayer is Jesus's 'report' back to the Father on how he has carried out the mission given him by the Father, and as such it is a report 'on the state of the church' at any time between the Ascension and the Parousia.

HOMILY NOTES

1. The period between the Ascension and Pentecost has been seen as one of the church waiting for the Spirit. Given that we have ritually observed, since the time of the writing of Acts, these two days, separated by the novena in which today falls, our reflection today has to express that sense of us as a longing people, a waiting people. It must be this notion that we are a waiting people, rather than just counting down to the coming of the Spirit, that has prominence or else we reinforce the notion that Pentecost is simply an anniversary rather than the celebration of a mystery.

2. So what is the character of this waiting: it is the time when we see in part and in shadows, have but glimpses of the majesty of God or the beauty of his kingdom, looking forward to our encounter with the Father 'face to face'. As Paul put it: 'For now we see in a mirror dimly, but then face to face. Now I know in part; then I shall understand fully, even as I have been fully understood' (1 Cor 13:12).

3. This is part of the difficulty of Christian faith: we place our faith in something that is yet to be, and must act as if it were already a fact in this world. This is what we mean by 'walking in faith' or the virtue of hope. This is quite different to the claims for assent that are made by many other religious systems: some make their claim on being a system that brings contentment or enlightenment, others that it interacts with the currents operating within the cosmos and so brings peace. Christ's demand is that we believe that all can be transformed wonderfully from what we see now, and that we must begin now with the transformation of the universe through love – but this is a process that moves us towards a future we cannot imagine. We always have to live with a tension: we believe that the kingdom is established in Christ's death and resurrection; yet we have to work as if we had to build the kingdom from scratch. Put another way, Christ's ascension to the Father has granted us access to the Father; yet we must lead lives that are free from sin and seek to do the good if we are to know the Father.

4. Over the centuries, we have tried to rationalise this tension by distinctions: Christ has opened the way to salvation potentially, but it must be actualised by a good life; or there was the resurrection and there will be the general resurrection. All these neat little systems fail to account for that mysterious element which is the intereface of human experience – temporal and fleeting – with the eternal. It is this, a mystery beyond words, that creates this tension which we must live with rather than try to puzzle out with a neat verbal solution. Christ is one with us, yet is with the Father; Jesus Christ shared our particularity – being limited by time and place – from the incarnation until the passion; now we proclaim him as ascended, still one with us but freed from human bounds and so equally present in all places and times. Christ is with us now, yet our being with him requires that we identify with him – not only in name and in inner intentions, but in the whole of our lives. The Father is always issuing an invitation to us in Christ, and we become united with the risen Christ in making our response.

5. It is this all-embracing invitation from the Father in every moment of creation, and reaching its high point in Christ, that is the theme of today's opening prayer ('Eternal Father, reaching from end to end of the universe ...'), which draws on the Wisdom literature for its imagery (see Wis 8:1), and which if recited again would form a doxology-style conclusion to the homily.

Seventh Sunday of Easter Year B

Introduction to the Celebration
See Year A

Rite of Penance
Replace with the sprinkling with Holy Water. The 'alternative' opening prayer ('Eternal Father', Missal, p. 272) is preferable.

Headings for Readings
First Reading
The Twelve chosen by Jesus collectively represent the scattered flock of Israel whom Christ was to gather home: this number had to be complete to be a symbol of Christ's saving mission and so we hear of how – in order to witness to Jesus – the gap in that number due to the defection of Judas had to be made good.

Second Reading
We are called to testify to the God who is love. 'No one has ever seen God,' but everyone should be able to see his nature, love, in the way we live our lives. Living lives of love is our witnessing to the God who 'has loved us so much'.

Gospel
Christ is our great High Priest – the one who goes into the presence of the Father and intercedes for us – and as we listen to these words we should remember that we are those for whom he is praying.

Prayer of the Faithful
President:
My friends, gathered as the body of Christ awaiting Pentecost, let us join our prayers with out great High Priest and ask the Father for our needs.

Reader(s):

1. That we may bear witness to the resurrection.

2. That we may forgive our enemies.

3. That we may care for the creation.

4. That we may seek the way of peace.

5. That the dead may rise in the Lord.

President:

Father, as you heard the prayers of the first Christian community, hear us now for we make our requests in our High Priest, Jesus Christ. Amen.

Preface

Ascension I (P 26) is preferable as it focuses on Christ as our priest.

Invitation to the Our Father

Gathered in prayer as the children of the Father, let us now say:

Sign of Peace

A gathering in prayer must be a gathering in forgiveness and love of the community. Let us express this in the sign of peace.

Invitation to Communion

The gathering of the disciples is the gathering to break the loaf which is Christ; behold that broken loaf, happy we who share in it.

Communion Reflection

Conscious that we are gathered here in prayer, like the gathering of Mary and the apostles between the Ascension and Pentecost, let us now pray as a community in silence.

The structured silence can then be broken by the Let us pray of the Prayer after Communion.

Dismissal

Blessing n 8: Ascension, Missal, p. 371.

COMMENTARY

First Reading: Acts 1:15-17, 20-26

This text, carefully shorn of vv. 18-19 which contain one of the more colourful variants (contrast it with the more sober suicide of Mt 27:5) of the fate of Judas, is a key scene-setting event for the second part of Luke's presentation of the Christian story. The Christ event (the new covenant) has been prepared for by God's providence from the beginning and has been announced in detail in 'the scriptures' – note how Luke not only cites the books belonging to the old covenant but expects that they can explain the lives of those who live in the time of the new covenant. Now this event involves scattered Israel being gathered together, and this is symbolised in 'The Twelve' – note this is a unique group who are not to be associated with either of the larger groups: 'the apostles' or 'the disciples' despite the fact that common memory uses phrases such as 'the disciples' when 'The Twelve' are meant, or 'The Twelve Apostles'. So, from Luke's perspective, if the message is now to move beyond Israel, this symbolic core must be complete, so a twelfth member, replacing Judas, must be chosen. Only as a complete group can they testify to what God has done in the history of Israel in raising Jesus from his tomb – a theme explored in several of the speeches Luke gives to Peter. And, just as God is constantly at work in history preparing for the Christ or in sending Judas to his fate, so he is miraculously involved in the decision making of the church so that election is by lots – in our terms, in the indeterminacy of the toss of a coin, God can effect his will.

Psalm

Use 'alleluia' as the response.

Second Reading: 1 Jn 11-16

One of the most moving and lyrical passages from the whole of early Christian literature. The sending of the Son is not just the love of the Father for his children, but it gathers us up into the mystery of God who *is* love, transforming us and challenging us to transform those whom we encounter.

Gospel: Jn 17:11-19

This is part of John's 'High Priestly Prayer' where Jesus intercedes for his people. By the time John wrote his gospel the paradigm for the weekly Eucharist had already moved from being
the special meal of Jesus with his disciples (as it is in the *Didache*)
to being the Christian Passover, and so linked specifically with
the Passover-meal of Jesus (what we refer to as 'the Last
Supper'). We see this in Paul (1 Cor 11:23-25) the Synoptics (Mk
14:22-25 and parallels) where this meal is presented as the origin
of the Eucharist. It is this shift in understanding that explains
why Christians have had a weekly Eucharist from the beginning, yet in the canonical texts this celebration is linked to an annual paschal meal which is adopted as the Christian paschal
meal. Therefore, since John places this prayer in his last supper
context – although there is no account of an 'institution' in his
account – he intended it to be heard by a gathering who would
understand it as Christ making his intercession for their
Christian Eucharistic assembly.

HOMILY NOTES

1. The time around the feast of the Ascension in one during
    which we as the People of God recall and celebrate the pres-
    ence of Christ in the church and the whole of creation. His
    coming among us is not confined to a single place / time, and
    in his resurrection he offers a new vision of the whole of real-
    ity: it can be transformed and brought to its completion in
    God. Developing a sense of this presence of Christ in the
    church, in human relationships and work, and in the natural
    world we inhabit, is a task we must confront today as never
    before.

2. A possible starting point in making ourselves aware of our
    belief in the cosmic Christ who is bringing the universe to its
    completion is to look at contemporary concerns over the en-
    vironment. Is the world around us simply a 'proving ground'
    for human beings – something that is only incidentally rele-
    vant to the divine plan – or is it part of the loving work of

God which was made through the Word (Jn 1:3 and the creed recited every Sunday) and which has been transformed – which we have just celebrated in Easter and Ascension? Alas, over recent centuries most Christians have taken the first approach: God is interested only in the 'spiritual bits', souls, and the rest is irrelevant. Indeed, this disregard for the integrity of creation was even made the motto of a Catholic religious order: *da mihi animas cetera tolle!* In this view, once the 'souls' are OK, then the universe is a just a testing ground to see if 'souls' pass the exam and can be found worthy of heaven. This approach looses all respect for creation, even those more sublime creatures 'the souls', for they are tested to destruction and the testing ground, the environment where we live, is no more important than the egg-shells are to the final omelette. We should note that this attitude is attractive both to those who like a more 'spiritual religion' and to those who make money out of the destruction of the environment. So we should not be surprised that conservative religious forces seeking an other-worldly message in Christianity, and those major stakes in industries that abuse the environment, often find much common ground upon which they can support one another!

3. However, Christian tradition sees the universe as showing forth its origins in the Logos whenever we discover systems within it: it is ordered in its materiality as it comes from the source of order. Athanasius spoke of the 'logicality' of the creation for it was shot-through with the marks of its maker, the Logos. In this vision we must respect the integrity of the cosmos as it is part of the entire loving design of God in which we too have our unique place: but we are unique *within* that plan, not superior to it.

4. Today we hear many voices being raised about the destruction of the integrity of the environment: unusual floods may be the result of our pollution; famines which result from abuse of soil; and a greedy lifestyle in the First World which if it were shared with every human being would require the

resources of four planets. All this then has impact on human beings – the inherent injustice of a few using the resources of many with its implicit operative belief that a life in the First World has the value of at least four humans anywhere else. All these voices are inchoately testifying to a truth about the creation which we Christians see as linked to the presence of Christ within it. If we think we can just 'use it and throw it' then we create suffering and injustice, something all humanity can appreciate, and we ignore the loving origins of nature in the Logos and his ascended presence within it – an appreciation that only comes through our belonging to the People of God.

5. If we have a task to appreciate the various presences of the risen ascended Christ, then we have an even greater task in being witnesses to Christ's presence before the world in which we live.

Seventh Sunday of Easter Year C

Introduction to the Celebration

By now, for most people, Easter seems a long time ago, so to create an emphasis stress that today falls between Ascension and Pentecost. We have a memory – as given in Acts 1:13 – that between these feasts the apostles along with Mary stayed together for nine days (the original 'novena') in continuous prayer. We, gathered today, must hold on to that image as a paradigm for our own Eucharistic assembly.

Rite of Penance

Replace with the sprinkling with Holy Water. The 'alternative' opening prayer ('Eternal Father', Missal, p. 272) is preferable.

Headings for Readings

First Reading

Stephen is the first martyr: witness to the resurrection is costly, but it is inspired by a vision of Christ, and characterised by forgiveness.

Second Reading

Our Easter declaration is that Jesus, in whom we live, is the Alpha and the Omega, the beginning and end of our lives.

Gospel

The risen Lord makes known the Father to us, for it is through our life in Christ that we are called into the mystery of God.

Prayer of the Faithful

President:

My friends, we have gathered like Mary and the apostles awaiting Pentecost, so now let us pray to the Father with one heart, and mind, and voice

Reader(s):

1. That we may bear witness to the resurrection.

2. That we may forgive our enemies.

3. That we may become people of prayer.

4. That we may seek peace and support all who work for it.

5. That the dead may rise in the Lord.

President:

Father, you listened to the prayers of the first Christian community; hear us, send the Spirit upon us, and be with us in Christ Jesus, our Lord. Amen.

Eucharistic Prayer

Ascension I (P 26) is preferable as it focuses on Christ as our priest.

Invitation to the Our Father

Gathered in prayer as the children of the Father, let us now say:

Sign of Peace

A gathering in prayer must be a gathering in forgiveness and love of the community. Let us express this in the sign of peace.

Invitation to Communion

The gathering of the disciples is the gathering to break the loaf which is Christ; behold that broken loaf. Happy we who are called to share in it.

Communion Reflection

Edmund Spencer's 'Easter', Breviary, vol 2, p. 608* (Poem 71).

Dismissal

Blessing n 8 for Ascension, Missal, p. 371.

COMMENTARY

First Reading: Acts 7:55-60

Luke draws together many bits of tradition here and welds them into his overall story. Stephen must have held some position of authority within the Jerusalem church (in 6:5 he is fitted into Luke's image of authorised apostolic authority by being one of the 'original' deacons) and clearly he was already venerated as the protomartyr. Luke takes this tradition and fits it into a pattern of witness to the resurrection in Jerusalem and Judea, and then with a single phrase moves the story forward by introducing Saul/Paul who will take that witness beyond Judea. So the death of the first witness forges a link to the next step in the plan of witness by which the resurrection is preached 'to the ends of the earth'.

Second Reading: Apoc 22:12-14; 16-17; 20

This is a part of the picture of the heavenly Jerusalem of the saints. Within Christian reading, as opposed to its apocalyptic original setting, it is the image of the eschaton which is anticipated in the liturgy – note the liturgical touches such as the washed/white robes of the baptised.

Gospel: Jn 17:20-26

This is the final part of the great prayer to the Father that John locates at the Last Supper. The context is the 'hour' of Jesus when he goes before the Father and offers the prayer which establish his people as the people of the New Covenant. Within Christian understanding all our prayer takes place 'in Christ' and here John portrays Christ presenting the whole of the church's prayer, as his own, to the Father.

HOMILY NOTES

1. Preaching to an average congregation about prayer is something we fear; some sort of moral message (e.g. 'Jesus loves you, so go and be nice to people you meet') seems to make more sense. However, if we do not speak of the need to be re-

flective, and on the human need to allow space in our lives to come to an awareness of the mystery of God, then we reduce faith to morality buttressed by cult – and into this vacuum step those who promote New Age fads promising 'increased consciousness'. This day, liturgically recalling the time of continuous prayer by the disciples in Jerusalem, is a suitable occasion to speak of the topic.

2. We believe that God has shown his face to us in the history of Israel and Jesus, and so has opened for us the possibility of dialogue in prayer. But prayer is never a simple matter. It is a personal matter in that it must arise from my heart; but since I discover God's face within the community of faith, it always involves the community. I must go off, like Jesus, on my own to pray; but I must also pray with others for it is when we gather in prayer that we have Christ's special presence with us. Equally, prayer is words and petitions and rituals – and so it has to be for that is the way we humans are as communicators; but prayer is not like a chat with a friend for we know that it goes beyond the rationality of human communication: the 'Father knows what' we 'need before' we 'ask him' (Mt 6:8), but ask him in words we must. Then again, we must reflect on the wonder of the creation, the mystery that surrounds us, and this should spill over into praise; but this does not 'add' to the divine glory for 'our desire to thank' God 'is itself' God's 'gift'. And there is still the problem of those who pray to whom bad things happen, while with all our prayer there is still evil, war, and greed. We cannot explain these paradoxes, rather we must live through them (this is faith) to glimpse the glory or hear the still small voice in prayer.

3. A practical model of what is involved is the Prayer of the Faithful at the Eucharist. Invite the assembly to reflect on what is happening in this weekly ritual. Start with the description given in the Missal, p. xxix, and read sections 45 and 46 (to the bottom of the page). It is an act of petition which involves each of us, but does so as the priestly people

interceding before the throne of God. It is at once a ritual, and something that is spontaneous, bringing in some themes every week (e.g. the need of the church for holiness) and others that relate to that day's news. It is the prayer of a group of Christians, but its concerns go out from ourselves to the larger society and to world needs. Prayer makes us conscious of our inner selves and our needs, but it must also draw us outwards in love and sympathy to all who suffer.

4. This would be a good occasion to make something special of the Prayer of the Faithful – a selection of readers, more silence, time for people to announce their own petitions. And, if you live where the bad habit of reciting the Hail Mary has crept in, then this is a chance to explain why it should be dropped, and to drop it. See the *Note on the Structure of the Prayer of the Faithful*.

Pentecost Year A

Note: the Vigil Mass

Today, most unusually, the Missal supplies a 'Mass for the Vigil' of the feast, and a 'Mass for the Day' of the feast, each with its own readings and prayers. This vigil Mass is understood as the vigil in preparation for the day, and so it assumes that those who take part in it, will also take part in the Mass during the day, 'when the day of Pentecost [has] come' (Acts 2:1). However, in most communities where there is a Saturday evening 'vigil Mass,' this is not understood as the beginning of a real vigil which would end on the day with another celebration, but it is the Sunday's Mass anticipated for the convenience of the assembly. Hence, those people who participate in the Saturday evening Mass *in lieu* of a celebration on Sunday morning will not hear the basic Pentecost readings nor experience the basic liturgy of this feast, if the Mass of the vigil is used on Saturday evening. Since that Saturday is really just 'Sunday early,' it is best to use the Mass of the day and its readings on Saturday evening – and leave the formal Mass of the vigil for those occasions when a real vigil (the Eucharist followed by the Liturgy of the Hours and concluding on the day) is being celebrated.

Introduction to the Celebration

Today we are celebrating a feast that was celebrated by many of the Jews who lived at the time of Jesus. Many of his early followers continued to celebrate it after the resurrection, and so it became part of the annual celebrations of all Christians. However, over the first few decades of the church, this feast took on a new meaning: Jesus has risen and ascended to the Father, but he promised us his Spirit. So today we rejoice that the Spirit is moving in each of our hearts making us a people, inspiring us to understand the mystery of our faith, and strengthening us to follow Jesus the Anointed One.

Rite of Penance

This great day ends the Easter season and the tone of the celebration should reflect its special status within our annual cycle
of celebration. Beginning with a Penitential Rite mars that tone,
so replace it with a period of silence invoking the Spirit to come
upon the assembly to empower it to be the priestly community
of Christ at the Eucharist. After the silence, use the third alternative opening prayer (Missal, p. 281) as an epiclesis, and then
move to the Gloria.

Headings for Readings
First Reading

The Spirit empowered the apostles in their ministry; he is now
empowering us in our ministries.
Or
This is the great account of the Spirit's coming down on the assembled church in Jerusalem and empowering them to preach
the good news to every nation.

(Vigil Mass, whichever reading is chosen:
This reading presents the spirit of God, which we Christians understand as the Spirit, as his power bringing life into the world.)

Second Reading

The Spirit is working now in our community, empowering all
who have ministries among us for our common good.

The Sequence: Veni Sancte Spiritus

This worked well when sung in Latin; simply read in English its
sounds pathetic. Moreover, since people are not expecting it,
they do not know whether to listen seated or standing, or
whether to join in or not. Its value is that it marks out this day as
special. If done with clear directions ('Let us stand for the sequence') and read by a small group (three / four female voices) in
the manner of a Greek chorus, interrupted regularly by a refrain
such as the Taizé *Veni sancte Spiritus*, it can be an excellent item

in the liturgy. If simply 'read' by the reader, it is just noise adding another brick to the wall of words that separate people from a sense of participation.

Gospel
The Spirit is among us offering us peace and forgiveness. We as the People of God must bring peace and forgiveness – often in the face of a worldly spirit of revenge and fear – and the Holy Spirit empowers us to bring this good news to the world.

Prayer of the Faithful
President:
We are gathered here by the Spirit; we are made brothers and sisters by the Spirit; we are enabled to pray by the Spirit, so now in the Spirit let us put our petitions to the Father
Reader(s):
1. That we, and all Christians, may hear the promptings of the Holy Spirit.
2. That the churches may be renewed by the Holy Spirit.
3. That all in public office may hear the Spirit's gentle voice prompting them towards the ways of peace.
4. That all humanity may enjoy the fruits of the Spirit in a world animated by forgiveness and reconciliation.
5. That all those who are seeking the truth may have the assistance of the Holy Spirit.
6. *Local needs.*
President:
Father, rejoicing in the presence of the Spirit who enables us to call you Abba, Father, hear our petitions and grant our needs, through Christ, our Lord, Amen.

Invitation to the Our Father
In the power of the Spirit, let us pray:

Sign of Peace
The Spirit's gifts are reconciliation, harmony, and peace; let us express our desire to make use of these gifts in the way we live.

Invitation to Communion
The Spirit lets us recognise the Lord in the breaking of the loaf; so, in the Spirit's power, behold the Lamb of God ...

Communion Reflection
There is so much already in today's liturgy, anything other than a period of silence can tend to 'overload' the celebration.

Dismissal
Blessing n 9 for Pentecost, Missal, p. 371.

COMMENTARY

First Reading: Acts 2:1-11
Here Luke presents a scene to convey his belief that the church carries out its mission in the power of the Spirit. See the *Note on Celebrating Ascension and Pentecost.*

At the vigil there is a choice of Gen 11; Ex 19; Ez 37; or Joel 3, all of which present the spirit of God, which we Christians understand as the Spirit, as his power bringing life into the world. These vigil readings focus on the Spirit's working in the world, which is an important part of the mystery we celebrate at Pentecost.

Psalm: 103: 1, 24, 29-31, 34; R/ v.30
YHWH's spirit is read in a Christian sense and identified with the Holy Spirit, and this Spirit is seen as renewing the creation and giving life.

Second Reading: 1 Cor 12:3-7; 12-13
A classic snippet of Paul on the Spirit: the Spirit brings unity, but is the source of a diversity of ministries that animate every church.

[*Vigil: Rom 8:22-27:* the Spirit is active always and everywhere, and he is active within our lives.]

Gospel: Jn 20:19-23
This pericope presents the Spirit as the source of forgiveness within the church, animating it to be the messenger/builder of forgiveness in the world.

[*Vigil: Jn 7:37-9:* The Spirit is the source of the living water which is life in Christ.]

HOMILY NOTES

1. The focus of Pentecost for Christians is as a celebration of, and a thanksgiving for, the presence and focus of the Spirit in our lives as Christians. The Spirit is the one who brings unity – unity with one another and with Christ, and so the church is 'his' work. Today is a thanksgiving for this gift, membership of the church, which we profess in the recitation of the Creed: 'we believe in one holy catholic and apostolic church'. Significantly, it is this gift of belonging to the People that made Christianity so attractive in the early centuries of its life where the emphasis was not on a set of peculiar doctrines which were shared by a group (e.g. the eastern mystery cults), but on belonging to a new community which had doctrines peculiar to it. We see this concern with belonging to the church in one of the simplest creeds that has survived from that time: 'I believe in God, the almighty Father and in his only-begotten Son, Jesus Christ, and in the Holy Spirit and in the resurrection of the flesh in the holy catholic church.' Belonging to this universal (i.e. catholic) group that cut across social, ethnic, linguistic, and political boundaries, was central to their self-understanding and was the on-going work of the Spirit.

2. If Luke wants us to use a festival fifty days after our Passover to recall the fundamental belief that the presence of God, the Spirit, dwells within and activates the church, how does he

imagine that presence? It is with this question we should look at his carefully crafted story in Acts 2.

The Spirit is the one who gathers us – all the different 'nations' are brought into contact with one another. Then the Spirit unites them into one church gathered around Jesus – so the followers of Jesus everywhere are linked through the apostles. The Spirit then inspires them and sends them forth to be the witnesses to Jesus to the ends of the earth. As Luke writes he has in mind the many individual churches where his work will be read and wants to ensure that each individual church recognises itself as a node in a great web that stretches not only across the empire (the *oikumene*) – 'visitors from Rome' – but even beyond its borders (Parthians and Medes) and so is universal.

3. We tend to think of 'the church' firstly as the worldwide institution and then of the local church as only 'the local office'. Hence we have tremendous concern with making sure that everything is the same universally – just look at the old arguments for a single liturgy in Latin or the present arguments over translations. This attitude blinds us to much of Luke's ecclesiology. He did not see unity as a unitary glut: but rather that the gospel could adapt itself to each nation – hence they did not hear the message in the *lingua franca* (in which he himself wrote) but in their own tongues. Unity between the churches is a gift of the Spirit, not a function of uniformity of practice. This reflected the real situation in which Luke wrote, where Christianity was already present (and this is pointed out in Acts) in, at least, four major linguistic areas: Greek (Asia and eastern Europe) and so Latin, Syriac (the spread of Christianity eastwards from Palestine), and the vernaculars of Egypt/the Nile valley. He assumed that they would each be different but would be bonded together not only by common rituals and books, but by a vision of themselves that was larger than their own Eucharistic group, region, nation, or any political boundary. While they would live and act locally, they would think globally, and so testify that the new

covenant meant Christ through them was offering his risen life to every human.

Pentecost Year B

Introduction to the Celebration
See Year A.

Rite of Penance
See Year A.

Headings for Readings
First Reading
See Year A.

Second Reading (for B option)
By the fruits of our lives we can know whether or not we are living under the guidance of the Holy Spirit.

The Sequence
See year A.

Gospel (for B option)
The Spirit inspires our understanding, gives light to our darkened minds, and leads us into the mystery of the truth.

Prayer of the Faithful
President:
My friends, the Spirit enables us to pray, and intercedes for us, so in his power let us put our needs before the Father:
Reader(s):
1. For the holy church, that the Spirit may be present in our lives.
2. For all who minister in this community, that the Spirit may make their work fruitful.
3. For all who need consolation, that the Spirit may strengthen them.

4. For all who are seeking the truth, that the Spirit may enlighten them.

5. For all who work for peace and justice, that the Spirit may empower them.

President:

Father, your Son promised us the Spirit to form us as your children of adoption, so now hear the prayers of your daughters and sons and grant us what we ask through Christ, our Lord.

Invitation to the Our Father

The Spirit reveals the Father's love to us, and so we pray:

Sign of Peace

The Spirit brings love, joy, peace, patience, kindness, goodness, trustfulness, gentleness and self-control. Let us show each other that we desire to build our community with these values.

Invitation to Communion

The Spirit lets us recognise the Lord in the breaking of the loaf; so, in the Spirit's power, behold the Lamb of God ...

Dismissal

Blessing n 9 for Pentecost, Missal, p. 371.

COMMENTARY

First Reading: Acts 2:1-11

See Year A.

Psalm

See year A.

Second Reading: Gal 5:16-25

Gal 5:16-25 is the Optional day reading for year B. The fruits of the Spirit who is dwelling in a community of disciples is contrasted with the opposite of life in the Spirit: a life of self-indulgence.

For the vigil reading see year A.

Gospel: Jn 15:26-27, 16:12-15

Jn 15:26-27, 16:12-15 is the Optional Gospel for Year B. This lection is a combination of two distinct passages in John, but the combination achieves a unity of its own that makes it a very fine reflection on our belief in the work of the Spirit in the members of the church. The Spirit reveals to us the fullness of the truth, makes us into witnesses, and enables us to pray glorifying Christ. The Spirit gathers us into Christ, and to be gathered into Christ is to be gathered into the Father.

For the vigil reading see year A.

HOMILY NOTES

1. In Luke / Acts, the author has a very definite plan of how the message of Jesus is to spread outwards to every nation (Luke thinks of the world populated by nations: related groups of people, rather than just individuals). The preaching will take place in three concentric circles. First, in Jerusalem; second, in Judea and Samaria; and then out to the ends of the earth. The Spirit at Pentecost initiates the process. Then later in Acts the Spirit intervenes to enable the preachers to move from the 'home nation' in Judea and Samaria out to the other nations, the gentiles, and in each new region he imagines that the Spirit has already been at work preparing the ground for the messengers of the gospel.

2. Earlier generations of Christians were terribly interested in when exactly in this great historical process the gospel first came to their own nation and how the Spirit has prepared their nation for its reception. We see this in the writings of Augustine for the Romans, of Gregory of Tours for the French, of Muirchú for the Irish, and Bede for the English. Each wanted to know when the gospel's power reached them for they imagined it as a ripple spreading over a pond: from Jerusalem the good news rippled out until it encountered them. Each of those writers wanted to study how the

Spirit was at work silently long before the people had heard the name of Christ, and they wanted to know how long before their own time this had happened for they were interested in how the Spirit was empowering each generation to hand on the gospel to the next.

3. This is a way of thinking that is very foreign to us. However, recalling it raises two questions: do we appreciate the Spirit's silent working in our world? Do we recognise our empowerment by the Spirit to hand on the gospel?

Pentecost Year C

Introduction to the Celebration
See Year A.

Rite of Penance
See Year A.

Headings for Readings
First Reading
See Year A.

Second Reading (for option C)
The Spirit makes us into children of the Father and sisters and brothers of Christ.

The Sequence
See Year A.

Gospel (for option C)
To help us appreciate the mystery of God, the Lord sends us the Holy Spirit who teaches us and enables us to enter into the life of Christ.

Prayer of the Faithful
President:
My friends, the Spirit enables us to pray, and intercedes for us, so in his power let us put our needs before the Father:
Reader(s):
1. For the holy church, that the Spirit may be present in our lives.
2. For all who minister in this community, that the Spirit may make their work fruitful.
3. For all who need consolation, that the Spirit may strengthen them.

4. For all who are seeking the truth, that the Spirit may enlighten them.

5. For all who work for peace and justice, that the Spirit may empower them.

President:

Father, your Son promised us the Spirit to form us as your children of adoption, so now hear the prayers of your daughters and sons and grant us what we ask through Christ, our Lord.

Invitation to the Our Father

The Spirit dwelling within us enables us to cry out 'Abba, Father' and so we pray:

Sign of Peace

The Spirit's gifts are reconciliation, harmony, and peace; let us express our desire to make use of these gifts in the way we live.

Invitation to Communion

The Spirit lets us recognise the Lord in the breaking of the loaf; so, in the Spirit's power, behold the Lamb of God ...

Dismissal

Blessing n 9 for Pentecost, Missal, p. 371.

COMMENTARY

First Reading

See Year A.

Psalm

See Year A.

Second Reading: Rom 8:8-17

Rom 8:8-17 is the Optional day reading for Year C. The Spirit makes us children of God, and note that his activity is not limited to the group of believers. There are no bounds to his work.

If you intend to focus on the Spirit as the animator of ministry in the community in the homily, then 1 Cor 12:3-7; 12-13 is a more appropriate text.

For the vigil reading see year A.

Gospel: Jn 20:19-23

Jn 20:19-23 presents the Spirit as the source of forgiveness within the church, animating it to be the messenger/builder of forgiveness in the world. This gospel, with its clear emphasis of the Spirit as the life force of the church's ministry, is to be preferred to the optional choice for year C.

Option for Year C: Jn 14:15-16; 23-26 presents the Spirit as the teacher who leads us into all truth. In John these promises form part of Christ's farewell prayer for the church.

For the vigil reading see year A.

HOMILY NOTES

1. There are two popular themes in preaching Pentecost that miss the point of this feast. First, that it is the 'feast of the Holy Spirit' as if this were analogous to 15 August as 'Mary's feast' or 17 March as 'Patrick's feast'. One cannot have a feast for a divine Person! Every feast, every day, every prayer is the Spirit's, or it is nothing! Just note how silly the phrase 'the Spirit's feast' is: which is the Father's feast, or do we imagine Mary is more important as she has more feasts? The implication of this approach is to use the homily for a user-friendly treatise on the Spirit. The second false trail is to say that this is the 'birthday of the church', on the supposition that birthdays are one of the few special times our culture understands. As a metaphor it can be quite useful, but it trivialises what is at issue by making it simply one of recalling the 'First [Christian] Pentecost.' Then the homily becomes a recollection of the Luke's idealised, imaginative picture of apostolic times. This not only perpetuates a false view of the early church, relies unwittingly on a fundamentalist scriptural hermeneutic, but misses the feast's central message.

2. Our belief is that the Spirit is coming upon us now, he who is

'Lord and giver of life', is descending now upon the church – at every moment, in every good thought and action, in every assembly – and giving us life and empowering us. We, in the congregation assembled, hold this feast to remind ourselves of this unseen presence in our lives, and to invite ourselves to call on him to empower and enlighten us. It is not the Spirit as the third Person of the Godhead, nor an event in Jerusalem long ago that we celebrate, but the Spirit as the life-giving core of our lives as a local church, gathered now for a meal to strengthen us to continue in our work of building the king-dom. We are celebrating someone who is already within us, or we would not be here are all.

3. How can we recognise the Spirit's presence? How should we imagine the Spirit? These are questions we all pose and are often asked. We have an image of 'the Father' as the old man with the beard – it is limited, but it is there; we all have an image of the Son for we have umpteen images of the Word made flesh; but how can we relate to the Spirit as a dove or a flame or a wind? The answer is that we can only relate to the Spirit in an act of reflecting upon our own lives and actions – it is the Spirit within us that provokes these very questions within each of us, spurring us to grow in the mystery of the divine love.

4. So how can we extend that action of reflection to see the Spirit's presence in our community? The Spirit's gifts are, in reality, the Spirit himself, so we should celebrate the various ministries that exist within the community. Obviously those who minister in the liturgy (the Spirit empowering us to prayer calling on the Father), and those involved in charity in the community (the Spirit as the source of love). But also all who teach – not only as catechists (the Spirit promoting the kerygma) but every teacher (the Spirit as the enlightener of minds). Then those who seek the truth in their work (e.g. journalists or scientists) for the Spirit leads us towards the truth. Then those who work of society's good be they police-men or social workers or whatever – for the Spirit brings for-

giveness and harmony. Then all who care for life, for the Spirit is the life-giver. One could keep going outwards to ever-wider circles until the whole community is included – for part of being a Christian is recognising that the Spirit is at work in every human heart. Wherever anything good, true, noble, or joyful happens, there is the Spirit at work. One of our tasks as the church is to discover how the Spirit is present and working in the world.

5. Instead of a discourse of words today, if you can think of some activity that would highlight how people in your community – in so many diverse ways – are animated for ministry by the Spirit, then you may have communicated the message of this day far more effectively than with a homily.